"In *Breaking the Marriage Idol* Kutter C̶   one
before. What Kutter has done for us is of   ical
exploration of culturally difficult, if not   our
culture *and* our churches live through ev̶   ̶̶ ̶̶̶ Callaway for
many years, and there are few in pastoral ministry or the academy who I respect
more. I wholeheartedly recommend this book for every Christian who is willing
to invite God into real life. Not because we all will agree, but because we all had
better join the conversation."

Chap Clark, professor of practical theology and youth, family, and culture at Fuller
Theological Seminary, author of *Hurt 2.0: Inside the World of Today's Teenagers*

"Kutter's right. Churches' marriage promise and allure of happily ever after has cast
many into a subclass existence. He carefully confronts Christians' assumptions about
singleness, marriage, community, and personhood and leads us toward a helpful
direction that is good news for singles, marrieds, young, and old. Kutter is being
more than a relevant theologian. He is a culturally in-tune thinker that possesses
the unique ability to reorient our categories of the popular and religious, the relevant
and traditional, the sacred and secular. This book bridges the gaps for needed
conversations that can help us escape the binary, anemic, and often hurtful views
that keep especially those in our faith communities from having generative conversations.
Whatever you do, do not read this book alone. Read it with your partner, your friends,
your community. Let it lead you into better conversations about faith, love, sex,
singleness, marriage, and community. We all know we need them."

Steven Argue, assistant professor of youth, family, and culture, applied research strategist
at Fuller Youth Institute, Fuller Theological Seminary

"Kutter Callaway has written and assembled a rich tool for reflection on marriage
and relationships in today's milieu. Its honest, provocative, and savvy engagement,
combined with biblical and theological considerations, makes it a strong resource.
Some of the additional voices—especially Joshua Beckett's—make it that much richer."

Mark Labberton, president of Fuller Theological Seminary

"I've been waiting for someone to write a book like this: a culturally astute, refresh-
ingly iconoclastic critique of evangelical Christianity's marriage myopia. Beyond
the shattered remnants of the marriage idol, singleness and marriage emerge as
equally and uniquely beautiful vocations within which followers of Christ can
steward our sexualities. I'm eager for you to read this book. I'm even more eager
for you to believe it."

Gregory Coles, author of *Single, Gay, Christian*

BREAKING
THE MARRIAGE
IDOL

RECONSTRUCTING OUR CULTURAL
AND SPIRITUAL NORMS

KUTTER CALLAWAY

IVP Books

An imprint of InterVarsity Press
Downers Grove, Illinois

InterVarsity Press
P.O. Box 1400, Downers Grove, IL 60515-1426
ivpress.com
email@ivpress.com

InterVarsity Press® is the book-publishing division of InterVarsity Christian Fellowship/USA®, a
movement of students and faculty active on campus at hundreds of universities, colleges, and schools
of nursing in the United States of America, and a member movement of the International Fellowship
of Evangelical Students. For information about local and regional activities, visit intervarsity.org.

All Scripture quotations, unless otherwise indicated, are taken from the NET Bible® copyright
©1996–2016 by Biblical Studies Press, L.L.C. All rights reserved.

While any stories in this book are true, some names and identifying information may have been
changed to protect the privacy of individuals.

Cover design: David Fassett
Interior design: Daniel van Loon
Images: © H. Armstrong Roberts/ClassicStock / Getty Images

ISBN 978-0-8308-4542-2 (print)
ISBN 978-0-8308-7406-4 (digital)

Printed in the United States of America ∞

InterVarsity Press is committed to ecological stewardship and to the conservation of natural resources
in all our operations. This book was printed using sustainably sourced paper.

Library of Congress Cataloging-in-Publication Data
Names: Callaway, Kutter, 1979- author.
Title: Breaking the marriage idol : reconstructing our cultural and spiritual
   norms / Kutter Callaway.
Description: Downers Grove : InterVarsity Press, 2018. | Includes
   bibliographical references and index.
Identifiers: LCCN 2018012238 (print) | LCCN 2018016436 (ebook) | ISBN
   9780830874064 (eBook) | ISBN 9780830845422 (pbk. : alk. paper)
Subjects: LCSH: Marriage--Religious aspects--Christianity.
Classification: LCC BT706 (ebook) | LCC BT706 .C29 2018 (print) | DDC
   261.8/3581--dc23
LC record available at https://lccn.loc.gov/2018012238

P   25 24 23 22 21 20 19 18 17 16 15 14 13 12 11 10 9 8 7 6 5 4 3 2 1

Y   37 36 35 34 33 32 31 30 29 28 27 26 25 24 23 22 21 20 19 18

To Jessica, Callie, Mattie, and Maeve

CONTENTS

Introduction   *1*

PART 1: THE CHURCH AND CULTURE AS EASY BEDFELLOWS

1 Disney Princesses, Taylor Swift, and *The Bachelor*:
Pop Culture as Premarital Counselor and Sex Therapist   *23*

2 The Internal Narratives of Contemporary Evangelicalism:
Waiting on True Love, Kissing Dating Goodbye, and Bringing
Up Princes and Princesses   *51*

PART 2: RECONSIDERING THE BIBLICAL WITNESS

3 Bone of My Bones and Flesh of My Flesh: The First Testament
on Marriage and What It Means to Be Human   *91*

4 Like a Virgin: The New Testament on Singleness and
What It Means to Be Sexual   *123*

PART 3: DEVELOPING A THEOLOGICAL FRAMEWORK

5 The Call of Marriage (or, Why Christians *Should* Get Married)   *159*

6 Desire in Singleness: Ascetics and Eternity (or, Why
Christians *Don't Need* to Get Married)—by Joshua Beckett   *193*

7 Sex, Saints, and Singleness: Practical (Re)Considerations   *213*

Conclusion: A Family Who Forgives Together . . .   *239*

Acknowledgments   *243*

Contributors   *247*

Notes   *249*

General Index   *263*

Scripture Index   *267*

VIGNETTES

1 Sitting at the Grownups' Table—by Jennifer Graffius   *21*

2 Running to Stand Still—by Lindy Williams   *48*

3 Battle Fatigue—by Michael Beardslee   *82*

4 More Than Just a Label—by Debi Yu   *87*

5 About a Christian Divorce—by Sarey Martin   *119*

6 Not Whole—by Anonymous   *150*

7 Cold Feet—by Claire Crisp   *155*

8 Single Not Solitary—by Colton Simmons   *190*

9 December—by Joshua Beckett   *211*

INTRODUCTION

I HAVE BEEN MARRIED for nearly twenty years. I am also the proud father of three young girls. As such, bedtime routines have taken on a kind of significance I never knew possible. My wife and I cherish these moments with our daughters, in part because we know they are fleeting. It's all fairly mundane really. We brush teeth, pray for one another, and, more times than not, read books together. But it's more than that. It is also a time when we get to imagine with them—to envision the world and their place in it not as it currently is, but as it one day could be. Seeing reality through their eyes is an experience in sheer possibility. When we read books together, it seems like every nook and cranny of existence is filled to the brim with potential, expectancy, and wonder. As we dive headlong into these imaginary worlds, nothing is impossible.

It is perhaps for this very reason that I am increasingly haunted by some of the stories we come across, even though my daughters are still unable to see beneath their surface. We recently encountered one such tale in an otherwise whimsical collection of children's stories written and illustrated by Richard Scarry. The title is innocuous enough: "Is This the House of Mistress Mouse?" But the story is far from innocent, for it paints a picture of the world that is as powerful as it is unsettling. Some may be familiar with this story already, but for those who are not, it chronicles a particularly significant day in the life of Mister Mouse:

> This is the house of Mister Mouse. He lived all alone and he was very lonely. One day he received a letter from Mistress Mouse. The letter said: "Dear Mister Mouse, I am very lonely too. Will you please come and visit me? Love and kisses, Mistress Mouse."[1]

Being the lonely bachelor that he is, Mr. Mouse responds to the letter from Mistress Mouse by searching high and low for her house. Because he doesn't know exactly where she lives, he decides to go from one door to the next, hoping that, at some point, he will find his soul-mouse. His search ends with a stroke of good fortune as he knocks on one final door:

> The door slowly opened. Sure enough! It WAS the house of Mistress Mouse! And they were soon married by Preacher Mole. Mister Mouse gave Mistress Mouse a golden wedding ring with a bright diamond on top. And from that day on they were never lonely.[2]

As someone with formal training in interpreting the meaning of cultural artifacts, allow me to offer a critical analysis of this "complex" narrative. If I understand it correctly, the moral of the story goes something like this: Single people are lonely. And marriage is the answer to their loneliness. Thus, if a single person is lucky enough to find someone who is equally lonely, they should marry each other immediately, because if they do, they will never be lonely again. Of course, for any of this to be possible, men and women need to remember their rightful place. Men must be willing to pursue the object of their desire with tireless effort; women must wait in passive anticipation for a man to rescue them from their isolated existence. It's just that simple, at least for mice anyway.

Given the way I have come to understand the story of Mr. and Mrs. Mouse, it is probably unsurprising to hear that when my daughters ask me to read it to them, I take the liberty of making significant revisions (for instance, rather than get married right away, the two mice befriend Mr. Mole and form a theater troupe that specializes in wedding re-enactments as a form of subversive performance art). I do this for a simple reason. In the span of a few short pages, this picture book presents a concise and compelling take on reality that cannot help but engage them on the level of their imaginations. It establishes a narrative framework that has the potential for shaping their vision of what is and is not possible.

More specifically, as it combines a straightforward plot with charming illustrations, Richard Scarry's *Best Storybook Ever* holds up marriage uncritically as *the* ideal paradigm for human flourishing. It is a vision of marriage that is embedded deep within the contemporary cultural imagination, which means that it is much more than a mere children's story; it is a way of envisioning the world. And if my assessment of the present situation is accurate, the tale of these two mice also represents the prevailing picture of marriage that is currently in operation within the life of the church—one that has so fully captured the church's theological imagination that we simply cannot see any other possibilities for how Christians might flourish in the modern world.

One of the reasons why stories like "Is This the House of Mistress Mouse?" are so powerful is that they function as the very means by which we weave the otherwise disconnected events in our lives into a meaningful whole. In the field of cultural studies, we would say that commonly held narratives of this sort are what embody and express a tribe's "norms," the spoken and unspoken "rules" to which all members of a society are expected to conform. In fact, so powerful are these guiding stories that they operate transparently. No other options are offered or even considered because this is simply "the way things are." The story of Mr. Mouse is therefore somewhat unique in that it makes explicit what is often rendered invisible. In doing so, it brings to the surface a particular norm that is typically in operation only in the background, guiding our thoughts and organizing our practices whether we are aware of it or not.

In Christian circles, this picture of marriage and singleness often becomes equated (and sometimes even conflated) with God's ultimate intentions for individuals and communities. In other words, it is not only socially normative but religiously normative too. As a result, it takes on a kind of spiritual significance that derives its authority from a different register of meaning altogether—the realm of unassailable dogma rooted in a particular interpretation of Scripture.

It is toward these seemingly unchallengeable assumptions that I am going to direct the core of my argument. In doing so, I am not simply questioning the viability of a number of long-standing beliefs. I am seeking to undo them altogether, or at least to challenge the unhelpful norms they have established. So even though my claim is fairly simple and straightforward, it is also potentially scandalous. In short, I want to suggest that marriage should *not* be the norm that orients the communal life of the church or determines what it means to be a faithful disciple of Christ. Because we've allowed marriage to function as the standard against which all other relationships are evaluated and understood, our vision of singleness, marriage, community, sex, and even celibacy has become distorted. And the time has come for us to construct a new vision, to develop new eyes to see and ears to hear.

When marriage functions as *the* normative vision for Christian life, and no alternatives for relational flourishing are made available, a kind of ripple effect takes place. On the one hand, the Christian community feels free to simply ignore matters of sex and sexuality, especially among young people and single adults. What should be a robust and ongoing conversation is reduced to pithy proscriptions like "just say no" or "true love waits." Because many within the walls of the church simply assume (wrongly) that every person is designed to be married and (rightly) that sex is to take place within the confines of marriage, there is little reason for anyone to give any thought to what it looks like to live faithfully as a single (that is, nonmarried) Christian who will still inevitably encounter the world in physical, sensual, and even erotic ways.

This normative story about marriage, singleness, and sex moves in another direction as well. Because the church is radically uncomfortable directly addressing the human person as a fundamentally sexual being (whether single or married), and because marriage is the *only* relational model we offer for Christians who long to experience intimacy, community, and family, we end up asking marriage to bear a burden it was never meant to bear. Marriage becomes the "answer" to a problem it simply isn't equipped to remedy.

Increasingly, though, as marriages within the church continue to dissolve as quickly and as often as those of the general population, these romanticized notions of marriage are proving inadequate. In fact, based purely on the odds, the majority of those who find their way into our offices for pastoral counsel are not going to have successful or healthy marriages. And yet, almost in spite of this glaring reality, we continue as both leaders of the church and as a church body to enact and reenact the same old story about singleness and marriage.

FINDING THAT SPECIAL "SOMEONE"

Whether anyone actually says these words aloud or not, when it comes to the Christian view of marriage, the church often operates with the assumption that for the single members of our community, God has chosen a spouse just for them. All they need to do is wait patiently for that special someone. Just as Meg Ryan's character confesses in *You've Got Mail*, even if there is no actual person out there in the real world, there is always the "idea of someone." In the meantime—in the absence of marriage—single Christians will remain forever unfulfilled and incomplete, forced to snuff out what everyone knows is an unquenchable yearning for sex by any means other than sex.

For those who are married or about to get married, the story remains largely the same. Marriage is a great way to address loneliness. It serves as a healthy and acceptable outlet for sexual expression and, even better, provides the means for resolving sexual confusions and dysfunctions. Marriage comes naturally for those who pick the right spouse. It is a mostly uncomplicated relationship in which our personal needs for love and respect are met. And this is why married people are just so much happier and why married life is so much more fulfilling.

There's just one problem with this narrative. For the Christian, marriage was never intended to be the universal norm. In fact, for all intents and purposes, it's the exception.

To be clear, marriage *has* functioned normatively within the Christian community for much of its recent history. It has been held up as the model to which everyone ought to conform, or at least ought to aspire. But I want us to consider an alternative: What if marriage were not the default category for understanding the Christian person—for our daughters and sons, for our "youth," for the increasingly large number of emerging adults entering adulthood as singles, and even for those who were once married but no longer are? What if marriage were neither the primary marker of adulthood, nor the "answer" for some lack or emptiness, nor the "outlet" for an unmet desire, nor the consummation of an idealized future?

What if, instead, marriage was a unique vocation meant only for those who are specifically called to an incredibly challenging but incredibly important task? And what if we could say the same thing about singleness? What if we held it up as an immensely difficult but equally important calling?

These questions imply another, somewhat more challenging, line of thought. What if singleness, and not marriage, were the primary category for orienting our individual and communal lives? Not singleness as a life of isolated autonomy, but singleness as being a person in communion. What if it were this kind of singleness—and not marriage—that set the norm?

Some may think that I am minimizing the significance of marriage by raising these questions, but I most definitely am not. Please don't hear what I am not saying. I am not suggesting we *privilege* singleness over and against marriage. Nor am I saying that Christians shouldn't get married (I'm married!). Instead, I want us to *prioritize* singleness and marriage differently—to develop internal language and devotional practices and organizing frameworks that allow both single and married persons to pursue their vocations as fully functioning members of the Christian community.

Put differently, I am hoping to offer a more realistic assessment of the on-the-ground realities of marriage and, for the Christian community at least, construct a more faithful vision regarding how singles might actually flourish rather than simply wait in the wings for their moment to arrive.

We will of course be encountering a number of deeply ingrained assumptions as we attempt to develop this renewed vision of marriage, some of which I am going to do my best to undo or move beyond. One of those assumptions has to do with how the Bible does or does not address the question of marriage and singleness. Part of my challenge will be to offer an alternate story about Christian communal life that remains faithful to the biblical narrative.

For example, it is certainly true that biblical authors employ marriage metaphors to describe the relationship between Christ and his church. But in the church's uncritical embrace of these metaphors, we overlook a fairly important detail. The biblical witness points to marriage as simply *one possible option* for the Christian. And if my reading of the text is even close to correct, this option is often the least advisable one.

In many (if not most) church circles, though, not being married is essentially a non-option. Rather than a vocation in its own right, singleness is approached (either explicitly or implicitly) as a kind of calling in incubation—a perpetual purgatory for those poor souls who haven't yet found their "better halves." In some cases it is even judged to be a deficiency, as if the single person simply doesn't have what it takes to find a mate. Marriage is touted as the ideal relational paradigm, and anyone who doesn't fit neatly within this framework is not only socially inept, but worse: they are not quite human.

When marriage functions as the dominant metaphor for understanding what it means to be a disciple, a member of the Christian community, or even a human being, we become blind to another equally important vocation: living in mutual interdependence as people called to embody singleness in community.

It isn't that our churches don't care about single people. After all, many have entire ministries devoted to them. It's just that our misplaced notions regarding marriage seem to dictate everything else we do, including the implied (and sometimes stated) goals we develop for people who are single. The unquestioned assumption is that everyone either wants to be married or at least should be married at some point, so rather than creating spaces designed for the development of a relational web of intimately committed Christians, "singles ministries" often function more like eHarmony or speed-dating services than anything resembling the body of Christ. In other words, because the norm for the Christian person and even for the human being is marriage, these ministries are not constructive sites for negotiating a robust identity as a person in community, but are rather services designed to move the "yet to be married" into a more appropriate (and "God-ordained") relational status.

The simple fact that singles are so often segregated from the larger body (of married people) says a great deal about how we understand the role of singleness in the Christian community. The thinly veiled message is that married people would rather not be bothered by the many foibles of single life. But this normative vision of marriage and the distorted vision of singleness it entails are, in my view, not actually reflective of the biblical witness. In some cases they stand in direct contradiction to the testimony of God's people through time. As such, these distortions are preventing the community of faith from addressing a number of interrelated issues that are not only dividing the church from within, but are also undermining its credibility as a witness in the public sphere.

And that, at its core, is what this book is about. I fully realize that I am making a claim that is countercultural on a variety of fronts. Beyond the life of the church, it is an argument that also runs counter to the cultural norms that exist within contemporary society. But I want to suggest that, in contrast to the more common visions of marriage currently available, the picture we will develop does a better job of addressing the unique (and increasingly urgent) demands of modern church life, primarily because it offers a more robust reading of the biblical text, the theological tradition, our contemporary cultural context, and the personal narratives of both single and married persons.

The book itself is therefore structured along these very lines. Part one focuses on the striking parallels between the church's views on marriage, singleness, and romantic love and the views embedded in contemporary cultural artifacts such as TV, popular music, and film. Chapter one presents a close reading of three media "texts" (Disney princesses, the music of Taylor Swift, and *The Bachelor* and *The Bachelorette*), each of which uniquely embodies the deep structures and mythic underpinnings of contemporary culture. Then in chapter two I connect these conceptions of marriage, singleness, and sexuality that dominate the contemporary cultural landscape with the internal narratives of evangelical Christianity. This chapter concludes by asking what is at stake for the church when it not only uncritically embraces these expressly cultural narratives about marriage, singleness, and sexuality but also identifies them as "God ordained" and "biblically faithful."

Part two shifts from critical assessment to a more constructive proposal for how Christians might renew their vision regarding marriage and singleness. Chapter three focuses on the narratives of the Hebrew Bible, asking in particular whether the biblical text understands marriage to be essential to our humanness. Chapter four then explores the relevant New Testament texts concerning marriage, singleness, and sexuality, focusing in particular on the concept of Christian discipleship as the right ordering of embodied desire. This is a biblical framework that has implications not simply for married or single life, but for our basic understanding of what it means to live as faithful disciples who are sexual creatures in a cultural context of confused and confusing sexuality.

Part three locates this conversation within a larger theological framework. In chapter five I offer a theological rationale for why Christians should marry and, when they do, how they might understand the theological significance of this covenant relationship. In chapter six I hand over the reins to Joshua Beckett, a Christian ethicist who is both single and same-sex attracted. As a complement to my thoughts on marriage (which are written from my perspective as a married person), Joshua makes a parallel move, but from the perspective of someone who is both single and committed to a life of celibacy. He explores the significance of singleness as a Christian vocation, focusing in particular on a theology of desire. Because Joshua is not simply in a temporary season of singleness that might one day come to an end, his proposals for life-giving practices of celibacy are necessary, challenging, and in my estimation downright inspiring. His is a call to faithful discipleship that invests the book with a kind of authority and weightiness that it would otherwise lack if authored only by me. All of us—whether single or married—would do well to listen to and learn from him.

The book concludes with a consideration of alternative ways of organizing the church's communal life. Synthesizing the biblical, theological, and cultural insights of the preceding chapters, the final chapter explores what it might look like if the Christian community were not stratified along the lines of those who are married and those who are not, but rather identified itself as the bride of Christ—a truly common vocation that functions as both a sign and a sacrament of the kingdom to come. This concluding chapter offers up several practical suggestions for how this paradigm shift might take root at the local church level.

MARRIAGE ISN'T FOR EVERYONE— AND NEITHER IS THIS BOOK

In his book *To Change the World*, James Davison Hunter makes the claim that public discourse in the contemporary world (especially in the United States) has been fully conflated with the political.[3] We have no real space for engaging in public conversations that are not already wholly political. Conversations about marriage suffer from this same problem. Whether it's marriage equality for LGBTQIA persons, passing legislation to define marriage as only between a male and a female, or addressing the role of fathers and fatherlessness among certain demographics, it seems that we cannot talk about marriage in a nonpolitical (much less nonpartisan) way. And the hard truth to face is that the Christian community is as guilty as anyone else in creating these conditions.

Consider this book an attempt to talk in public about marriage not in a nonpolitical way, but in an intentionally nonpartisan way. How am I going to accomplish this? Well, the first step is admitting that, just like everyone else, I too am a political actor, and I have personal opinions about all the matters we are discussing here. But I am laying these perspectives on the table for all of us to engage critically. And I am asking my readers to do the same.

In addition to assuming a self-critical posture, my approach entails a second dimension that is perhaps even more important. This book is written to and for the Christian community. It is an internal conversation. On the one hand, this means that I am making no claims about how marriage should function in broader society. It may very well be helpful for those who do not identify with the Christian tradition. But this book is not about identifying a set of timeless "principles" for marriage that can then be used to coerce culture into conforming to the preferences of the Christian community. Heaven help us if it were anything of the sort.

On the other hand, because this book is written to and for the Christian community, it is self-consciously addressed to my own tribe— a group of people with whom I often disagree but am nevertheless called to love and to learn from. As a result, I have taken great care to incorporate the voices of those who do not necessarily see things in the same way that I do. I want readers to hear the other side of the argument, especially because the other side in this case is actually composed of internal voices. With this goal in mind I have included throughout the book nine autobiographical vignettes written by people who have encountered—both explicitly and implicitly—the normative expectations regarding marriage and singleness that are present in a variety of ecclesial contexts. I have done so not simply to pile up evidence for my claims regarding the unintended consequences of ecclesial norms, but rather to help readers *feel* themselves into the situation—to engage the problem on an affective, intuitive, and embodied level. For this is the primary mode in which norms most fully exert their power in our lives, shaping us in ways that are not always brought to the level of conscious awareness.

These personal stories demonstrate how the normative picture of marriage is not isolated to a single context (for instance, a particular church, denomination, or Christian subculture). They also serve to carve out a space in the book in which diverse (and sometimes contrasting) voices might be heard. What this means is that the hard truths we are trying to discern are fundamentally dialogical. I hope to offer a corrective to the paradigm for marriage that has captured our collective imagination. And I hope I am convincing. But in no way will this be an attempt to construct an unassailable argument. No one learns much of anything from that approach anyway. Instead I am inviting us all into what I hope is a mutually enriching dialogue—a conversation that very much depends on the wisdom, insight, and perspectives of those with whom we might occasionally disagree.

"FAMILY VALUES" AND THE "BIBLICAL" VIEW OF MARRIAGE

If this community-wide conversation has any chance of being more than a one-off, those of us who identify with the Christian tradition need to start by being honest with ourselves. Simply put, marriage isn't working, at least not for most people. Ask any sociologist or statistician: marriage is not an incredibly successful endeavor—not in the least. If the measures for a successful marriage were the same as for a middle school math exam, Americans would be, to put it mildly, underperforming.[4]

Among Christian marriages, however, things are even worse. Christians themselves divorce approximately at or just above the same rate as the general population. But in one of life's great ironies, it seems that Christians are the ones who most often (and most loudly) tout the importance and centrality of marriage, not only for the Christian community but also for the sake of the world. A flourishing society hinges on the presence and cultivation of strong marriages, or at least that's how the story goes.

In fact, for many Christians, "family values" (which are believed to be perfectly embodied by a married couple with children—a "nuclear family") are the fundamental moral grounding for society at large. In America, Christian leaders, politicians, and even legal experts point to marriage as if it were the foundation on which the whole of Western civilization is built and sustained.[5] It is of course impossible to separate this notion from other nationalistic ideologies, but the message remains clear. When marriage is not the fulcrum for common life, things get very bad very quickly.

And yet, from a purely statistical standpoint, it would seem that the very people who claim that this "institution" is the lifeblood of a healthy and thriving society are no more or less committed to marriage than anyone else. This is not to say that the church's imperfect track record completely undermines its claim that marriage can be a societal good. Rather, it is to say that the Christian community's fairly radical inconsistency on this matter (some might even call it hypocrisy) reveals a lack of either commitment or understanding (or both) on its part. But why is this the case, especially when marriage is purported to be so vital to our collective well-being? Let me offer a few possibilities that we will explore in greater detail throughout the book.

The Christian community doesn't take marriage seriously enough. If marriage really is that important (and I think it is), then we should be a community that refuses to conceive of marriage as simply an outlet for sexual desire or a solution to loneliness or a requirement for people to be included as fully functioning members of the community. Marriage is far too significant to be reduced to a panacea for the anxieties of modern life.

When we approach marriage as if it were simply the default for everyone, we actually diminish the significance of this relationship and risk sweeping the profound tragedy of broken marriages under the rug. It's almost as if marriage were a relationship that people can try on for size. If it doesn't work, it's not much of a problem. The parties involved probably just didn't choose the right person. They'll have better luck next time. Rarely is a thought ever given to the possibility that perhaps some people shouldn't be getting married to anyone—even if they are lonely or burning with desire or want a baby.

The sometimes thoughtless and often flippant ways Christians enter marriage suggest that at best we lack a critical self-awareness and at worst we are guilty of covering up a deep and abiding hypocrisy. Before we can claim any sort of moral high ground or presume to speak as a credible voice on the importance of this "institution" for society, we have to pause for a moment and ask ourselves a much more difficult question. Do we really value marriage, or do we simply lack the courage to imagine new possibilities for human life?

Consider the numbers again for a moment. We know from the raw data that nearly half of all marriages will not last. From this view the suggestion that marriage should not function normatively for the Christian is really not a scandalous claim at all. It is already the case that a sizeable number of those who have experienced wedded bliss have decided at some point that it was not for them. They either chose to be single again or, depending on the (often tragic) circumstances, had the decision made for them.

It's as if the institution itself is crying out for reassessment. Like wisdom personified in Proverbs, marriage calls to us from every street corner: "Hey now—wait a minute! You all can't just do this willy-nilly!" The tragedy is that we are refusing to listen. Only a small fraction of marriages are truly flourishing, and an even smaller percentage actually stand the test of time. Knowing this reality, why then do we treat marriage as if it were everyone's destiny?

The Christian community doesn't take singleness seriously enough. Let's do some more number crunching. There are presently about 240 million Americans over the age of eighteen. Of those, only about half are married (120 million or so). If the statistics play out, nearly half of those marriages will end in divorce (divorce rates for subsequent marriages are higher, so this figure is an average of all marriages). That leaves us with only 60 million people in America who will stay married—one-quarter of the adult population.

So even though a majority of men and women still say they would like to be married at some point, the marriage relationship itself seems to be sustainable only by a minority of people. In other words, the claim that marriage should not be normative is simply a better way to describe reality.

The good news is that divorce rates are actually trending downward in the United States. But the primary reason is not that spouses have suddenly decided to be more fiercely committed to one another. Rather, it is because fewer people are choosing to get married in the first place. This trend shouldn't be surprising to us, but it is. Divorce rates drop when fewer people assume marriage is simply what "everyone does" and, at the same time, there is a viable option for living a full and flourishing life as a single person.

The faith community doesn't take this possibility of lifetime singleness seriously enough, in large part because it operates with a vision that assumes every individual is designed for marriage. It's the default position. We say we want to do something about rampant divorce within our churches and within society at large, but little thought is given to one of the best ways of generating a greater number of strong and healthy marriages: encouraging single people to stay single.

If nearly seventy-five percent of adults are single or are soon-to-be single again, the Christian community has an obligation to support singles *as intrinsically valuable members of the body of Christ* and foster an environment where one's ministry and vocation is not shackled by external expectations that are both unrealistic and, dare I say it, "unbiblical."

The Christian community doesn't take the Bible seriously enough. I put "unbiblical" in quotes above because I am almost always wary of arguments that claim to be "biblical" or accuse someone else of being "unbiblical." It isn't that I am unconcerned with what the Bible says. My concern has to do more with the lack of recognition (especially among many of my fellow evangelicals) that we are always already in the process of interpreting how the Bible relates to our present circumstances. This process evolves in the context of community and with the guidance and direction of the Holy Spirit, which means that being "biblical" is not a matter of simply lining up biblical data to support or discredit a previously held notion. Rather, it means that the Bible interprets us. It challenges our core assumptions and reveals our blind spots. Being biblical means entering into an ongoing conversation with the larger narrative scope of Scripture and the larger historical tradition of interpretation to which we are indebted.

When it comes to the question of the Bible and marriage, it is not uncommon to hear people (and those people's political representatives) talk about the "biblical" definition of marriage or the "biblical" notion of the nuclear family or the need to be "biblically" faithful while advocating for or against marriage reform. We don't need to rehearse the content of these arguments here. I only bring them up as a way of exemplifying the strong currents of "biblical" marriage that I am swimming against.

In contrast to what is often said about the Bible's "view" of marriage, I want us to reconsider what the Bible actually says about marriage and singleness. In fact, so committed am I to the biblical text that we will spend two entire chapters on this topic alone. I am an unabashed evangelical, which means that, along with all those who also lay claim to this label, the Bible really does matter to me.

However, I say "in contrast to" because it strikes me that in many instances the "biblical" notions of marriage that are bandied about in the public sphere are not so much the result of faithful engagements with the historic community of interpretation as they are religious window dressing for a political agenda. The pictures that hold us captive both shape and set the boundaries for any interpretation, and at present, the primary image holding us captive is drawn not from the biblical witness but from a larger web of cultural, commercial, and political stories.

This is of course not always the case, and there are numerous faithful and well-meaning Christian interpreters of the biblical text who will still disagree with my particular understanding of marriage and singleness. Again, I am offering here one possible option for consideration. However, as will become clear, my primary argument is that our picture of marriage as the sole avenue for the flourishing of the human-being-in-relationship and the Christian disciple is not, in the end, "biblical." What I mean is that such a view (1) uncritically favors certain texts, (2) reflects a number of cultural assumptions about the human being that are not present in the text itself, and in some cases (3) simply disregards or dismisses passages that clearly articulate a position to the contrary.

When all is said and done, whether or not we change each other's minds or simply agree to disagree, of one thing I am sure. As people who are outspoken in our commitment to biblical authority, we need to take the biblical witness more seriously and not less. When it offers a picture that radically or even slightly challenges our convictions, we need to develop the eyes to see and the ears to hear its rebuke. We also need the courage to respond accordingly. And that is one of the goals of this book.

WHAT THIS BOOK IS REALLY ABOUT

At the end of the day, this book isn't simply about marriage or singleness. It's really about my daughters. Actually, it may be for their children. Truth be told, most of us adults are hopelessly lost. I am not sure we can habituate ourselves quickly enough to shift the tide in any meaningful way in my lifetime.

But I am hopeful that we can begin cultivating a different space for my three girls—one that affirms them in all their breathtaking beauty whether they ever meet the "person of their dreams" or not. In fact, if I am being truly honest, my hope is that the Christian community might become a space not where their dreams about marriage come true, but where their dreams about the people of God are enlarged. I hope they grow up in a community where their imaginations are reshaped on a fundamental level, not around a potential spouse, but around the One whose bride is the church. And in the final analysis, that is what this book is about.

PART ONE

THE CHURCH
AND CULTURE
AS EASY
BEDFELLOWS

SITTING AT THE GROWNUPS' TABLE

By Jennifer Graffius

It came in the mail at my parents' house. A big fancy envelope addressed to "The Graffius Family." It could only be one thing—a wedding invitation. My parents had been cordially invited to my cousin's upcoming nuptials. And sure enough, I was their "plus-one."

As I thumbed through the rest of the mail, I found a second festive invitation. It was addressed to my younger sister and her husband, two people who just so happened to be living in my parents' guest house at the time.

If the first envelope was frustrating, then the second was infuriating. The message was loud and clear: I am not a real adult, and I won't be until I get married. Because as we all know, it is not until a woman is married that she is deserving of her own invitation to a family wedding. Forget about the fact that she no longer lives with her parents and that she may very well want to invite a plus-one of her own to the blessed event. It doesn't matter. When it comes to weddings, the "unmarrieds" can only be put in one of two places: the kids' table or the old maids' table.

Why is marriage the mark of a fully formed adult? I have been asking myself this question for a while. Is there not a better set of criteria by which we can evaluate one's maturity and success? I mean, anybody can get married, and yet somehow marriage is seen as the gateway to real adulthood. It doesn't even really matter if one's marriage is healthy or not. To be a true grownup, all that matters is that it exists. When did marriage become the achievement of all achievements?

I never saw myself as the person who would be asking these questions in my thirties. I'm one of those overachiever types. I was always a little "mature" for my age. I tried to do everything right. I worked hard in school and got good grades. I went to church and was the gold-star youth group kid. I never thought I'd be wondering whether I counted as a legitimate adult.

But here I am—a woman in my late thirties who holds a master's degree from a prestigious institution and is working on a doctoral degree at yet another prestigious university. I have a great job. I have been a professor for several years. And I have traveled the world. What's more, I have amazing friends and even a dating life! All of these things add up to a pretty vibrant and fulfilling life. And yet I continue to encounter a world—both inside the walls of the church and outside them—that tells me I just haven't made it yet. In my current state, I am incomplete. Maybe I will understand what I'm missing when I am married . . . *if* I am married. Sigh.

None of this is meant to suggest that I don't really care about being single. I do care. I care a lot. It hurts at a depth that I can't easily articulate. And it hurts because underneath it all is a subliminal message that says there's got to be something wrong with me: "You're not only single, you're broken." But surely I'm not any more broken or incomplete than anyone else simply because of my marital status. Is it possible that I could be single, in my thirties, and healthy? Might there be a way for me not only to flourish, but also to contribute something substantive to society even though I haven't walked down the aisle?

I certainly hope so, but then again, I'm still waiting for the arrival of my invitation to sit at the grownups' table.

1

DISNEY PRINCESSES,
TAYLOR SWIFT, AND
THE BACHELOR

POP CULTURE AS PREMARITAL COUNSELOR
AND SEX THERAPIST

BEFORE ANYTHING ELSE, this book is a work of theology and cultural criticism. It is not a how-to book. Anyone hoping to find the keys to a successful marriage in these pages might as well call it a day right now. While it's true that my wife and I have been together for nearly twenty years, I am by no means a marriage expert, nor am I in a position to offer anyone relationship counseling. There are far better resources out there for that.[1] It's not that having a happy and healthy marriage is unimportant. It most certainly is. But my primary concern here is ecclesial rather than conjugal. I want us to take a long and hard look at the church. More specifically, I want us to ask some potentially unsettling questions about the normative picture of marriage that presently orients the common life and practice of the people of God.

Before we can even hope to identify, much less undo, the norms that orient and organize the community of faith, we first must be able to describe and assess with some measure of accuracy the broader cultural circumstances in which we find ourselves—that is, our "cultural moment." As Jonathan Grant rightly suggests in his book *Divine Sex*: "The question we must first address is contextual. . . . We need to know where we stand before we can plan our journey toward the place we want to be."[2] In other words, in order to critically engage the view of marriage that has captured the church's imagination, we first need to develop a more robust theological understanding of culture.

I have chosen as our starting point a series of contemporary cultural artifacts. We will focus on the princess films produced by Disney Animation Studios, the music of Taylor Swift, and the television programs *The Bachelor* and *The Bachelorette*. This is by no means a comprehensive or exhaustive list, nor is it intended to be. Each of these pieces of media will serve as a representative type that is directed toward one of three key demographics (children, young adults, or adults). As we consider each type, we will be operating with the assumption that these pop-cultural products both embody and represent the deep-seated desires, longings, and values of contemporary persons. As such, they serve as mirrors of who we are and models for who we might become, both reflecting and giving shape to our collective imagination regarding what it means to be married, single, and sexual.

In theological terms, I am primarily interested in discovering how the Spirit of God is present and active in the contemporary world. This is not my way of suggesting that every cultural product is good or true or beautiful. Nor is it to say that every piece of culture is worthy of our time and attention. But it does mean that, rather than simply critiquing culture according to some abstract notion of Christian truth, we would do well to consider whether certain cultural products and projects might have the potential for serving as manifestations of God's ongoing work in the world.

Our objective is not so much to pass judgment on these individual cultural forms, but rather to discern the broader cultural impulses embedded in them, considering how they might be helping people make sense of their life and the world. Of course, as I hope to make clear both here and in the next chapter, popular culture presents a rather problematic vision of marriage, singleness, and sexuality for the Christian. But it isn't *The Bachelorette*'s somewhat distorted vision of romantic love that should be worrisome. What should trouble us is that the church's vision looks nearly identical to the one we find on a reality TV show. In fact, these cultural artifacts are in some ways the products of the Christian imagination itself. So the real force of my critique is not directed toward any one pop-cultural form, as if movies and TV were solely responsible for society's (or the church's) many ills. Rather, I am far more concerned with the Christian community's tendency to uncritically embrace (and thus unwittingly produce) certain visions of human flourishing that are at best misleading and at worst destructive.

SOMEDAY MY PRINCE WILL COME

One such vision might strike many as innocent enough, and it can be summed up by the lyrics of a well-known song: "Someday My Prince Will Come." The movie that features this song is *Snow White and the Seven Dwarfs*, which was Walt Disney's first foray into feature-length filmmaking. Most readers will be familiar with this song (and could probably hum the tune if pressed) because of *Snow White*'s immense popularity. This is the film that made it possible for the Walt Disney Company to emerge as one of the most significant cultural forces of the past century, both in the United States and globally.

Far more than a movie studio, the Walt Disney Company is one of the most profitable and pervasive multinational media conglomerates in the world. In addition to its films and related theme parks, media, and merchandise, it owns ABC broadcast television and numerous other networks such as ESPN and ABC Family (formerly Pat Robertson's Christian Broadcasting Network).

Yet Disney's cultural influence (as well as its ongoing profitability and viability as a corporation) is due to more than simply its large share of the modern media landscape. It has far more to do with the power of its stories. Standing at the heart of the entire Disney enterprise is the construction and dissemination of world-shaping narratives—the mythic resources from which contemporary persons draw in order to form a coherent whole out of the disparate elements of their lives. To catch a glimpse of this world-making power in action, all we have to do is take a stroll through the hallowed halls of Disney's pantheon of princesses.

The classics. Snow White is the paradigmatic Disney princess, in part because she was the first, but also because every princess who has followed in her wake is in some way grappling with both Snow White as a character and the mythological setting of her story. Which is why it's all the more interesting that her particular story turns not so much on the question of romantic love, but on the question of youthful beauty. Snow White's prince does indeed come to the rescue in the end, so he certainly has a part to play in the progression of the plot. But the reason her life is in peril in the first place and the reason the prince has any desire to rescue her at all is because the magic mirror woke up one day and decided to deem Snow White "the fairest of them all." Unsurprisingly, the princess herself has no say in the matter. Why would she? As everyone knows, decisions about who is the most beautiful in all the land are best left to talking pieces of reflective glass (or *People* magazine). Nevertheless, it is Snow White's physical attractiveness that not only makes her worthy of the prince's affections but, perhaps more importantly, establishes the young princess as her stepmother's mortal enemy.

Snow White and her evil stepmother are thereby thrust into an epic battle for something that neither of them can actually possess, much less maintain: eternal youth. Interestingly, of all the princesses in Disney's pantheon, Snow White's age is the most ambiguous. Both the pitch of her voice and the shape of her figure suggest that she is quite young. But the content of her speech (in the form of both lyrics and dialogue), along with the fact that the prince takes her immediately to his castle in the end, would lead us to believe that she is perhaps older than she appears at first blush. Yet regardless of her actual age or the age of her stepmother (who also appears quite young when she is not assuming the form of an old hag), the narrative pits these two women against one another in terms of this rather vague notion of nubile beauty. In this way, "beauty" isn't something that one simply prizes or even possesses, but it functions as a kind of sacred object with near-magical powers. We are never told exactly why the wicked queen is so desperate to maintain her status as "the fairest of them all," but her unrelenting pursuit of this prized possession is what serves as the central tension driving the entire plot of the story.

Because these two women (or rather this woman and this girl) are caught in a kind of mythic struggle for the title of "most beautiful," the only one who can save them from themselves is of course the prince. "True love's kiss" is all that is required, and we can be sure that this (nameless) prince truly loves Snow White because, well, just look at her. She's not simply pretty—she's the fairest of them all! It doesn't matter that the prince isn't otherwise involved in the narrative. It is simply self-evident that the kind of beauty embodied by Snow White will always evoke a love that is deep, mature, and genuine. So it makes perfect sense that it's only by means of the prince's erotic and truth-filled touch that Snow White rouses from her apple-induced slumber (note the allusion to the primeval Garden). And once she does, the smitten pair are finally able to enter into the great beyond—that timeless realm more commonly known as Happily Ever After.

Interestingly, the story of *Snow White* comes to a close without making it entirely clear whether "happily ever after" involves a wedding or not, although it is certainly implied. The same cannot be said of *Cinderella* and *Sleeping Beauty*, films in which marriage is an essential element of their fairy tale endings. Like Snow White, Cinderella suffers at the hands of a jealous stepmother, but she must also endure the machinations of two stepsisters whose lack of external beauty is meant to reflect the ugliness that resides within the core of their being. Cinderella, who we soon discover is truly beautiful both inside and out, dreams of one day being free from her tormentors. But she is utterly helpless on her own to do anything about her grave circumstances. She has no other choice but to wait for the day when she will be rescued.

In the meantime, she bides her time with equal parts housecleaning, daydreaming, and pining. Oh, and making clothes for mice.

In contrast to Cinderella, Prince Charming is the sole author of his fate. Although the king just wants his son to marry someone (anyone!), the prince is determined to find the love of his life. And while he and Cinderella are together for no longer than the length of a single dance, that is all the time he needs to know that they were meant to spend the rest of their lives in each other's embrace. "So this is love," Cinderella sings on the morning after. Here are two souls, each destined for the other, falling hopelessly in love at first sight. Motivated by this revelation, Cinderella waits expectantly for her prince to rescue her, and he doesn't disappoint. After the prince fits Cinderella with the glass slipper that she lost on her way out of the ball, they marry immediately. And just like Snow White and her prince, they go on to live happily ever after. Fade to black.

Sleeping Beauty follows this same narrative pattern, but with one slight difference. Rather than the story ending with a wedding, Princess Aurora and Prince Phillip are betrothed at the very beginning. In other words, these two aren't destined to be together at some point in the distant future. They already are. They just don't know it. And lest we become too worried about whether an arranged marriage of this sort could ever involve real, true, genuine love (that is, romantic love), Aurora and Phillip are separated at birth, only to stumble upon each other as teenagers. Luckily, they fall in love without either of them knowing the other's true identity (phew!). Yet much like Snow White before her, Aurora is put into a magical slumber. The sleeping beauty now must wait—passively, silently, and unconsciously—for true love's kiss. Thankfully, Prince Phillip is willing to pursue the object of his affection to the ends of the earth. Driven by nothing more than the power of his love and armed only with the "sword of truth" and the "shield of virtue," he slays the wicked fairy Maleficent, who summons "all the powers of hell" in her defense. In doing so, Prince Phillip breaks the curse that had been cast on both his princess and the entire kingdom.

The renaissance. Taken together, the three films from the classic era of Disney's myth-making project serve as the archetype for all those that would follow, even (and perhaps especially) when subsequent princesses call this paradigm into question. In the late '80s and early '90s, Disney animation experienced a time of creative rebirth when it released *The Little Mermaid* (1989), *Beauty and the Beast* (1991), and *Aladdin* (1992) in the span of a few short years. Each film was a huge success in its own right, both economically and in terms of critical acclaim. More importantly though, each film also featured princes and princesses that directly challenged the prevailing societal norms regarding marriage and romantic love.

It isn't that Ariel, Belle, and Jasmine have no romantic inclinations or that they don't want to get married—quite the opposite. In fact, they may be even more driven by the ideals of marriage and romantic love than their predecessors. It's just that they cannot abide the notion that anyone or anything would determine for them who is or is not the appropriate object of their passionate longings. To marry for any reason other than romantic love is a near absurdity for these princesses, so much so that they are willing to risk being ostracized or even excommunicated from their tribe of origin if that is what their love demands.

As a consequence, rather than evil stepmothers, the primary antagonists for these young women turn out to be their own fathers, men who undoubtedly love their children but nevertheless expect their daughters to conform to their (outdated/patriarchal/oppressive) vision of what it means to be a princess and, by extension, who it is they ought to marry. In certain respects, then, their desire to find their one true love expresses an even deeper yearning for independence and self-determining agency. Or in the words of Ariel:

Betcha' on land, they'd understand.
Bet they don't reprimand their daughters
Bright young women, sick of swimming
Ready to stand.[3]

As bright young women who are ready to stand on their own, Ariel and Belle dare to cross the societal boundaries that discourage humans from loving nonhumans and vice versa. For her part, Jasmine chooses to disregard class distinctions (and her father's directives) altogether in order to "follow her heart." In other words, in contrast to the passive, silent, and frequently unconscious characters that preceded them, these modern princesses are nonconformists to their core. They are as independent, intelligent, and strong as they are beautiful. And this represents a decisive shift in Disney's films that we can affirm and even celebrate. As Belle's story makes clear, the broader community still sees their refusal to conform to traditional gender roles as "strange—no question." Nevertheless, Ariel, Belle, and Jasmine all remain steadfast in their rejection of the status quo and the rigid expectations that have been foisted on them both by their fathers and by society as a whole.

Each of these characters indeed exposes and challenges many stereotypes that have long been associated with the paradigmatic princess. Significantly, though, not a single one of their stories finds resolution or completion until the moment when the lovelorn princess is finally joined with her unlikely soulmate, a union that most often culminates in marital bliss. They are not fully themselves—not whole—until they discover and marry their prince (or their prince discovers and marries them). So Jasmine chooses Aladdin, the former "street rat" who, now by association, gets to become a real prince. And Belle's love for the Beast changes her prince back into human form and so paves the way for Belle to become a princess herself.

Indeed, Belle's story is somewhat exceptional in this regard, for it begins with her clearly yearning for a more intellectually stimulating context, but it ends with nothing of the sort. While she is identified as being a bit of a book worm at the beginning of the film, the book that Belle is in fact reading is a *fairy tale*:

Here's where she meets Prince Charming
But she won't discover that it's him till chapter three.

So even though Belle claims to want intellectual stimulation and to experience "adventure in the great wide somewhere," her character arc would suggest that her deeper desires have already been shaped by the stories in which she is immersed—stories that look suspiciously like those of the classic Disney princess.[4]

Ariel's story is perhaps even more troubling. For Ariel, becoming a whole human being through marriage is more than merely symbolic. It is quite literal. In fact, up until the moment when her romantic love is enacted, she is not even subhuman. She isn't a human being at all. In the end, she must literally cast off her identity as a mermaid if she wants to be "part of your world."[5] For Ariel, the decision to marry does not simply bring about a change in her relational status. Rather, it effects a fundamental transformation of who she is. As she marries Prince Eric, she becomes—for the first time—a human being. And we recognize the ending of this story as "happy" because it brings about the exact scenario that Ariel has desired all along. Rather than enduring another day as a radically incomplete half-human, she is now fully human—thanks in no small part to the power of romantic love. And rather than be subject to the dictates of a tone-deaf father, her story concludes just as we always knew it would—in wedded bliss with the one she loves.

The revival. If classic Disney films understand romantic love to be a kind of destiny or fate that can only be realized in marriage, and the films of the early 1990s picture romantic love as one's inalienable right, then the new wave of princess movies could be said to conceive of romantic love as a reflection of a deeper and indeed far more significant source of fullness: familial love.

As contemporary retellings of well-known fairy tales, *The Princess and the Frog* (2009), *Tangled* (2010), and *Frozen* (2013) depend on the tropes of classic princess narratives while also reimagining them. As such, they serve as not-so-thinly veiled critiques rather than full-blown subversions of the princess paradigm. Interestingly, instead of evil stepmothers or overbearing fathers, these films feature heroines whose parents are either dead or entirely cut off from their daughters. As a result, rather than pursuing romantic love and marriage as a way of expressing their personal autonomy and freedom from cultural norms, the primary motivation for this group of princesses is their desire to reclaim the wholeness that they once knew but now can only intuit— a longing rooted in the absence of a family.

As their stories unfold, these objectively beautiful (and once again ambiguously youthful) women attract the attention of a number of would-be suitors. The implication of course is that they could not do otherwise. But the romances that eventually develop are more happy accidents than integral elements of the plot or their character arcs. These princesses never really imagine that any man (prince or otherwise) could ever completely satisfy their deep ache for wholeness. In fact, the very notion of "love and marriage at first sight" is explicitly parodied in these movies. One can even detect a faint hint of cynicism regarding the possibility of romantic love.

For instance, instead of breaking an evil spell, Tiana herself is turned into a frog when she kisses her frog prince. Likewise, Rapunzel agrees to collaborate with Flynn (a.k.a. Eugene) not because she is attracted to him (at least not at first) but because it is a pragmatically expedient way for her to see the mysterious floating lanterns that have long captivated her imagination. And Princess Anna, sister to Queen Elsa, not only declares her love for Prince Hans within moments of their meeting, but also agrees to marry him. With a wink and a nod to the long history of "love at first sight" fairytales, Prince Hans and Princess Anna cannot help but break into song ("Love Is an Open Door"), making clear both to themselves and to the audience that

> Our mental synchronization
> Can have but one explanation
> You and I were just meant to be.[6]

That Anna discovers shortly thereafter her fiancé's plan to seize control of her kingdom only underscores the absurdity of their premature declaration of love—something Kristoff is quick to ridicule as well.

It's important to note that Anna's story is technically the "b-plot" in *Frozen*. Elsa's transformation, which has nothing to do with romantic love, is the primary focus of the narrative. It's a redemptive journey in which fear and isolation give way to a deep sense of integration and belonging. Still, given the amount of screen time dedicated to Anna and her misguided romantic impulses, it is difficult to say that the movie is "about" one or the other sister. In actual fact, it's about both Elsa and Anna. So it is significant that, just like Tiana and Rapunzel before her, the initial spark of romantic love (or passionate lust) that Anna experiences turns out to be both distorted and deceptive. Rather than orienting and energizing her quest, it functions as a character flaw that is fundamentally misleading and not to be trusted. Rather than her ultimate destiny (as with Cinderella) or the object of her desire (as with Ariel), Anna's romanticized longing to marry a charming young prince is the very hurdle that she must overcome.

None of these contemporary princess stories elevates marriage or romantic love to the level of a pristine ideal, which is why it is all the more significant that they still end in marriage, or at least the promise of marriage. Tiana marries her prince in the narrative itself (and thus becomes a princess), but in *Tangled*, we are told through Flynn's voice-over narration that the wedding is taking place sometime after the story proper, in the "happily ever after" to come. And even though it seems that princess Anna would have learned her lesson about following her heart's desire too quickly, she and Kristoff formally announce their romantic relationship at the end of the film with a passionate kiss . . . only days after meeting Kristoff and agreeing to marry another man. Just as Kristoff's family of trolls assumed when they first met Anna, the narrative leads the audience to believe that marital bliss awaits the two lovers at some point in the immediate future. So while these films begin with a profound yearning that is born from the absence of family, they end, once again, with professions of romantic love and pronouncements of "husband and wife."

The franchise. Along with Anna, Elsa, Rapunzel, and Tiana, all the Disney princesses now reside in a mythical land known as Happily Ever After. Significantly, in this place of eternal wholeness, every single one of them is married. We know this because Disney's narrative work does not end with its films. It continues on unabated by way of a massive integrated marketing campaign known as the Disney Princess media franchise. To understand the way this franchise both reflects and shapes the broader culture, it is of course important to consider the individual movies in their own rights, just as we have done. But we cannot overlook the commercial strategies of Disney's myth-making project. The Princess franchise represents Disney's most coherent and consistent vision of romantic love, marriage, and human flourishing. Because it draws on the entire catalog of Princess films at once, this transmedia franchise also embodies one of Disney's most powerful narratives, especially when we consider the fact that its primary con-stituency is children.

One notable outlier in the princess pantheon is Merida, the central character from Pixar's *Brave* (2012). The tumultuous story of her induction into the royal court offers a helpful illustration of the Disney metanarrative—one that not only frames but also reshapes how we ultimately understand the individual stories we encounter in each of the films. Besides being the only princess from a Pixar film, Merida is also the only one who does not have a love interest, which really shouldn't be all that surprising. After all, her entire character was meant to break the mold of the prototypical Disney princess. Yet, as part of her official "coronation party," Merida got a makeover. In the artwork that the Disney Consumer Products division used on its official website and merchandising, the color of her fiery red hair was muted and its wild curls were straightened. Her freckles were removed, her dress was cut much lower, and her waist shrunk a few inches. Her breasts even grew by a couple sizes. It seemed that someone at Disney believed this "mold breaker" needed to be remolded.

When both John Lasseter (chief creative officer at Disney Animation) and fans of the film rightly called foul, Disney recanted and removed the made-over version of Merida. But the overarching message had already come through loud and clear.[7] Apparently, to fit in as one of Disney's princesses, this young woman needed a little more sex appeal. How else would she ever find a prince, much less fulfillment or satisfaction in her new life in the land of Happily Ever After?

Merida's coronation story is in many ways emblematic of the pop-cultural ambivalence regarding singleness, sexuality, and marriage. For example, on the one hand, the successful rebirth of Disney animation in the early '90s and its revival in the early twenty-first century hinged in part on a direct critique of the classic princess narratives. In addition to Merida, all Disney's modern princesses are, in their own ways, mold breakers. Rather than passively waiting for their prince to come, they are strong and independent, unrestrained by societal expectations. Not only are their relationships with other women often brought to the foreground, but they are also frequently placed in the position of the ones who are actively pursuing the desires of their hearts. Their stories reveal and critique how the maintenance of marriage norms most often serves the interests of powerful men who care very little about things like "romance" or "love."

Yet, on the other hand, none of these films ever fully subverts the conventions of the genre. And even when they come close to doing so, the larger narrative work of the Disney Princess franchise tends to reinterpret them along the lines of the status quo. So while we may never know if Happily Ever After is really a heavenly hereafter or more like a perpetual purgatory, what we do know is that, when taken as a whole, the princess myth that Disney has constructed envisions the individual as free and autonomous, but also wholly incomplete in the absence of their one true love. It's a bit of a mixed message.

In addition, while the women in these films are no longer silent and passive, the men are still expected to actively pursue their romantic impulses, even if at first they don't succeed. In this way, both the princess herself and the love she represents become objects. This objectification is demonstrated perhaps nowhere more clearly than in the various ways these stories idealize youth and sexualize young women. Whether it's Snow White's fairness, Ariel's voice, or Rapunzel's hair, a princess's youth, beauty, and sexuality function as sacred objects—literal talismans that convey power to the one who possesses them.

So if these young single women are not quite fully human until they are wed to their soulmate, and the primary means by which they are able to find and secure their partner is rooted in the expression of their sexuality, then it makes perfect sense why the mythic world of Disney films envisions marriage as the culmination of a life quest rather than the start of a shared journey. It is not simply "The End" of this particular story. It is "the end" in a far more ultimate sense. Marriage can only ever truly exist in the timeless realm of Happily Ever After because it represents the *telos* (that's a theological term for the ultimate purpose or end) toward which the whole of the created order is moving, including our individual lives. This Disney-fied take on marriage, singleness, and sexuality has come to define reality for many if not most of us, especially for those living in North America at the turn of the twenty-first century. Or to put it somewhat differently, all of us are, in one way or another, waiting for that fateful day when our prince too will come.

LOVE STORIES AND BLANK SPACES

To be fair, it's not all Disney's fault. It's true that their films offer a concrete distillation of the contemporary cultural imagination, and there is little question about how widespread they have become. In this respect, Disney's animated films—both the classics and their modern equivalents—function as a shared narrative for a society that has all but lost any sense of a common story. But it's difficult to say whether Disney's films are responsible for creating the vision of marriage and singleness that has come to define the contemporary cultural outlook or whether they are simply reflecting what is already in the water. They are very likely doing both.

Despite Disney's cultural prominence, their movies make up only one piece of the cultural puzzle we are putting together. An equally significant piece is popular music, a deeply formative and increasingly pervasive form of mediated culture. In fact, given the proliferation of digital technologies that grant users access to a nearly unlimited supply of music at every moment of every day, commercial pop music has become one of the most influential forms of life in the modern world. It is at once an art form, a commodity, a marketing tool, and a way of life. And it is especially significant for youth and emerging adults. In fact, historically speaking, pop music has both given shape to and been shaped by the emergence and growth of youth culture in the United States—from the Beatles to the Backstreet Boys to Beyoncé. For this reason, many of the songs produced by pop artists over the years have been concerned with youthful expressions of romantic love (or angst regarding one's lack or loss of romantic options).

I could make the same point with just about any pop artist or pop song, but I have chosen the music of Taylor Swift because it serves as one of the more prominent examples of our contemporary moment. Over the course of her professional career, Swift has piled up numerous critical accolades, including multiple Grammys (in 2016 she became the first woman ever to be awarded Album of the Year twice). Her songs are incredibly popular, routinely finding their way onto the Billboard Top 100 list. Here we will only have time to consider her seven number-one songs. Part of her popularity, especially among younger listeners, has to do with the relationship she has built with her fan base. Swift frequently interacts with fans on social media as if each one of her millions of followers ("Swifties") were actually her BFF.

Swift's songwriting is pretty good too. Ryan Adams, an acclaimed musician in his own right, recorded an entire cover album of Swift's *1989* (released in 2014). It is hard to imagine a greater compliment for a young singer-songwriter. As one of the *New Yorker*'s music critics noted, Adams "took songs that, due to their popularity, belong to the world, and made them his own."[8] The capacity to make mass-marketed songs "our own" is part of the reason why pop music functions so significantly in our lives (not to mention why we can't seem to get some tunes out of our head!). We incorporate these songs into our bodily know-how as they shape not only how we see and understand the world but also our very being in the world. And as demonstrated by Ryan Adams's cover album, Swift's music has also demonstrated its ability to connect with a much broader demographic than was perhaps originally intended.

But even though Baby Boomers are now able to tap their feet and bob their heads to her music, Taylor Swift is a particularly significant artist for young and emerging adults. Swift released her first album at the age of sixteen, received a lifetime achievement award at twenty-three, and received the Album of the Year Grammy at the ripe old age of twenty-six. In other words, as both a musician and a public figure, she has quite literally grown up along with her listeners, and they too have moved from adolescence to adulthood (or extended adolescence) while listening to her music.

Swift's music is helpful for our purposes in part because of its cultural reach, but also because it serves as a bridge between those who primarily consume Disney princess movies (children) and those who primarily consume *The Bachelor* and *The Bachelorette* (adults). Her music charts the process by which our collective consciousness concerning singleness, sexuality, and marriage has come of age.

Take, for example, her first number-one hit, "Love Story." If we ever needed to make a case for how the princess paradigm has set up shop within the contemporary cultural imagination, this song would be Exhibit A:

> Romeo take me somewhere we can be alone
> I'll be waiting, all there's left to do is run
> You'll be the prince and I'll be the princess
> It's a love story, baby just say yes.[9]

It isn't difficult to imagine Ariel, Belle, or Jasmine singing a word-for-word rendition of this song. In fact, it's a little too on the nose—

derivative even. Besides explicitly referencing princes and princesses, the lyrics are written from the perspective of a young woman whose freedom from her authoritarian father depends exclusively on the arrival of a prince. The expression of their love for one another will do more than simply solve the problem of their loneliness—it will save them. And of course, throughout the entire course of the song, it is simply assumed that this love story, if it truly is a love story, can have one and only one outcome: marriage. Sound familiar?

Swift released this song on her first album, which means that it debuted when she was only sixteen years old. Given her age, it makes sense that the music she was writing at the time would reflect a vision of singleness and romantic love that is strikingly similar to the one depicted by Disney's slate of princess films. But the point is not simply that a young woman wrote a hit song based on a romanticized notion of love. What is far more significant is that even as her music has matured (and as she too has matured), it has remained fully committed to the underlying assumptions of the classic princess paradigm. Much like Swift's earlier work, her more recent music describes a world in which romantic love is fulfilling in an ultimate sense and indeed is a requirement for human flourishing. The only difference is that whereas the "love stories" she once sang about ended with a fairytale wedding between a prince and a princess, they now become an endless string of sexual relationships. If the development of Swift's music is any indication, then the princess has become a serial monogamist.

The beginning of this shift is seen in her 2012 number-one single, "We Are Never Ever Getting Back Together."[10] Right there in the title is a young woman's declaration that, no matter how passionate they once might have been, certain relationships simply cannot be reconciled. Yet Swift's concern with sexually intimate relationships that inevitably end in irreconcilable differences did not reach its full expression until the release of *1989*, an album featuring no less than five number-one singles. Much like "Getting Back Together," the chart-topping songs from *1989* simply assume that passionate, romantic love is a self-justifying good. Indeed, the psycho-sensual force of one's initial infatuation with another person is seen as sufficient to energize and sustain every other aspect of the relationship.

As Swift suggests in her song "Style," each of us is driven by a seemingly unquenchable desire for that special guy or gal to "take me home, just take me home." And even though this impulse to ravish and be ravished by the object of our affection almost always comes "crashing down" on us, we "come back every time" to pursue these sexually intimate relationships because they constitute the source of all our passionate longings. Indeed, they "never go out of style."[11] And if that original spark of passion does in fact fizzle out, it signals not a new stage in the development of a relationship, but its dissolution. In other words, in the absence of an all-consuming, erotic love, no human relationship is ultimately viable—it is simply a dead end. Naturally, for the sake of our own well-being, we must name and discard these unproductive relationships so that we might find one with real sustaining power.

There's more to the story, though. In the terms established by these songs, every person is indeed driven by an insatiable need for human intimacy and sexual expression. While women certainly feel the effects of these basic urges, men are especially susceptible (and so particularly culpable). But we are no longer so naive as to believe that there is such a thing as "happily ever after." Or as Swift puts it in "Wildest Dreams," "nothing lasts forever." Still, because we never stop being red-blooded mammals, it's impossible to ignore the fact that

He's so tall and handsome as hell;
He's so bad but he does it so well.

In other words, succumbing to our carnal desires is a foregone conclusion. It's almost as if we cannot help ourselves. We have no other choice but to get "tangled up with [each other] all night," even though we both know that the relationship itself is going to end badly and will soon exist only in our memories—in our "wildest dreams."[12]

According to Swift, though, our memories are rarely generous, much less dreamy. It is far more likely that, given the depth of intimacy that our relationships demand, their unraveling is going to produce a significant amount of "bad blood." Even though we may have once described a particularly meaningful relationship as a kind of "mad love,"

> Now we got problems,
> and I don't think we can solve them.
> You made a really deep cut.
> And baby now we got bad blood.[13]

When she released the album *1989*, Swift hinted that she originally wrote "Bad Blood" with a female friend in mind, but because she intentionally kept the lyrics of the song ambiguous, listeners have tended to interpret it in terms of a romantic relationship. So, much like her other singles, the song simply takes it as a matter of fact that all human beings long for sexual intimacy and romantic love. In fact, these forms of sexual expression are an essential means to self-actualization—to living a fully realized human life. In some cases, they are also the only possible means for experiencing self-transcendence. Nevertheless, long after these moments of intimacy have passed both parties are left with little more than a collection of open, festering wounds.

And this is the point where Swift's music assumes a more tragic shape (which becomes even more poignant in Ryan Adams's cover version). The kind of emotional, physical, and psychological vulnerability that allows our relationships (romantic or otherwise) to be meaningful in the first place turns out to be the very thing that wreaks havoc in our lives when these relationships come to an end:

> Did you think we'd be fine? Still got scars on my back from
>   your knife
> So don't think it's in the past, these kinda wounds they last
>   and they last.[14]

We are fated (or perhaps doomed?) to pursue the desires of our heart (no matter the cost) because we are trying to satisfy a hunger or an ache that we just can't seem to shake. But if our concrete, lived experience of heartache and heartbreak has taught us anything, says Swift, it's that we can no longer hold on to the misguided (and naive) notion that our love story will have a happy ending.

The song that perhaps best captures this sentiment is "Blank Space." In this piece, Swift effectively distills the vision of singleness, marriage, and sexuality that permeates contemporary culture into a catchy (and über sing-able) hook:

> So it's gonna be forever, Or it's gonna go down in flames
> You can tell me when it's over, If the high was worth the pain
> Got a long list of ex-lovers, They'll tell you I'm insane
> 'Cause you know I love the players
> And you love the game.[15]

To put all this in far more prosaic terms, human beings yearn for a passionate love that will be "forever," but the realities of modern life are such that this love, no matter how bright it burns, is likely to "go down in flames." So rather than allow our "long list of ex-lovers" to discourage us from pursuing romance, it's best to leave open a "blank space" for the next person who will attempt, but will ultimately fail, to fill the void in our hearts. In other words, sex and romance are necessary for human life, but they inevitably end in pain and disillusionment. And in light of this undeniable reality, we can either wallow in despair and self-pity or, as Swift urges, "shake it off" and move on.[16]

BACHELORS AND BACHELORETTES

We don't need to spend too much time with *The Bachelor* and *The Bachelorette*, in part because the picture of marriage, sex, and singleness they construct is nearly identical to the previous two forms of culture we have analyzed, but also because there really isn't much substance to be found there. Everything exists on the surface, like a veneer with nothing underneath. It's a world that's almost entirely superficial, artificial even—and intentionally so. But this is exactly why it's important for us to consider how it is that reality television shows like *The Bachelor* and *The Bachelorette* hold such sway over the contemporary imagination, especially given the increasing amount of quality TV that is now available to us.[17]

For anyone who isn't already familiar with these programs (or for anyone who isn't willing to admit that they occasionally succumb to this guilty pleasure), both shows follow a rather predictable formula. The names and faces change from one season to the next, but audiences are pretty much watching the same program over and over again. Each new season starts with one lucky guy (*The Bachelor*) or gal (*The Bachelorette*) who hopes to find the love of their life—their soulmate—among the twenty-five potential suitors who are also looking for love. Each week the bachelor or bachelorette joins these suitors on both individual and group dates to determine which couplings generate some kind of relational or sexual "chemistry" and which do not. Because everyone on the show seems to agree that sexual compatibility is a prerequisite for successful long-term relationships, the contestants often explore various levels of sexual intimacy with one another.

The kind of conflict created by dating (and being physically intimate with) numerous people at the same time is exactly as one might imagine. During each episode any number of frivolities ensue, including drunken brawls, tearful confessions of infidelity, revelations about unknown spouses, children, or ulterior motivations, and even at times sincere professions of love and affection. And that's exactly what makes it great reality TV. Being the consummate consumers of media that we are, if there weren't any drama—however fabricated it might be—we would simply change the channel.

In the midst of all the theatrics, there is always one constant. Every episode concludes with "The Rose Ceremony"—a weekly ritual during which the bachelor or bachelorette winnows down the group by offering a rose to a select few and saying goodbye to the unwanted or undesirable.

The season comes to an end when only one lucky guy or gal remains. If all goes well, the show's climactic moment involves a proposal (and one of the "losers" is announced as the bachelor or bachelorette on the next season). But if all goes *really* well, numerous other media outlets continue to follow the newly engaged couple, either as they enter into the happily ever after of wedded bliss or as their relationship crashes and burns as quickly as it started.

This is of course a very skeletal description of the two shows, but to enter into the gritty details of any particular episode or season would be to risk losing the forest for the trees. Far more important for our purposes is not only the basic formula the show employs from one season to the next, but also the question of why audiences find this vision of singleness, dating, marriage, and sexuality so compelling. *The Bachelor* began in 2002, and *The Bachelorette*, the first of the franchise's many spinoffs, debuted in 2003. It is now one of the longest running reality TV shows in history, and in a time when most reality TV shows were either being canceled (for instance, *American Idol*) or scaling back on airtime (for instance, *So You Think You Can Dance*), the nineteenth season of *The Bachelor* (which aired during the 2014–2015 TV season) not only had a boost in ratings but also added more airtime. Not only that, but it continues to capture the coveted eighteen- to forty-nine-year-old demographic and, in a fittingly dramatic fashion, is skewing younger as it ages.[18]

Given the sheer number of people who routinely consume these shows, certainly something about *The Bachelor* and *The Bachelorette* has captured the contemporary imagination. We of course need to be careful not to make too much of audience share (because even though millions of people are watching, there are still hundreds of millions who are not). Nevertheless, it is impossible to ignore the fact that *The Bachelor* and *The Bachelorette* are not only mirroring but also modeling a take on reality that resonates with a sizable group of contemporary people. For instance, "the vast majority of emerging adults—94 percent in one survey—want their marriage partner to be first and foremost a 'soul mate.'"[19] Considering this fact, it's not surprising that this same group of people connects so readily with a show that dramatizes their desire to meet and marry one's soulmate.

Before we get too far, though, we need to take a step back and remember that this soulmate narrative is nothing new, nor is it isolated to a single television franchise. As we have already noted, it's embedded deep within the princess mythology of Disney films and is equally present in the music of Taylor Swift. *The Bachelor* and *The Bachelorette* are not creating something from scratch. Rather, they are tapping into an already existing narrative that pervades the contemporary cultural imagination. One obvious example of this is that despite slight variations to the formula from one season to the next, these shows almost always frame the bachelors and bachelorettes as real-life Cinderellas and Prince Charmings—lonely individuals on a search for "the one" who will not only save them but also complete them. It is simply assumed that the contestants are all destined for (and even designed for) marriage. But the only way they will be able to find their future spouse (and one true soulmate) is by wading through a sea of seemingly infinite choices until they discover the one that produces the greatest amount of sexual chemistry.

To quote Mrs. Potts from *Beauty and the Beast*, this well-worn narrative about soulmates is a "tale as old as time." Yet, with all due respect to such a beloved teapot, the timelessness of the story doesn't make it any less of an illusion. Taylor Swift herself has said as much, only with an extra dash of cynicism:

> I think there's actually sort of a realism to my new approach to relationships, which is a little more fatalistic than anything I used to think about them. I used to think that, you know, you find "the one." And it's happily ever after, and it's never a struggle after that. You have a few experiences with love and relationships, and you learn that that's not the case at all. . . . If I meet someone who I feel I have a connection with, the first thought I have is:

"When this ends, I hope it ends well. I hope you remember me well." Which is not anything close to the way I used to think about relationships. It's that realization that it's the anomaly if something works out; it's not a given.[20]

Swift is articulating here the very same notions about singleness, romantic love, and marriage that we can see at work in every episode of *The Bachelor* and *The Bachelorette*. The primary difference is that in contrast to the way pop music works, reality TV takes the somewhat abstract idea that there are an infinite number of potential mates from which to choose and makes it concrete and explicit. It constructs scenarios in which bachelors and bachelorettes quite literally increase their odds of finding the "right" person (and their odds of winning) when they actively pursue multiple (often sexual) relationships, one right after another.

In more ways than one, *The Bachelor* and *The Bachelorette* typify what Jonathan Grant calls "the soul-mate search"—the modern quest to find "the one" that "perfectly fits" us and will therefore make us whole.[21] This is significant in its own right, but what is perhaps even more important to note is that these two TV shows are drawing from the same cultural narrative that not only produced Taylor Swift's conception of serial monogamy and sexuality as self-actualization, but also made possible Disney's take on the single princess as an incomplete human who is fated to marry, and thus be made complete by, a prince. Which is another way of saying that, no matter our age or the kind of media we consume, this is the story that holds us captive, so much so that we simply cannot imagine things being any other way.

FRAMING REALITY

If these three pieces of media are in fact representative types and not simply isolated incidents, then taken together we might say that they embody the mythic underpinnings of contemporary culture—those deep structures that both mirror who we are and offer models by which we might live. Pop music, movies, and TV collectively frame reality for us and so reveal certain aspects about what it means to be married, single, and sexual in the modern world. But this picture of marriage and singleness also has the capacity to distort and even hide certain realities from us, which is why it is incredibly problematic to operate as if our particular take on reality were absolute.

This is especially the case for the Christian community when we spiritualize certain paradigms as an expression of "God's perfect will" or as "*the* biblical model," and therefore can no longer see how these norms might actually be *mis*leading us. We fail to recognize that ours is but one way to frame reality and that there might be other, far more constructive (and in some cases, far more faithful), alternatives. And as the next chapter will make clear, I believe this is exactly what has taken place within American evangelicalism. We have not only un-critically adopted a distorted and distorting vision of marriage, singleness, and sexuality from our cultural environs, but we now organize our entire common life together as if this vision were normative for everyone within the Christian community. As a result, we are no longer aware of all that is hidden from our view. We are wearing blinders, but have mistaken them for spectacles.

Needless to say, I include myself among those who have become blind to our own blindness. When it comes to how we understand singleness and marriage, none of us is innocent, which is why it is vital that we engage routinely in the process of self-critique. More specifi-cally, we would do well to consider the many ways that we as the church are currently operating with certain assumptions about human life and flourishing that are rooted far more in popular music, film, and television than in the historic Christian tradition. In fact, it would behoove all of us who identify as Christians to acknowledge our ten-dency to adopt certain ways of being in the world that are often at odds with our faith commitments. We may not have even realized anything was blocking our line of sight, but we need to address the log that is firmly planted in our own eye rather than the speck in our neighbors'—the beam of wood that not only obscures what we can see but also prevents us from knowing what we can't see. In other words, if we are to develop a more constructive and life-giving vision of marriage and singleness, we must turn our critical attention toward the internal dynamics of the faith community. And it is exactly this task that we take up in the next chapter.

RUNNING TO STAND STILL

By Lindy Williams

I grew up in a home that encouraged me to be whatever I wanted to be. I had the full support of both parents to pursue anything and everything, which is how I found myself at West Point not long after my eighteenth birthday. It was perhaps the first place that I really encountered disdain for something outside my control: my gender.

I entered West Point during a time when women were welcome, but there was still a sense of isolation. It was slightly better for me since I was on a sports team. I had fifteen other women who were like built-in friends. Outside of athletics, though, there was always the subtle feeling that nothing I did was good enough, and every failure reflected poorly on the other women trying to succeed. I had to do everything better, but it would never be enough. I was constantly fighting the idea that as a woman in a man's world I had taken a qualified man's spot. Since it was assumed that I would likely get married and get out of the service, or at least get pregnant and not deploy, being a West Point graduate would mean little to me in the long run.

What emerged from this hostile environment—both for me and for an insanely high number of the other female cadets—was an eating disorder that eventually hospitalized me and cost me most of my college friends and my army career. It grew out of a debilitating need to prove myself and be considered worthy. The pressure felt a great deal like being a hamster on a wheel that never stopped spinning. It was exhausting.

Perhaps the most troubling part of my journey, including my ongoing recovery, is that my path has led me away from the church community rather than toward it. Sadly, many of the same destructive messages that clouded my West Point experience pervade my church experience, and they are actually more destructive in the church. In fact, the strange confluence in our churches of issues around identity, beauty, and sexuality make it a difficult place to be a single woman.

Yet the primary message that I hear as a single woman is that my identity stems from a good marriage. A man who stopped by the Fuller Seminary office where I am currently employed found out I was working on a PhD in Old Testament. He said, "You know, you should really think about getting married. The two of you would be quite a team. I mean, with your scholarship he could really . . ." He trailed off at this point, but the message was clear: as a woman, it doesn't matter how accomplished I am if I am without a husband. True ministry happens as a pair (really it happens as a man with a good supportive wife), and until I pair up I can only ever be partially effective. So what might help me get married sooner so I can be effective?

The answer that seems to be most common is that, first and foremost, I need to make myself more sexually desirable. I need to have flawless skin and perfect makeup. I need to be thinner and look forever young. I also need to project a confidence and a level of sexuality that matches a man's.

A recent dating experience of mine offers a telling example. I was introduced to a man through an online dating site, which means that I had never met him in person. But he was Catholic and seemed nice enough. He randomly asked me to meet for coffee after work one day. I'm fairly blunt, so I said I could do that as long as he knew that I had ridden my bike at lunch and hadn't showered yet so it might not be the best first impression. He responded that first impressions are important and in this case would be particularly helpful for him because he would really be able to see "what he was getting." Within an hour of meeting me he was talking about a sexual relationship, mostly because he needed to see if we were compatible before moving any further. So there we were, two Christians, with this seemingly insurmountable wall in front of us. I was supposed to look a certain way in order to entice him because I was the commodity he was "getting." I was also expected to approach sex in the same way he did. It all felt so self-motived—perverse even—which made me wonder how much of his attitude was supported (and even perpetuated) by the church community he attended.

Being a single woman in the church often feels like a rerun of my exhausting West Point experience. From the church's perspective, I take up space that could be better utilized if I were in a pair. If I could somehow strike the perfect balance of theological conviction, physical appearance, and sexual drive in order to catch the right guy, I would finally be valuable. And just like that, the hamster wheel starts to spin once again. I don't seem to be going anywhere.

2

THE INTERNAL NARRATIVES OF CONTEMPORARY EVANGELICALISM

WAITING ON TRUE LOVE, KISSING DATING GOODBYE, AND BRINGING UP PRINCES AND PRINCESSES

As a teenager, my perspective was that church leadership seemed to take most of its cues about sex from Reagan's war on drugs. As if it were crack-cocaine (only slightly worse), we were told to "just say no." I readily admit that my views were colored by the adolescent hormones coursing through my veins at the time, but the basic (albeit mixed) message about the connections between married life, single life, and sex that I received from my faith community went something like this: "Sex is a *beautiful* gift from God. But it will most certainly *destroy* you. So don't think about doing it, talk about doing it, or watch TV or movies where someone is doing it. And *definitely* don't do it yourself! Until you get married, of course. At that point, something . . . magical . . . happens. In fact, if you can just 'save yourself' for marriage, your sex life will pretty much take care of itself. But if you fail in your all-important pursuit of purity, well, we don't even want to think about that, so we won't. Again, it's all very simple: *Just. Say. No.*"

And that was that. In the interim, we weren't advised to *do* anything with our sexuality as single people, other than suppress it through sheer force of will. Well-meaning adults and youth pastors would often invoke

Song of Solomon 8:4: "[Don't] awaken love until the time is right" (NLT). But what they didn't talk about was what it meant for us to live as sexual creatures, whether we were married, formerly married, or waiting to get married (in what felt like a state of permanence). We never considered how we might integrate our basic sexuality into our lives as a matter of Christian discipleship.

Don't get me wrong. "Just say no" does have some practical value. In fact, it's pretty solid advice for those considering whether or not to experiment with illicit narcotics. But I'm not so sure it works the same way when it comes to sex. It's thus no small wonder that, along with many of my contemporaries, I began to see marriage as a kind of Christian loophole—the only religiously sanctioned site for experiencing the ultimate (and otherwise forbidden) human pleasure. Marriage became the solution to the problem of one's sexual angst, the cure for a lifetime of loneliness. As if by some kind of mysterious alchemy, marriage was capable of transforming sex from an act that was inherently destructive and even life-threating into one that was productive and life-giving. The lone requirement was to utter the magical incantation "I do"—a small price to pay for having all of one's sexual desires fulfilled, not to mention a housemate who could do the laundry *and* split the cost of video game purchases. And why wouldn't we believe that marriage and sex worked in this way? I mean, as anyone who's ever been married knows, marriage is exactly the kind of relationship that all thirteen-year-old boys imagine it to be.

I am intentionally being playful here, but it is not an exaggeration to say that the marriage-as-antidote-to-sexual-promiscuity narrative I inherited from my church community shaped my awareness of the world on a fundamental level—that is, on the level of my imagination. And as I hope to demonstrate, my experience is not at all unique. In fact, as the remainder of this chapter unfolds, it will become increasingly clear that the vision of marriage, singleness, and sexuality that I am describing here—a picture of reality that not only captured my imagination as a young person but also made its presence known during my time in pastoral ministry—is the same one that is currently holding the broader community of faith hostage. Like most fairytales, it's a story that is simply too good to be true. But it's also more than that. In its own insidious way, it's a lie.

EXPOSING THE LIE ONE STEP AT A TIME

In the previous chapter, we explored a series of pop-cultural artifacts in the hopes that we might develop a deeper understanding of the vision of marriage, singleness, and sexuality that currently pervades the public sphere. But this kind of critical engagement with culture represents only the first step toward our goal. Our next step, which is equally crucial, is to shift our attention from culture more broadly conceived to the unique ways the church itself is enculturated. So what I'd like to do now is consider whether and how the church in North America at the turn of the twenty-first century has (perhaps unwittingly) adopted and produced the very same conceptions of romantic love as those expressed by Disney films, contemporary pop music, and reality TV shows. I'd also like us to reflect on what's at stake when Christian communities (and the individuals who make up those communities) operate as if this romanticized picture of marriage, singleness, and sexuality is not only normative for all Christians but also biblically justified and thus divinely authorized.

In this chapter, then, we turn toward a few specific examples of the marriage norm at work within the church. One of the problems we will immediately face is that norms of this variety are notoriously difficult to address, which is due at least in part to their numerous, overlapping associations. For instance, in some cases the church's normative picture of marriage primarily concerns our understanding of how to live as a faithful disciple of Christ (spiritual formation) and by extension what it means to be a member of the Christian community (ecclesiology). In other cases, though, it has more to do with what it means to be a human being (theological anthropology). The challenge is to expose and explore these numerous aspects of the marriage norm without separating them entirely or treating them as if they were one and the same, especially when one (for instance, ecclesiology) so often follows directly from the other (for instance, anthropology). Because I want us to consider the variety of complex ways the marriage norm functions in our faith communities, I will generally have all these dimensions in mind as we proceed, but at certain points I will draw out the distinctions between them for the sake of clarity.

Another difficulty is that because these norms are so deeply ingrained in the fabric of a community's lived experience, they often go unspoken, which means that they exert their influence implicitly rather than explicitly. It's in their very nature to be both silent and invisible. In fact, if we were to poll the members of any given church in America, it's likely that few if any would actually come out and say that marriage is the absolute pinnacle of human flourishing and that single persons are therefore less-than-fully-realized human beings. Nor would they be likely to acknowledge that the practices of their own church are organized in ways that encourage and even expect all its members to pursue marriage as the divinely endorsed avenue for living an authentic human life.

Even so, it would be a mistake to conclude that the marriage norm was any less real or exerted any less of an influence within the Christian community. That's because some of the most powerful and effective messages are those that no one has to put into words at all. We simply feel them in our gut, which makes them both incredibly compelling and, at the same time, nearly impossible to undo. Like fish that have never known anything but the ocean, we can't step back and critically reflect on the water in which we swim because it constitutes the very conditions of our existence.

LOST IN THE MAIL?

I realize that for some readers my claims about this invisible but ever-present norm at work within the church are obvious to the point of being self-evident. They are simply a matter of fact. Indeed, when the topic of this book has come up in casual conversation, most people have responded as if I were describing something that they always sensed on an intuitive level but never quite had the words to express. Their eyes typically widen, and they say something along the lines of: "Yes! That's *so* true! The church definitely needs to address this problem. In fact, let me tell you a story you would not believe . . ."

However, I also realize that not everyone will be so easily convinced. So for anyone who remains unsure, let me offer some low-hanging fruit. Consider for a moment any of the numerous blogs written by people who have recently tied the knot. To make a molehill out of a mountain of examples, here's but one:

> I don't have an exact statistic, but I would wager to say that 90-95% of the marriage and dating advice I was given growing up directly or absorbed indirectly through example and culture was a heaping, steaming pile of shameless and unadulterated lies. Almost nothing was like "they" said it would be.
>
> I've struggled with who exactly "they" are. Parents? Teachers? Pastors? Friends? Authors? Bloggers? Probably all of them with some degree of culpability or another. But it's not even solely the fault of specific people or institutions. There's also a culture at large that prizes—worships, maybe—marriage and being in a state of "partnered relationship," to the point that it seems like being attached to another person in some official capacity is the end-all, be-all of the human experience, and those that fail to form such an attachment are sub-humans, missing out on the best that life has to offer.
>
> One way or another, I received these messages. Whether they were intended the way I received them or whether they, as Derrida says, "got lost in the mail," is hard to say. But at the end of the day, I went into dating, relationships, sex, engagement, and marriage with a whole host of unspoken assumptions about the way things would be. And the more they turned out to not be that way, the angrier I got.[1]

Like so many others who are now married, or were once married, or who hope to one day be married, this blogger can't directly identify the source of the messages about marriage that she came to internalize over time. Was it a pastor or a parent, a teacher or a friend? Maybe all of the above? It's probably the case that no one ever actually said these specific words to her. And yet, somehow, she is able to articulate with a great deal of precision and critical insight the content of a message that, at least from her perspective, everyone (and everything) in her life was communicating to her loud and clear. In no uncertain terms, the message she received was that marriage is the "end-all, be-all of the human experience," and anyone who is not married is "sub-human" and is missing out on "the best that life has to offer."

In more ways than one this blog posting serves as a helpful example of how norms work. As an interrelated set of implicit values and ideals, norms are constantly operating in the background of a community's shared life whether the individual members of that community ac-knowledge them or not. Interestingly enough, this particular blogger is quick to point out that the misguided assumptions she brought into marriage were not handed to her from a single authority or source. As the remainder of her blog makes clear, the church played a key role in shaping her understanding of marriage, but she isn't simply "mad at the church" for selling her an illusion. Rather, her picture of what mar-riage would and should be gained traction over time. It developed as a kind of composite that she pieced together from a number of over-lapping sources—religious leaders, teachers, parents, friends, and even (or perhaps especially) culture as a whole. In certain respects, no one in particular is to blame for her disillusionment. At the same time, everyone is.

"Everywhere," says Andrew Marin, "we act out the sexual images and ideas provided for us, projected upon us, by others."[2] When it comes to marriage, singleness, and sexuality, our imaginations are in-exorably shaped by the larger cultural context in which we live and move and have our being. And much like individuals, the community of faith is also a fundamentally enculturated entity. The church (and its norms) cannot be separated out from the larger culture in which it is set. It does not exist "alongside," "above," "within," or even "on the margins" of culture. Rather, culture creates the very conditions for the church to exist. Or, to put it differently, the Christian community does not go about its business in a hermetically sealed bunker. Instead our devotional practices and various other forms of life draw from a shared set of cultural resources that we have simply "made odd," and this is especially true of those practices that are in one way, shape, or form related to marriage.

So what I am not intending on offering here is a critique of contemporary culture as if it were a distinct entity from the church. But neither do I intend on trying to justify the Christian community's wholesale embrace of the modern myth of romantic love. Rather, my intentions are far more modest. I simply want us to name the internal narratives that most clearly express what has become the normative view of marriage within evangelical circles. This is, of course, no easy task, in part because it requires us to reflect critically on how we have contributed to the problem. But it is necessary if we have any hope of moving beyond these narratives and the norms they underwrite.

HOW DID WE GET HERE?

In case the above anecdotes don't make it clear enough, let me pause for a moment and underscore my own culpability in all of this. This chapter (and the book as a whole) is as much about my own failings as a pastor and Christian leader as it is an assault on the normative view of marriage. It's important for me to be up front about this because, in order to avoid the perception that I am making gross generalizations or rash inferences based purely on my own limited experiences, I now need to provide some concrete evidence for us to consider. I will need to interact with a few of the more prominent voices within evangelicalism that have fueled the spread of this particular take on marriage and singleness. In other words, I need to name names.

However, I in no way desire to blame any of the individuals involved. No one person is at fault here. This is a communal problem, and the answer to our problem cannot be simply to scapegoat some collection of Christian leaders just because their books happened to sell more than others. No. What we need to do is ask how certain norms and rules came to exist in our lives in the first place, or, to use a turn of phrase from philosopher Charles Taylor, how they became "values made flesh." As a community, we need to ask: How exactly did we get here?

According to Taylor, norms typically emerge through a two-stage process. Before anyone articulates them in verbal form, we first embody them. We could even say that we learn to "embody the point; or to enact it bodily."[3] Indeed, like so many other emerging adults, this very much describes how I first came to "know" that marriage was the ideal model for human flourishing. But this kind of bodily enactment is never simply an individual endeavor; it is largely communal. So, for instance, we as a church enact these commonly held norms every time we segregate our communities into groups of "singles" and "married couples," every time we participate in wedding rituals that have no meaningful analogue for single persons, and every time a pastoral search committee chooses to hire a married person over equally qualified single candidates. In short, when it comes to communicating norms, actions definitely speak louder than words.

But words still matter, especially when it comes to the words a community uses to talk about its guiding norms. In fact, says Taylor, to bring a norm to speech

> makes it exist for us in a new way. It comes into focus for us. It acquires clarity for us, and sometimes as a result has greater force. This in turn can bring about two kinds of reactions. On one hand an articulated good [i.e., a normative value] can work on us more powerfully, and motivate us more than before; on the other, getting clear on what is involved here may make it possible for us to break away from it, and repudiate a value which we had learnt to embody.[4]

Taking a page from Taylor's book, we could say that the marriage norm has become a powerful motivating force within the church at least in part because our communal practices have trained us to embody it expressively. We'll come back to this point in a later chapter, but for now it is enough to say that we have practiced and rehearsed this norm to such an extent that it is now a part of our daily habits. It is not simply an "idea" that we "believe"; it is a value that shapes who we are as individuals and as a community.

In addition, though, this norm has also drawn its power from the various rules that certain (usually influential) members of the faith community explicitly teach about, write about, and thereby disseminate. And as Taylor suggests, when we are able to identify and name these explicitly articulated values, we can see the norms they underwrite with a greater sense of precision and clarity, which leaves us in a somewhat unsettled (and unsettling!) predicament. On one hand, this kind of clarity can actually make a norm more powerful, thereby compelling us to embrace it with even more gusto than before. On the other hand, it can help us see that some of our commonly held values actually run counter to the deeper set of convictions by which we claim to live and thus provide us with the means for rejecting and renouncing what we have learned to embody.

So I would like us to do just that—to render the marriage norm visible by pointing out where it is explicitly stated in the hope that we might break away from it completely. With this aim in mind, I want us to consider briefly three internal narratives within the evangelical community that have to do with marriage, singleness, and sexuality. I have chosen to group these narratives into three general categories: purity culture, the princess paradigm, and Christian courtship.

It's important to note, however, that because evangelicalism covers such a broad and diverse set of loosely affiliated Christian churches, institutions, and individuals, no single narrative has been taken up universally by everyone who identifies as "evangelical." Nor is it the case that all these categories are in operation in all places simultaneously.

Indeed, to claim the identity of evangelical in the United States is to enter a deeply contested space, and the same can be said of claims about what constitute evangelical norms.

In addition, I want to highlight the fact that the influence of these particular normative values has waxed and waned over the years, and in fact seems to have waned recently. But the values are important to explore nonetheless because, while their immediate influence has certainly diminished, no other narrative resources have filled the void. As a result, they continue to operate as base-level assumptions within the church, even when no one is making them explicit.

PURITY CULTURE: WAITING ON TRUE LOVE

Our first category has to do with a number of related movements, ministries, and initiatives that focus on the sexual "purity" of both individual Christians and the faith community as a whole. It is perhaps unsurprising that the bulk of these ministries are primarily concerned with the sexual lives of teenagers and young adults—those members of the church who are still "waiting" on marriage. But equally important in the development of this evangelical purity culture are the various networks, organizations, and events that involve adult men and women, both married and single.

For instance, in a recent article published in the *Journal of Contemporary Religion*, sociologist James S. Bielo presents his ethnographic study of the Acts 29 network, which investigates the moral commitments of this conservative evangelical men's movement in terms of its social engagement. Drawing on his own field research, Bielo's study concludes that evangelicals tend to use whatever cultural materials are at hand in order to conceptualize and articulate their common values. What makes this assessment both interesting and revealing is that it clearly identifies how evangelicals develop their norms by drawing from prevailing "cultural scripts" rather than theological or biblical resources.[5]

Tellingly, the cultural script that Bielo identifies among the various congregations, proceedings, and published documents affiliated with the Acts 29 movement operates according to what he calls an "individualist" rather than "structural" logic. To put this in more accessible language, Bielo is suggesting that, in general, evangelicals understand both the problems that we face (whether moral, social, or ecclesial) and the solutions to those problems in terms of the responsibilities and actions of lone individuals. So, for example, whether I am married or single, sexually active or celibate, sexual ethics is a private matter. Living with sexual integrity as a Christian is first and foremost *my* problem, and *my* success or failure has principally to do with *me*. Rarely are larger structural or systemic problems even considered.

In addition to this individualist logic, Bielo also notes that within many evangelical communities (especially those associated with the Acts 29 network) "men are constantly and solely positioned as the necessary key to a successful, healthy future for marriage, local congregations, and the universal Church."[6] What this means is that, according to this prominent evangelical narrative, the task of advancing and sustaining the moral well-being of both the church and society (not to mention the health and vitality of the institution of marriage) is uniquely the responsibility of Christian men.

According to this way of framing things, the problem isn't—as one might suppose—that women are effectively eliminated from the picture altogether, robbed of both their agency and their voice (much like a young mermaid we discussed earlier). Rather, according to this particular script, the real problem is that all men suffer from an inescapable desire for sex. Indeed, so fundamental is the male sex drive that even as it concerns widespread social problems like human trafficking, both the causes and the solutions are couched in terms of individual male desire and moral failure. For instance, rather than consider the larger structures or systems that create the conditions for sex trafficking (such as excessive poverty, globalization, or objectifying and overly sexualized images of women in mass media), Tony Anderson, the executive director of Unearthed (a film ministry that partners with Acts 29), suggests that "at the root of sexual exploitation is a demand, and it's driven by men. . . .

Men in our country, in our cities, in our backyards, in our churches . . . fuel the global sex trade."[7]

From this point of view, sex is both an unyielding biological imperative and an active agent that is out to destroy men. Indeed, as the title of the popular book and related curricula suggests, the struggle to live with sexual purity as a Christian is best understood as "every man's battle."[8] But it is also far more than that. When combined with the notion that marriage (and by extension the nuclear family) is the foundational institution not only for the Christian community but also for human life more broadly, male sexuality becomes the hinge on which the entire project of modern society turns.

It is for this very reason that many evangelical leaders believe that the primary problem facing the church and society today is a "man problem."[9] Or to quote Tony Anderson again: "We know when men's hearts are restored back to wholeness, when men are healed [from sexual brokenness], their family, their workplace, and everything around them changes as a result of that."[10] According to this script, rather than assuming their rightful place as leaders of the church, men are abdicating this role, choosing instead to remain in an extended adolescence, allowing their base sexuality to go unchecked through rampant pornography consumption and the like. If Christian men could just get their sexual drive under control and "man up" by getting married and staying faithful to their spouses, not only would the church experience much-needed healing, but the people of God would also be freed to change the world. In other words, marriage is capable of solving the problem of male desire and, by extension, is the key to society's well-being.

Or at least that's how the story goes. And to be clear, it's a story that the Acts 29 network and its various ministry partners have inherited. They neither created it nor are they solely responsible for perpetuating it. Instead, these ministries are simply operating with a picture of marriage, singleness, and sexuality that has long held the evangelical imagination captive. Indeed, the concern (obsession even?)

among evangelicals about masculine sexuality and its connection to the well-being of marriage and society can also be found in numerous other parachurch ministries, such as Promise Keepers, which both preceded Acts 29 historically and established a well-worn pathway for its proliferation.

In more recent years, though, this interest in sexual purity in general (and male sexual purity in particular) has found unique expression among a number of ministries and initiatives that focus on the sexual lives of youth and young adults. Chief among these is the True Love Waits campaign and Silver Ring Thing events.

For those who are not already familiar with True Love Waits, it is an abstinence campaign that began in the early 1990s as a means for promoting sexual purity among Christian teenagers—an admirable mission indeed. In the early days of the movement, hundreds of thousands of young adults signed commitment cards, pledging to remain sexually abstinent until they entered into a "biblical marriage relationship." Although the impact of the initial campaign has diminished, LifeWay Christian Ministries, its sponsoring organization, recently relaunched the True Love Project, which aims to continue the legacy of True Love Waits by "helping students understand issues pertaining to sex and purity through the lens of Scripture."[11] At their core, both the True Love Waits campaign and the True Love Project approach the sexual lives of single Christians in terms of a fairly straightforward equation: abstinence equals purity. It's clear, precise, and memorable, even if it is a bit overly simplified.

A distinct but closely related initiative is Silver Ring Thing, a live stage performance that is equal parts rock concert, sketch comedy act, and motivational seminar. Even though these events promote abstinence along similar lines to the True Love Waits campaign, they do so by doubling down on the untold pleasures of sex. For example, participants often join in a collective "sex is great!" chant, which no doubt makes the whole event particularly attractive to youth and young adults.[12] After getting everyone amped up on the life-altering nature of sex, these gatherings culminate with individuals pledging to abstain from sex before marriage. In addition, much like the teenagers and college students who signed True Love Waits commitment cards, those who attend Silver Ring Thing events often don a "purity ring" as a sign of their commitment to abstinence. In doing so, they collectively express in symbolic form the equating of sexual purity with abstinence.

It may be unsurprising to some, but both of these movements have received a fair amount of criticism. In her book *Making Chastity Sexy: The Rhetoric of Evangelical Abstinence Campaigns*, Christine Gardner outlines a few of the most common critiques:

> The campaigns [True Love Waits and Silver Ring Thing] borrow the forms of concerts and comedy clubs from the secular sexualized culture. The message of abstinence focuses on great sex in marriage.... This positive, even sexy, portrayal of abstinence is more than a mere spoonful of sugar to conceal the unsavory medicine of prohibited sex: it is a fundamental shift from a solely God-centered approach to a self-centered approach to behavioral change. Although purity may be a God-centered approach to abstinence in that purity is described as a lifestyle standard created by God, the underlying reason offered for pursuing purity is that it is a lifestyle that is most beneficial (and pleasurable) to the individual. The argument proceeds this way: a life of purity, including sexual abstinence until marriage, is God's plan, and God's plan is the best plan for young people, resulting in great marital sex in the future and the absence of unintended consequences such as pregnancy or STDs in the present. God's plan is best not just because it is God's plan, but because it has great benefits for the individual.[13]

Gardener's claim is that this kind of rhetoric is ultimately destructive because it reinforces selfish desires for gratification that set people up for divorce or dissatisfaction in marriage.[14] While I find her analysis convincing in many respects, especially as it concerns how these initiatives risk setting young people up for an incredibly disappointing reality check when they finally do get married, my take on purity campaigns is a bit more sympathetic than Gardener's. As a former pastor to middle school and high school students, I simply cannot fault anyone for attempting to provide young people with legitimate avenues for pursuing sexual integrity in the modern world. Being a teenager is difficult enough as it is, and these difficulties are only amplified in our sexually saturated cultural context.

That being said, my bigger concern with evangelical purity culture is that while ministries like True Love Waits and Silver Ring Thing claim to offer a "Christian" or "biblical" alternative to the visions of sexuality, marriage, and single life that are swirling about in the public sphere, they are actually using nearly identical scripts. And the same can be said for similar initiatives that have adult audiences in mind. Books and multimedia curricula like *The Wait: A Powerful Practice for Finding the Love of Your Life and the Life You Love* by Devon Franklin and Meagan Good and *God Where Is My Boaz? A Woman's Guide to Understanding What's Hindering Her from Receiving the Love and Man She Deserves* by Stephan Labossiere are two obvious examples. In these instances and so many others like them, the starting assumption is that sexual expression in the form of romantic love is primary and foundational. Even though marriage is understood to be the only context in which one's sexuality can be fully realized, sex is pictured as the animating force for the whole of life—an ultimate good. Or to use the language of the Silver Ring Thing chant, "sex is great" in an unqualified sense. As such, sex becomes the gateway through which we enter the "life we love," an experience that every man and woman not only desires but also deserves.

Sexual expression is thus pictured as the essential ingredient for an individual's self-actualization, which is why so many evangelical leaders urge their fellow Christians to recognize that sex is well worth "the wait." In fact, because true (that is, "Christian") love is a love that fundamentally waits (on sex), the truth of one's love is best measured in terms of sexual activity (or the lack thereof). So while it certainly has the potential for being destructive (especially outside of marriage), sex nevertheless functions as the primary gauge for authentic human relationships.

Recalling our discussion in the previous chapter, what these examples highlight rather clearly is that evangelical purity culture is operating with many of the same assumptions that currently pervade popular culture. In fact, when framed by an individualist logic and a corresponding conception of sex as a biological necessity, these events, ministries, and initiatives are constructing and disseminating a particular narrative about marriage, singleness, and sexuality that is strikingly similar to the one embodied by the music of popular artists like Taylor Swift. The key difference is that whereas Swift chooses to direct her sexual energies toward serial monogamy, evangelicals direct their erotic desires toward marriage. Nevertheless, the end result is that, as Gardner rightly points out, "These groups are using a savvy rhetorical strategy: They are using sex to sell abstinence. They are using the very thing they are prohibiting to admonish young people to wait. They are saying, 'If you are abstinent now, you will have amazing sex when you are married.' The argument then becomes a promise of marriage."[15]

If this all seems like a somewhat convoluted way to speak about abstinence and its relationship to marriage, that's because it is. But this promise of a sex-filled marriage as both a reward for abstinence and a solution to the problem of one's sexual desire only becomes more complicated when princesses get involved.

THE PRINCESS PARADIGM: WOMEN CAPTIVATING MEN WHO ARE WILD AT HEART

The numerous parallels between purity culture and popular culture are not always immediately apparent, even if they seem obvious now that I have made those connections explicit. However, when it comes to princess narratives, what's so interesting (and indeed troubling) is that many Christian authors and thought leaders explicitly identify these stories as the ideal paradigm for articulating a Christian vision of marriage, singleness, and romantic love.

Two of the more prominent and influential voices in this regard are John Eldredge and his wife, Stasi Eldredge, both of whom have authored and coauthored a series of books and workbooks that explore what it means to be Christian men and women in the modern world. The titles of their two most popular books, *Wild at Heart* and *Captivating*, are perhaps revealing enough, but at their core the Eldredges are making two closely related claims about what it means to be a human being made in the image of God. First, "in the heart of every man is a desperate desire for a battle to fight, an adventure to live, and a beauty to rescue."[16] Because these three desires are what make men "come alive," they are the essential ingredients for the realization of one's manhood. Second, "every woman in her heart of hearts longs for three things: to be romanced, to play an irreplaceable role in a great adventure, and to unveil beauty. That's what makes a woman come alive."[17] In other words, God created men to be princes and likewise created women to be princesses. And according to the Eldredges, if we refuse to acknowledge this fundamental aspect of what it means to be a (gendered) human, we deny both men and women any chance of ever being fully themselves.

In making these claims, the Eldredges are not alluding to fairytale narratives as if they were simply helpful illustrations. Rather, they are explicitly framing their theological anthropology in terms of the princess paradigm—the exact same vision of singleness, marriage, and romantic love that we explored in Walt Disney's most popular film franchise. For instance, in one of their follow-up books, titled *Your Captivating Heart: Discover How God's True Love Can Free a Woman's Soul*, all the artwork features women dressed as princesses, riding bareback on stallions, and being swept off their feet by dashing men. In addition, every chapter employs language that intentionally invokes this same paradigm (as in chapter titles such as "Damsels in Distress," "Who Is This Prince?," and "Between *Once Upon a Time* and *Happily Ever After*").

Without saying anything else, this would be ample evidence to suggest that some of the most prominent narratives within evangelicalism are constructed from the resources of popular culture. But *Wild at Heart* takes this one step further, not simply borrowing from the princess paradigm but proactively advancing this narrative as one that is fundamentally Christian. I feel the need to quote Eldredge at length here to ensure readers that I am not taking anything out of context:

> Once upon a time (as the story goes) there was a beautiful maiden, an absolute enchantress. . . . But this lovely maiden is unattainable, the prisoner of an evil power who holds her captive in a dark tower. Only a champion may win her; only the most valiant, daring, and brave warrior has a chance of setting her free. . . .
>
> Every little girl knows the fable without ever being told. She dreams one day her prince will come. Little boys rehearse their part with wooden swords and cardboard shields. And one day the boy, now a young man, realizes that he wants to be the one to win the beauty. Fairy tales, literature, music, and movies all borrow from this mythic theme. Sleeping Beauty, Cinderella, Helen of Troy, Romeo and Juliet, Antony and Cleopatra, Arthur and Guinevere, Tristan and Isolde. From ancient fables to the latest blockbuster, the theme of a strong man coming to rescue a beautiful woman is universal to human nature. It is written on our hearts, one of the core desires of every man and every woman. . . .
>
> Don Henley says, "We've been poisoned by these fairy tales." There are dozens of books out there to refute the myth, books like *Beyond Cinderella* and *The Death of Cinderella*.
>
> No, we have not been poisoned by fairy tales and they are not merely "myths." Far from it. The truth is, we have not taken them seriously enough.[18]

In more ways than one, the above passage offers a distillation of my entire argument in this chapter. To use Charles Taylor's language, Eldredge is presenting here an explicitly articulated norm. He is bringing to speech a specific set of values and ideals that govern the beliefs and practices of the Christian community. And he is unabashed in his claim that the primary source for these normative values is the myth of romantic love.

But John and Stasi Eldredge are not alone in their embrace of the princess paradigm. In his book *Bringing Up Girls*, James Dobson follows a nearly identical line of reasoning, but applies it to young girls. He quickly dismisses "feminists" who are troubled by how princess narratives shape our understanding of women and girls, marriage, and sexuality. He suggests instead that the primary reason for the popularity of the princess fantasy is that "every little girl shares her mother's love for romance, and there is always a romantic twist to the princess dream. It gives expression to their inner yearning to love and be loved and to live 'happily ever after.'"[19] But it's also more than that for Dobson. The princess movement, he claims, is ultimately about the development of Christian virtue:

> Modeling virtue is one of the reasons I like the movement. In a subtle way, the Disney stories present a wholesome image of virginity until marriage and then lifelong love thereafter. They also promote femininity, kindness, courtesy, the work ethic, service to others, and "good vibes" about one's personhood. Where else in the popular culture do you find these values represented in such an attractive way?[20]

For the sake of transparency, I must admit that I have significant problems with how Dobson and Eldredge understand gender distinctions.[21] In fact, their troubling views about gender are likely both the product of and the primary reason for their enthusiastic embrace of these princess narratives in the first place. But we need to bracket these specific concerns for now because they are actually secondary to the larger point, which is simply to highlight another of the many ways the evangelical community has uncritically adopted the princess myth and openly embraced this narrative as normative for Christian life and practice.

As I suggested in the previous chapter, princess stories conceive of the single person—the single woman in particular—as profoundly incomplete. In fact, in the terms established by the fairytale narrative, princesses are not fully themselves unless they are passively waiting to captivate a "manly man" with their beauty. Likewise, princes are not fully themselves unless they are actively in pursuit of an adventure that ends with their rescuing of a "girly girl." Given this radical state of incompleteness and these gender-specific yearnings, stories about these princes and princesses naturally culminate in wedded bliss—the happily ever after for which they both long and by which they are finally made whole.

And that's all fine and well as far as fairytales go, but here's where things get theological. According to John and Stasi Eldredge and James Dobson, the princess paradigm offers us an authentic picture of human flourishing or, in their words, what it looks like for the hearts of men and women to "come alive." And according to these authors, all of this is so—that is, it is fundamentally true—because God made men and women this way. Thus men "need a deeper understanding of why they long for adventures and battles and a Beauty—and why God made them *just like that*. And they need a deeper understanding of why women long to be fought for, to be swept up into adventure, and to *be* the Beauty. For that is how God made them as well."[22]

From this perspective, to claim that we are all princesses and princes is simply another way of saying that we are made in the image of God. The male desire to go on a wild adventure and rescue a damsel in distress is a universal urge that was given to us by our Creator, and so too is a woman's longing to be captivating, to be romanced, and thus to be made complete. As such, the narrative is now fully baptized by Christian theology, so much so that the theological claim can no longer be separated out from the story in which it is set. It thus follows naturally that marriage would be seen as the ideal relational model to which everyone in the church is encouraged and expected to conform because it is the only real means by which we are able to realize our full humanity. Here then is a perfect example of how ecclesial practices and personal discipleship emerge directly from our theological anthropology.

Of course, if it's true that finding a woman to rescue or a man to captivate is central to who we are as human beings, then it would seem that in the absence of either we are not quite fully who we were created to be. To address this obvious concern, John and Stasi Eldredge are quick to say that their equating of the princess paradigm with the image of God should not be taken to mean that single people are incomplete or that women exist merely to satiate male desire: "We did not say that a woman is prized only for her good looks. We did not say a woman is here merely to complete a man, and therefore a single woman is somehow missing her identity."[23]

Fair enough. But this kind of caveat still doesn't address the significant problems that are present in their understanding of romantic love. For instance, in spite of their protests to the contrary, the Eldredges *do* in fact say that not only do men and women complete each other in and through their expression of romantic love, but this truth lies at the heart of reality itself:

> And that is how life is created. The beauty of a woman arouses a man to play the man; the strength of a man, offered tenderly to his woman, allows her to be beautiful; it brings life to her and to many. This is far, far more than sex and orgasm. It is a reality that extends to every aspect of our lives. When a man withholds himself from his woman, he leaves her without the life only he can bring.[24]

A second problem follows from the first, and it has to do with the way that narratives work. To make reference to any portion of a narrative is to invoke it in its entirety. That's why stories are so powerful. They aren't simply collections of discrete events—they are world creating. Fairytales are no exception. In fact, fairytales are prime examples of the totalizing power of narratives. This is important to recognize because if, as Dobson and the Eldredges claim, stories about princes and princesses do indeed reflect the deep structures of the world—the way reality truly is and was created to be—then we have to take responsibility for everything that comes with them, especially if we are claiming that these narratives resonate with God's intentions for the created order.

In other words, we can't have our cake and eat it too. Narratives just don't work that way. We simply cannot escape the fact that when cast in terms of the princess paradigm, singleness is a state of radical incompletion, romantic love is a self-justifying good, and marriage is an end in itself.

So the problem here isn't simply that evangelicals are using cultural materials to talk about the significance of singleness and marriage. As I mentioned above, both individual Christians and the church as a whole are always already fully enculturated, so we really haven't any other option. Rather, the real problem is structural, which means that even when the Eldredges and Dobson are not explicitly or formally perpetuating these structural commitments, implicitly and materially they are. The tragedy then is that they don't even realize what they are actually saying because they have uncritically adopted certain narrative frameworks as if they were straightforward expressions of a universally applicable Christian norm. Making matters worse is their subsequent labeling of these stories and the norms they underwrite as "biblical" and "divinely inspired" when they are anything but.

CHRISTIAN COURTSHIP

The final category—Christian courtship—features many of the same impulses found in purity culture and the princess paradigm, but takes them to their logical conclusion. Although the concept of courtship is certainly not new, in 1997 a young man named Joshua Harris published a book called *I Kissed Dating Goodbye: A New Attitude Toward Romance and Relationships*. His book not only brought about a marked shift in the dating practices of many young adults who were part of the evangelical subculture at the time (even if only temporarily), but it also reflected just how difficult it is for someone who has been indelibly shaped by a norm to critique it, much less move beyond it.

The book's primary argument is fairly straightforward and perhaps for this reason was even a bit scandalous. In short, Harris dared to suggest that dating might be a less than ideal practice for single Christians, especially for those who either have no intention of getting married or are not ready to pursue marriage. But even more shocking was his claim that not only is it possible to flourish as a single person, but singleness is a gift from God.[25]

To be sure, Harris's call for single Christians to "kiss dating goodbye" clearly ran counter to the common practices of both the Christian community and broader society. But at the end of the day, his "new attitude toward romance and relationships" was not a critique of the church's conception of marriage and romantic love, nor was it ever meant to be. In fact, for single people who, like Harris, chose to avoid dating altogether, marriage still served as both the primary point of departure and the organizing principle for understanding the significance of their own singleness, not to mention their (eventual) marriage. So rather than mapping out a viable way of life for single Christians, to "kiss dating goodbye" was mostly about avoiding sexual indiscretions while waiting for marriage to (inevitably) occur. In other words, Harris's project was not an attempt to break down the marriage norm, but a way of encouraging single Christians to live faithfully within it.

In many ways, Harris's approach (and those like it) actually reinforces the normative view of marriage all the more. After all, Harris wasn't swearing off marriage—only dating. And to operate as if one could meet a future spouse without dating (or something like dating) only served to underscore the notion that God has designed a "perfect someone" for all of us and in due time will reveal who that person is. In the meantime, like Rebekah in Genesis 24 going daily to her well to draw water, we don't have to do anything other than be prepared.[26] We simply have to ensure that we don't mess anything up (by having sex) as we patiently wait for God to reveal our soulmate to us. It is once again marriage rather than singleness that functions as the default status for the Christian person. In fact, there really is no such thing as "singleness" when things are framed in this way. There are only married people and pre-married people.

Harris offers a helpful illustration of the ways this normative view of marriage not only shaped his personal understanding of singleness, but also became an inescapable reality:

> Being of "marriageable age" and single is a precarious condition. Even if marriage isn't at the forefront of your mind, it's guaranteed to be on the minds of those around you. My family proved this to me when I turned twenty-one. In my family, we have a tradition of writing letters to each other on our birthdays. The letters I received on my twenty-first birthday really caught me off guard. Why? Because of the consistent references to the "special someone" who evidently, in the opinions of my parents and younger brother, would pop up any day. . . . [My dad's letter] picked up the marital theme: "Finally, expect to meet her someday soon, if you haven't met her already. She will be prepared for you by God because 'a good wife is from the Lord.' When you know you have found her, be patient—you needn't rush. But neither should you need to delay things. Marry her within the year and count on God to help you take care of her."[27]

At the end of the day then, rather than offering a critique of the soulmate theology that is pervasive within evangelical Christian circles, *I Kissed Dating Goodbye* advises single Christians simply to delay the inevitable (marriage) for the sake of maintaining one's sexual purity. The question is not *if* God will deliver that perfect someone to those who are faithful. The question is simply *when*. Singleness is thus pictured as a season of waiting designed to prepare the single person, not for a life of faithful Christian discipleship per se, but for marriage.

As a twenty-one-year-old who had endured a series of painful breakups, Harris's decision not to date was a matter of genuine Christian conviction. So I certainly want to affirm both his personal resolution and his willingness to encourage others to do the same. Like so many young adults who have encountered similar circumstances, the time was just not right for him. But when the time *was* right and Harris met the woman he would eventually marry, his prior decision to kiss dating goodbye immediately ran up against the numerous assumptions and expectations that have come to define the evangelical community's approach toward marriage and romantic love.

Harris addressed this inherent tension in his follow-up book, *Boy Meets Girl*, by making a case for Christian courtship. Although it did not receive as much attention as his previous book, *Boy Meets Girl* was part of an avalanche of books written by Christian authors who were staunch advocates for the practice of courtship. Beyond Harris's books, Eric and Leslie Ludy's *When God Writes Your Love Story* is perhaps the most well-known of these.[28] According to these and other authors, courtship isn't just another (more "holy") name for dating, but is rather "a season for two people to grow in friendship, to get to know each other's character, and to see how they interact as a couple. . . . Courtship isn't a form of preengagement. It's a time to consider the possibility of marriage and to seek to make a wise choice."[29]

What's important here is not to determine whether courtship is, in the final analysis, a theologically justifiable approach to dating. I have no doubt that it has served as a helpful and welcome alternative for numerous Christians. Instead, I am calling attention to these books about Christian courtship in order to demonstrate another way the Christian community has found itself

> in the grip of a powerfully seductive fantasy in which the two main characters are Cinderella and Prince Charming. The drama is all about "falling in love" and the action consists primarily in an elaborate wedding followed by a ride into the sunset. . . .

Indeed, it is its affinity with broader cultural ideals of individualism and consumerism that gives the fantasy of romance much of its power over the American imagination, including the American Christian imagination.[30]

Rooted as it is in the myth of romantic love, the Christian community's normative picture of marriage does more than simply encourage individuals to pursue (or wait patiently for) their "perfect someone." It also shapes on a fundamental level the way we read and interpret Scripture, thereby further justifying its status as a *Christian* norm. For example, in the preface to *Boy Meets Girl*, which functions as a kind of biblical and theological introduction to courtship, Harris offers up a creative, noncanonical story about Adam, the first human. Harris imagines Adam and his granddaughter having a conversation about Adam's relationship with Eve:

> You ask these questions because you yourself long to meet your soul's match.... But you miss someone you've never met. You want to run through time and glimpse that first meeting. You want to know how you'll know him. But you need not fret.... When the Maker brings you your husband, you'll be aware that it was He who made you for each other and He who planned your meeting. And in that moment, just as we did, you'll want to sing a song of praise to Him.[31]

While the characters and setting are certainly inspired by biblical material, the dialogue itself is not a far cry from what we often hear during any given episode of *The Bachelor* or *The Bachelorette*. The only notable difference is that instead of a consummate reality TV host like Chris Harris delivering the lines, it is an aging Adam. Nevertheless, the point is crystal clear: As human beings, we are all missing our soulmate—the one for whom we were made and ultimately long. But on that blessed day when—not *if*—God reveals to us our "soul's match," we will finally be made whole. All of our individual needs for romance, for sex, and for companionship will be met in this person—the true object of our desire. Which means that none of us need bother asking whether or not God has called us to be married. The only real question is, how long must I wait?

SO WHAT'S REALLY AT STAKE?

I have located each of these books, conferences, devotionals, and campaigns into one of three broad categories, primarily for the sake of organizing our discussion into something more manageable. But in real-world terms, these projects are all interrelated. In fact, when taken together, it becomes increasingly evident that they are offering up a fairly coherent and compelling narrative that both explicitly and implicitly identifies marriage as the norm for the Christian community and by extension for all Christians. But as I hope this chapter has made abundantly clear, there is far more to this story than meets the eye, for even though these numerous, interrelated narratives claim to offer a "biblical" and thus divinely endorsed alternative to broader cultural ideals about singleness, sexuality, and marriage alike, they have in fact adopted a nearly identical set of assumptions and commitments. And as it turns out, the bulk of these commitments run in direct opposition to the historic Christian tradition. As a consequence, some of the most prominent narratives within evangelicalism not only fail to offer a robust theological accounting of what it means to be either married or single, but they actively contribute to and help sustain the many relational dysfunctions they are seeking to resolve.

However, let me reiterate once again that none of the individuals I have named is solely responsible for creating or perpetuating this convoluted narrative. Rather, they collectively embody and express an entire church culture, the totality of which cannot be reduced to a singular author or even movement. In fact, these pastors, authors, and ministry leaders are all, for their part, intending to tell a very different kind of story—a distinctly Christian story that might serve as a constructive alternative to the relational fragmentation of modern life.

Yet all these projects end up promoting the very same normative values they are intending to replace. This raises a question: What is at stake when the community of faith uncritically adopts a romanticized picture of marriage, singleness, and sexuality as normative for its life and practice?

We can answer this question by first pointing out the many ways these internal narratives radically recast our picture of single life. The whole meaning of "singleness" is reduced to a matter of sex, or more accurately, not having sex. As such, single Christians are understood to be living in a fundamentally preparatory state—one that is not meaningful in its own right but only insofar as it prepares nonmarried individuals for the day when they will be married. In the meantime, they are waiting not only for their partner, but also for their life to begin.

From this perspective, singleness functions as a kind of extended purgatory. At best, it is a time of sexual purification that one must endure or suffer through. At worst, celibate singleness is understood to be simply impossible, especially when this season of refinement by fire extends later into life. Indeed, because faithful Christian discipleship demands that the single person abstain from that which is taken to be ultimate (sex), singleness simply cannot be seen as a gift or a calling. It can only be a curse.

Singleness is thus envisioned as a state of radical incompleteness. It is a condition that can only be "fixed" or "solved" by denying sexual desire until the moment when God reveals the object of that desire— the soulmate. And so that I'm not misunderstood, let me make this point painfully clear. To understand single life in terms of waiting for a soulmate is to treat one's imagined future spouse as both a fetish and an idol. It is sub-Christian. When framed by the myth of romantic love, marriage can only ever be an arrangement that caters to the individual needs of the consumer. Its apotheosis is not self-giving love but rather self-realization.

These misleading notions about singleness also lead to a distorted picture of marriage. Much like they do with our understanding of single life, the most common evangelical narratives reduce the entire meaning of the marriage relationship down to sex. Marriage is held out for the Christian as the divinely sanctioned solution to the problem of sexual frustration. According to this very clearly articulated message, sex is incomparable—ineffable even—so if single people can just wait until marriage, they will finally be able to engage in all the mind-blowing sexual activity they could ever want without having to worry about sin, or guilt, or unforeseen complications. Which means that, in addition to being a "solution" to the "problem" of sex, marriage also functions as a reward for abstinence. Indeed, the longer and more grueling the wait, the more (sexually) fulfilling the marriage relationship is sure to be.

As we have seen, this way of understanding marriage, singleness, and sex does not represent a fringe point of view within evangelicalism. Rather, it is the norm—the model by which everything else is accepted, understood, and evaluated. Which is why it is so very important for us to acknowledge how deeply problematic this model truly is. In more ways than one, it simply reproduces modern society's chief confusions and obsessions. As if the Christian community's only resources were the Top-40 Billboard charts, we tend to conflate and confuse *the things we do* sexually with *who we are* as sexual beings. We not only artificially elevate what we do (copulate) to unrealistic heights, but we also leverage that supposed "transcendence" to secure a specific kind of moral action, especially among young people and single adults.

But this largely behavioral approach to marriage and sexual ethics in the name of "Christian purity" actually has two somewhat unintended consequences. In the first place, it discourages single people from doing anything constructive with their sexuality because it effectively de-sexualizes all (nonmarried) life. Second, though, by boiling the whole of human sexuality down to nothing more than the sex act between spouses, neither single people nor married people are left with any other spaces for cultivating a robust notion of human sexuality—one that involves the entirety of our lives in the world, and not just those few isolated moments when we are engaged in the act of sex.

When marriage and singleness are framed in these terms, should it really surprise us to discover that many Christians are filled with anxiety about being single for the rest of their lives and therefore obsessed with finding a spouse? Is it at all shocking when Christian newlyweds experience their married life as a monumental letdown, or worse—a mistake? And is it any surprise that so many Christian marriages collapse due to some form of sexual dysfunction or outright infidelity? Given the way we talk about it in our churches, seminars, and curricula, one could easily conclude that marriage somehow eliminates any prior struggles with sexual integrity and at the same time fulfills all our deepest longings.

Yet, as every married person knows, sex only constitutes a very small portion of what it means to be married. It's not that sex is unimportant in marriage. It's just that it isn't of primary importance (and in some life stages it's not even of secondary or tertiary importance). So it is downright misleading and unhelpful to imply that marriage is primarily "about" sex, or that it could ever "solve" something as textured and complex as sexual desire.

Truth be told, getting married solves nothing. If anything, marriage amplifies our many dysfunctions (including sexual dysfunctions). It tills the soil of our lives, bringing to the surface what we would rather keep buried deep within us or ignore. In some cases, this upheaval can be the very thing that spurs spouses to grow, forcing them to address certain issues in constructive ways within the context of a loving and supportive relationship. In other cases, though, it is a recipe for disaster. It can easily become an unwelcome intrusion, especially for those who entered marriage primarily for the sake of their own fleeting sense of personal happiness. The number of people who struggle with pornography addiction before, during, and after marriage is evidence enough that marriage doesn't "solve" our self-serving inclinations, sexual or otherwise.[32]

Yet, to borrow a phrase from Gary Thomas's *Sacred Marriage*, marriage isn't about making us happy; it's about making us holy. Which is why it is also unhelpful (and possibly even destructive) to talk about marriage as if it were some kind of a reward for abstinence. But if marriage isn't about making us happy, then it isn't about sexual gratification either. Instead, it's about a daily, sometimes moment-by-moment commitment to being emptied of our constant need for self-satisfaction. It is for this very reason that Christine Gardner finds the rhetoric of evangelical purity culture so potentially damaging. Abstinence campaigns like True Love Waits and Silver Ring Thing talk about sex and marriage in completely individualistic and self-serving terms, and then go on to suggest that single Christians will be able to find this kind of individualized, personal gratification in an iron-clad covenant that hinges on mutual submission and self-giving love—a relationship that has literally nothing to do with self-serving pleasure.

So if we really value marriage to the degree that we claim, then it will simply no longer do to treat it as a bribe for sexually frustrated Christians. To continue to do so is simply to perpetuate a norm that almost inevitably leads to disillusionment and disappointment. Indeed, it has already produced a whole generation of single people and newlyweds who basically feel they have been not only duped but set up for failure, much like the blogger quoted earlier who said that everything she was told about marriage was "a heaping, steaming pile of shameless and unadulterated lies."

We would also do well to address the structural and systemic dynamics that shape our approach toward marriage and singleness. As a community of faith, we need to rethink how we organize our common life together, developing shared practices that do more than simply encourage people to abstain from sex while they wait for marriage. In other words, we need not only preparatory practices, but sustaining practices as well—common forms of life that allow both single people and married people to flourish in and through the hard realities that are unique to each calling.

But we can say more. If we are indeed as biblically faithful and theologically orthodox as we claim to be, then we also need to do something about the utter absence of single people held up as models of Christian faith within contemporary evangelicalism. As I mentioned before, many of the narratives we have explored in this chapter are declining in influence. But they continue to function as standard operating procedure because there are currently no commonly accepted alternatives that might serve as their replacements. More recently, some have attempted to push the evangelical community in the right direction by raising critical questions about the marriage norm and its implications for the people of God. And it should come as no surprise that the ones who are often voicing these critiques are the people whose very lives are already serving as models of faithful Christian singleness— thought leaders such as Wesley Hill and Christena Cleveland.[33] As a community of faith, we need to not only take their critiques seriously, but also find ways to ensure that their leadership is no longer the exception that proves the rule.

Of course, now that we have identified these problems with our internal narratives and the normative picture of marriage they express, the challenge before us is to move from a posture of critique to construction. But this is no small undertaking. After all, it's not too difficult to point out what's broken. The real trouble arises when we try to put the pieces back together. And it is to this central task that we now turn.

BATTLE FATIGUE

By Michael Beardslee

Some conversations are so burned into memory that recalling them is something like virtual reality. One of these for me involves a dear friend years ago. The details are vivid: the time of day, where we sat, how the night looked, the vitriol in my face, the hurt in her eyes. I recall it with no small degree of shame.

This friend, who we'll call "M," was a close friend of many years, and at one point a longtime crush, maybe even a first love. Our conversation that evening followed the typical aimless path, finally reaching a point of confession. M, some two years before, had sex and, by implication, had been occasionally active since.

The effect on the evening's jovial tone was catastrophic. I drove her back to her car in silent judgment, seething anger and hurt, while she begged for some response from the passenger's seat. I can still hear the pitiable tone in which she said my name. Her heart was breaking, and I in some sense was happy for it. It felt like vindication. This is how we ended the night, just before her return to college for the new term.

At the same time, I was a small-group leader in my home church's youth group. A number of popular Christian books were in fashion and pronounced in the youths' impressionable minds. These easily identifiable works by mostly evangelical authors were little theologies of romance, aimed at a high school and college demographic. Their marketing was successful, and their words were inducted into the common grammar of the hundred or so kids we oversaw. Yet even then, when my evangelical fervor was at its most zealous, I found myself outside the gravitational pull of their allure. Not that I disagreed with them, but I did wonder at their effect, and if they roused unnecessary obsession over sex. Well, more than puberty already does.

Regardless of my lack of interest, a similar ethos shaped my approach to sexuality. Among my friends, I was a relative latecomer to faith, but I was eventually inducted into all the same cultural norms: music, books, conversational lingo (such as "I'm really wrestling with . . ."), and social standards. Being both a sincere evangelical Christian and an adolescent in the hormonal throes of late puberty, I, like many of my peers, thought long and hard about how to handle sexuality and the relative availability of sex. I participated in studies that involved in-depth readings of *Every Man's Battle* and the like. Exhortations and encouragements were offered, along with many prayers. Sexuality was seen as something of a battlefield, and to forfeit one's virginity was to give the upper hand to the enemy, or to quite simply lose the battle. Game over.

Now, this was not a wholesale demonization of sex, for sex was described as good and something to revel in, eventually. The result was that sexuality in general was something to combat until vows were taken. It was a qualified demonization of sex. As I now see it, this produced a line that was drawn between two types of people: those who have heroically abstained from sex, and those who have fallen on the battlefield. And this line was horizontal, creating a hierarchy with the heroes on top and the fallen on the bottom.

So while my reaction to M's confession came partly from emotional places, it was informed and (in my mind) justified by a distinct theological order—one I likely couldn't have articulated but was still deeply entrenched in my self-understanding.

My own virginity, like many (even many evangelicals, I suspect), was handed over in less-than-ideal circumstances. It happened long before marriage and with someone I wouldn't marry. There was initial shock and existential crisis, followed by resignation. Yet my binary understanding of sex remained my basic understanding, and my only recourse. Thus for the months following, sex was riddled with pain and guilt; other times it was careless. I saw myself on the fallen end of the hierarchy, resonating somewhat with Jack in the movie *Fight Club*—deconstruction through self-destruction: "I wanted to breathe smoke."

Ultimately, the relationship ended, and thus began a surreal period of reconstruction. What did it mean to live and think faithfully about relationships and sex now? My core narrative of sex, that basic understanding, simply could not provide any means to rediscover my Christian sexual identity. If anything, I now resonated with those who, like M, were prosecuted while sitting in someone's passenger seat. I had conversations with heroic Christians who hadn't grappled with the existential crisis that premarital sex brings about, and who thought I hadn't either. The insight this provided was profound. When it came to sex, the doctrine of grace was perceived as tame and anemic. Here there was little room for affirming one's genuine faith and one's fallenness. Something was deeply amiss.

During my period of reconstruction, I found myself again hanging out with M. I reciprocated the brokenness I saw from her that night years before and apologized with painful sincerity for judging her so. She graciously forgave with a smile. She told me more about her own circumstances for losing her virginity. I learned that it wasn't consensual. It was forced. And for some time after, sex was her way of coping with that trauma.

The "sex-as-a-battlefield" theology I was fed as a young Christian had little space for conceiving of such a thing.

PART TWO

RECONSIDERING
THE BIBLICAL
WITNESS

MORE THAN JUST A LABEL

By Debi Yu

In my late twenties, my mother and I were speaking about my calling and ministry, what it meant for me to be a faithful disciple of Christ. She was my best friend and my greatest supporter, so her answer rattled me a bit. With nonchalance, she explained that my most important calling in life was to be a helper for my brother, who had the real calling and anointing of God.

It stung and I spent the next several hours that evening questioning my own personal value, wondering if all I was valuable for was to be an adjunct to someone else whose life had true meaning and purpose. I could say much here about my mother's cultural worldview, but the simple conclusion is that she had not considered that God might have a ministry prepared for her daughter apart from her son.

Add to that the fact that I am still single at forty—unmarried and without children— and the story becomes a bit more muddled. In discussing my part in my church's ministry, my pastor said to me, "I don't know what to do with you." Ouch.

Of course, much of the context behind that statement can't be explained in the short space I have here, but the statement is telling. I don't belong anywhere according to the pastor's statement—I was not a college student, not a young adult, not married, not a single male pastor. I wasn't ordained, wasn't a deacon, didn't want to be part of the hospitality committee, and yet I was educated with a seminary degree in theology. I had a voice in people's lives, but I was a quandary because I couldn't be categorized in the conventional ways.

All this sounds like complaining, and perhaps it is to a small degree. But really, my thoughts hinge on how I and other women like me can survive and thrive in a church setting that really does not know what to do with us.

I once thought that unless I was married, God would not be able to use me because I was incomplete. True, I believe marriage is a great institution to learn unconditional love and sanctification. But perhaps marriage should be understood as a meeting of equal minds, two people coming together to unite rather than to complete each other.

Using that paradigm, I find that I am specifically gifted with wisdom and understanding of my own person. My whole identity is bound up in who the Father says I am in him: loved, accepted, needed, and protected.

Living in the United States, people often ask others what they do for a living as a way of getting to know them. We are teachers, pastors, engineers, and missionaries. Perhaps it is fair to say that what we do is so bound up in who we are that when we are attacked professionally, we also feel attacked personally.

Maybe one good way to talk about identity is to consider those things that offend us, the things we feel that we need to protect or defend. We are offended when our intelligence is questioned, when our income is ridiculed, or when our senior pastor doesn't acknowledge our hard work and dedication.

For me, the offense I feel is a marker that my ministry has become my identity, that what I do has become who I am, and that an affront to my work is a direct affront to me.

So what is my task as a single, unmarried woman in ministry? I was dissuaded from teaching in my church so that I don't become a competing voice in the congregation. In a setting where I feel marginalized, unappreciated, and misunderstood, the temptation is to grasp after my rights, to defend my talents, and to assert my God-given abilities.

As a single woman, I often feel that I don't have someone unconditionally on my side, a husband or boyfriend who can stick up for me and defend me. So the temptation is to stick up for myself, assert my own worth as a woman, protect myself, and aggressively ensure I have a voice.

But I've seen that as I stop trying to grasp for things—as I let go of the tight-fisted clutch on my own personal rights and entitlements—God opens doors for new realizations and new ministry opportunities. By no means am I saying that single women should let go of their rights, or let people walk all over them. Maybe what I'm saying is that people will inevitably misunderstand and exclude. I think that's just the human condition.

But even when that happens, I can choose to continue living out my gifts with wisdom and courage, trusting in God's pleasure and presence with me, even in the midst of hurt and exclusion. Lately I've been trying to live with open hands. It's strange, but people who I've never met have somehow found me, asking me to come and be an instructor.

Ultimately, the story I want to tell is the story of God. When I linger on the injustices of being a woman—and a single woman at that—I become defensive and protective of my rights and privileges. Don't get me wrong, I am an advocate for women to have greater levels of authority in the church. But perhaps what we ought to strive for is being a little less defensive in promoting our own personal story.

It hurts that my mother did not believe in my ministry. It hurts when my pastor and my church don't know what to do with me. It hurts when people pity me for being single. I suppose I have many reasons for being defensive, but what if nothing true can be said about God in my ministry because the message is muddled with my own defensive causes?

The church needs to change, and I see already that there are changing attitudes toward singles and women in the church. As the wheels of change are in motion, perhaps we can prayerfully and humbly contribute to that change through living out our identities with the fear of God as our guide, so that we can say something true about God from a posture of love.[1]

3

BONE OF MY BONES AND
FLESH OF MY FLESH

THE FIRST TESTAMENT ON MARRIAGE
AND WHAT IT MEANS TO BE HUMAN

THE SWISS THEOLOGIAN KARL BARTH is often quoted as saying that preachers should always have the Bible in one hand and the newspaper in the other. It's a great image to keep in mind. His point was really about the contextual nature of the Christian faith. The people of God need to be constantly reimagining what it means to be faithful disciples because the context in which they live is always changing. And according to Barth, without at least a passing awareness of what's in the "newspaper" (or in our day, television, film, and digital media), there would be no real way for Christians to relate the Word of God to their daily lives, or vice versa. It is for this very reason that we spent so much time in chapter one exploring a series of popular films, songs, and television shows to discern what their vision of marriage, singleness, and sexuality might be.

But in thinking about our cultural context (the "newspaper"), let's not forget what's in Barth's other hand: the Bible. For Barth, the Bible matters. And on this point I couldn't agree more. Indeed, as a theologian who identifies as an evangelical, I consider the biblical text to be an authoritative source for the life and practice of the Christian community. But as the last two chapters made abundantly clear, the question remains as to exactly *how* the Bible matters. The question concerns the process by which we move from an understanding of what the Bible says to how it informs and gives shape to our basic awareness of the world. We may very well be holding a Bible in one hand and a newspaper in the other, but what does it look like to bring them together in an act of faithful obedience? That's the question we take up in this chapter and the next.

Of course, anyone paying even the slightest bit of attention to the numerous conversations about marriage and human sexuality taking place within evangelical Christianity right now (many of which are fiercely contested) can attest to the fact that there is a great deal of diversity within Protestant Christianity in general and evangelicalism in particular regarding how the Bible relates (or doesn't relate) to the rest of our lives. Yet, whether these contested conversations take place in the church or in political spheres, all of them have at their core a common question: What does it mean to be human? As I suggested in chapters one and two, many well-meaning people of faith would (and in fact do) answer this question in a way that equates being married with being fully human. In other words, marriage operates as the normative category for the Christian community because, in the minds of many, it offers us a picture of what it means to be a human being.

As a governing norm, this vision of marriage does more than merely influence how the church understands the human person, whether as an individual or in relationship with others. It also affects how faith communities organize, prioritize, and even evaluate the significance of those relationships. Which is why it is important to note that the normative view of marriage did not originate with the various ministries, authors, and church leaders we named in the previous chapter. Rather, they inherited a particular take on marriage that has been deeply imbedded within the Christian tradition of biblical interpretation. For instance, even the iconic Martin Luther, one of the key Reformers credited with repositioning Scripture as the final authority for Christian faith and practice, understood marriage to be an essential component of what it means to be fully and authentically human: "Whoever will live alone undertakes an impossible task and takes it upon himself to run counter to God's Word and the nature God has given and preserves in him. . . . Stop thinking about [marriage] and go to it right merrily. Your body demands it. God wills it and drives you to it. There is nothing you can do about it."[1]

In no uncertain terms, Luther articulates a conception of singleness and marriage that is pervasive within the church but often goes unspoken and unseen—the notion that marriage is the ideal type to which all good Christians ought to conform and, apparently, are incapable of resisting anyway. To be fair, Luther was pushing hard against the medieval church's disparagement of married life as a kind of second-class spirituality, and his eventual marriage to Katharina (a former nun) was a demonstration of how marriage had become a way for former priests and nuns to show they had embraced the Reformation.[2] But in the process, he goes too far. And given the fact that his statements about marriage are coming not from some anonymous blogger but from Luther himself, they underscore just how much of an uphill battle we are truly facing, both historically and theologically. If Martin Luther of all people thought that singleness runs counter to God's Word and that marriage is an essential component of our human nature, then who are we to suggest otherwise?[3]

With all due respect to our kindly theological forebear, that's exactly what I intend to do. In fact, what I am suggesting runs counter not only to Luther and the great many people of faith who have followed in his wake, but also to contemporary political theory and most expressions of popular culture. In addition to the various internal narratives of evangelicalism we have already addressed, a strong and diverse set of voices—ranging from lawyers and political philosophers who are chiefly concerned with the development of public policy to Christian ethicists like Max Stackhouse—support what appears to be a general consensus that marriage is necessary for the right ordering of civic life and that Christians are therefore obligated to preserve marriage as the norm.[4]

So the story I am telling is most certainly the minority view. Yet, to borrow from Luther himself, "Here I stand, I cannot do otherwise. God help me."

As it concerns the development of a robust theological anthropology, my central claim is that for Christians, marriage should not be the norm for understanding what it means to be human. This means that the church should neither operate as if marriage were essential for human flourishing (whether individually or collectively), nor organize itself in a way that privileges marriage as the ideal relational model for all Christians. In other words, we need to separate the question of what it means to be human from what it means to be married.

Following from this basic line of thought, the suggestion I want to make in this chapter is potentially even more scandalous. If we read the biblical text with a set of lenses that are no longer framed by this normative picture of marriage, what emerges is a picture of humanity as a community of persons living in intimate and mutually inter-dependent relationship with each other and God—a vision of life that most decidedly does not see marriage as "essential" to our humanness. From the perspective of the First Testament, marriage is a genuine good and should be celebrated as such. But it is not the pinnacle of what it means to be human, nor is it a generic human calling for all people. Rather, every human being is called to pursue particular types of relationships with specific people, each of which has its own unique set of structures, commitments, and obligations.

THE FIRST TESTAMENT'S TAKE ON MARRIAGE

I use the word *scandalous* to describe my read of the biblical text only because to some it may very well be. But I am simply drawing on the wisdom of others. Numerous Christian leaders, biblical scholars, and theologians—whether writing for academic or popular audiences—have acknowledged that the Christian community operates too often as if marriage were normative for everyone.[5] Almost in spite of what is found in the biblical witness, the church tends to elevate marriage in ways that are not supported by its central authoritative texts. The result, as Old Testament scholar David T. Lamb suggests in his engaging book *Prostitutes and Polygamists*, is that our understanding of marriage has become profoundly distorted.[6]

So what I am doing here is simply calling to our attention the cognitive dissonance that presently exists within the Christian community—an unacknowledged tension rooted in the stark contrast between what we find in Scripture and the ways we live. Indeed, the very fact that my claims regarding singleness and marriage will be unsettling to certain readers is evidence of the marriage norm at work. So rather than attempt to diminish the uneasiness that some readers may feel as this chapter unfolds, I am going to lean into the discomfort in an attempt to pierce through our collective numbness. For even (and perhaps especially) when the Bible challenges our preconceptions, it is imperative that we listen to what it actually says. We must allow the text to speak on its own terms, all the more so when it makes us uncomfortable and disrupts our modern sensibilities.

This disruptive power is on full display in the First Testament (more commonly known as the "Old Testament" or "Hebrew Scriptures").[7] We begin with the First Testament because, well, it came first. Of course, as Christian interpreters, we cannot separate our understanding of the Hebrew Bible from what we find in the New Testament and in the person and work of Jesus Christ. But the New Testament cannot (and should not) wholly dictate our engagement with the "Old." Nor does it render the prior narratives of God's working in the world irrelevant or obsolete. We remain obligated to the whole of the biblical text, even when it generates more questions than answers. Truth be told, if we could ignore the First Testament altogether and simply focus on the New Testament, I would have an easier time making my point. As will become clear in the next chapter, Jesus and Paul don't pull any punches when it comes to how their vision of marriage conflicts with the status quo. But the very fact that Jesus and Paul were themselves so fiercely committed to Scripture (which, in their case, was the Hebrew Bible) should be encouragement enough to follow suit, entering courageously into conversation with the text no matter the outcome.

For our purposes, I have grouped a number of biblical passages into a few broad categories (descriptions, prescriptions, and metaphors) rather than attempting to provide a comprehensive account of every reference to marriage in the First Testament. Yet, as we briefly consider each category in a bit more detail, it will be important for us not to lose sight of the larger point: the First Testament does not hold up marriage as the normative model for humanity in general or even for God's people in particular. Rather, it simply assumes that marriage is a cultural given. It is part of the "facts in the ground," the basic "stuff of life" with which God works.

Many readers might assume that the most natural starting point for this discussion would be the opening chapters of Genesis, where the Garden of Eden serves as the site of the first destination wedding between the first husband and wife. We will return shortly to a more detailed interaction with Genesis, but as will become clear, part of the case I am trying to make is that we have mixed things up. We tend to read the Genesis accounts as if they were about marriage when they are actually about what it means to be human, and we tend to read all the texts that are actually about marriage as if they don't really count or matter. So before we get too far ahead of ourselves, we need to consider where and when the First Testament actually speaks about marriage.

Descriptions of marriage. The first category concerns the various narrative descriptions of marriage found in the biblical text. To make sense of these, we could look at the stories of David, Solomon, or any of the numerous kings of Israel (many of whom had multiple wives and married outside Israel). We might analyze what the Bible says about Joseph in Genesis 41 (who married an Egyptian rather than a Hebrew), or Moses in Exodus 2 (who also married outside the covenant community). We could examine the highly dysfunctional relationships between Judah, Tamar, and Onan in Genesis 38 (who all had sex with each other rather than get married), or the other Tamar (King David's daughter), who in 2 Samuel 13 is raped by her half-brother Amnon and forced in her desperation to ask him to marry her (as outlined in Deuteronomy).

In all these cases, though, marriage (or the refusal to marry) is functioning as part of the story's backdrop. The biblical authors are describing something that simply is. What they are not doing is outlining an ideal type to be emulated. If anything, it's just the opposite. These stories about marriage in the First Testament often serve as depictions of God's unrelenting grace in the midst of seriously misguided human decisions. So we must be careful not to equate or conflate biblical *descriptions* with *prescriptions*. At the same time, we must also be careful not to elevate certain descriptive texts over others simply because they more easily align with our preconceptions regarding what marriage ought to look like. Again, these stories are not presenting us with ideals for marriage. No ideal could ever account for the many textured and complex ways the biblical text displays faithful obedience.

Our primary concern is not whether the biblical authors did in fact have an ideal scenario in mind regarding what a marriage should look like or how it ought to function. Instead, we are concerned with whether these texts are in any way suggesting that marriage is the ultimate relational paradigm for being and becoming human—the norm to which human beings ought to conform. So perhaps a better way to focus our energies would be to consider the marriages of Abraham, Isaac, and Jacob, if for no other reason than these patriarchs often serve as paradigmatic exemplars for Yahweh's chosen people—for good, for ill, and for everything in between. If there were an ideal type to which all of us ought to conform, surely we would find it in the narratives that depict the marriages of these seminal figures.

Indeed, we don't need to look far beyond the stories found in Genesis 12–50 to get a fairly clear picture of how the First Testament understands the significance of marriage. Significantly, though, when it comes to their nitty-gritty details, none of these stories are straightforward or simple. But it's not because God has no intentions for marriage or that the biblical witness fails to articulate what a faithful marriage might be. It's simply because these stories are not responding to the particular anxieties that modern people have about marriage. They aren't principally about our contemporary concerns. Instead, the narratives regarding Abraham, Isaac, and Jacob are about God's undying commitment to God's promise. And it just so happens that God's promise hinges on one thing: making babies. More specifically, it has to do with giving birth to sons.

It should not be surprising that these ancient narratives about the patriarchs' marriages are so focused on having (or the struggle to have) children. After all, producing a male heir was an absolute necessity for surviving in the ancient Near East, which meant that marriage functioned as the basic social and economic arrangement that ensured a family would be able to make ends meet—either by having a male heir of their own, or through a mutually beneficial exchange of goods with a family that already had a male heir. In fact, so central was marriage to the economy of ancient Near Eastern society that marriage contracts are the subject of a great many of the surviving legal documents we have.[8]

When we take this cultural context into account, it becomes clear that marriage functions in the First Testament primarily as a social mechanism through which God works. Again, this is not to say that God does not value marriage or that it is unimportant to God how marriage partners relate to each other. It's just to say that the chief focus of these narratives is not marriage per se, but rather God's covenant promise brought about by birthing male heirs.

For example, the story of Abram (later Abraham) in Genesis 12 begins not with a wedding or the search for a wife, but with a different kind of calling altogether. Abram is to be the father of a great nation that Yahweh will bless so that they might bless the world (Gen 12:1-3). When God first calls Abram, he is not only already married, but he happens to be married to his half-sister (Gen 20:12). While an incestuous marriage of this sort would surely trouble us today, the text gives no indication that it was a departure from God's ideal. In fact, it goes one step further. The text points out that Abram's moral failure was not that he married his half-sister, but that he denied being married to her at all (Gen 12:10-20).

But there's more. Abram also marries more than one woman. As the story goes, he takes his concubine Hagar to be his wife (Gen 16:3-5). Again the text gives no indication that either having a concubine in the first place or Sarai's decision to give Hagar to Abram "to be his wife" was wrong. What is wrong is that Abram and Sarai attempt to bring about God's promise of an heir through some other means.

Of course, as is the tendency with these kinds of arrangements, things get messy pretty quickly. In a jealous fit, Sarai demands that Abram send Hagar and her son Ishmael away (that is, divorce her), but even though their love triangle dissolves, the biblical author passes no judgment on the marriage relationship itself. In fact, God promises to provide for Hagar and Ishmael, once again suggesting that the issue here is not plural marriage, but Sarai's misguided machinations (Gen 16:9-15).

Needless to say, Abram's marriages are a far cry from what we might expect from the father of God's chosen people. So to suggest that this story or others like it are somehow setting out "principles" for marriage, or that it elevates marriage as an ideal to which all human beings are called, is to seriously misread the text and to miss the larger point entirely. The point of the story is that God will do what God promises to do—no matter how improbable it may seem. And what God promised to do for this now elderly man, Abram, and his aging wife, Sarai, was to give them a son.

That son's name was Isaac, and, truth be told, he doesn't say much. Isaac's general reticence in the narrative makes some sense given his personal experience. After all, his father did agree to kill him as a sacrifice to a strange and unwieldy God that no one seemed to know except his dad. Still, it is interesting that as the story about the search for Isaac's wife develops in Genesis 24, Isaac remains completely silent. We of course could (and often do) romanticize the story of Isaac and Rebekah as the meeting of two "soulmates," destined from a time before time to be married. But that's not how the story goes. Isaac has literally no voice in the matter. He may have very well met his "better half" in Rebekah, but we're given no indication one way or the other if this is actually the case. In fact, it's almost as if his marriage is not about him at all. Unlike other couples, Isaac and Rebekah's nuptials are no run-of-the-mill arranged marriage. They are orchestrated not by the parents of the bride- and groom-to-be, but by Yahweh—the God who is faithful in bringing about God's promises.

So Isaac marries Rebekah (Gen 25:19-26), and soon thereafter Rebekah gives birth to twins, Esau and Jacob (who later becomes Israel). Much like his father and grandfather before him, Jacob lives out a story with a well-worn pattern. God's promise first comes under threat, and then the patriarch and his wife (or in this case wives, Leah and Rachel) respond by taking matters into their own hands. Yet every time God not only remains faithful to God's promise but also makes on-the-fly adjustments when the plans cooked up by these models of faith don't turn out quite the way they intended.

For instance, just as God provides for and blesses Hagar and Ishmael, God also provides for and blesses all of Jacob's children, whether those children are born to his first wife, Leah, his second wife, Rachel (Leah's sister), or one of his two concubines, Zilpah and Bilhah (each of whom was given to Jacob "as a wife" by one of his other wives in Genesis 30). Once again, while Jacob's polygyny generates its own unique set of relational difficulties, just as any plural marriage would, we are given no indication that the marriages themselves were in any way illicit. If anything, God responds to Jacob and his wives not by punishing them for their marital indiscretions, but by blessing them all the more. Each of his sons becomes a forerunner and namesake for the twelve tribes of Israel, which only underscores the fact that the text sees these children as part of God's promise to Abraham. In fact, as Jacob returns to meet his brother, Esau, in Genesis 33, he describes these women and children not as the products of his past mistakes, but as "the children whom God has graciously given your servant" (Gen 33:5).

So what's the point of rehearsing these details? In the first place, as I stated above, when we look at the actual biblical data, it becomes increasingly evident that the biblical authors saw marriage not as an ideal type, but as a cultural given. Marriage was a taken-for-granted contractual agreement in the ancient Near East that was designed to produce male heirs and thus ensure a family's survival. It also had to do with the safety and well-being of women and children, which means that marriage was not primarily (if at all) about romance or sex or even personal fulfillment. This is not to say that Isaac did not truly love Rebekah or that Abraham was not genuinely in mourning when his lifelong spouse, Sarah, died. Nor is it to say that sex was not a major part of these marriages (just ask Jacob!). But before it was anything else, marriage was about producing a male heir. Its purpose was procreation and societal stability, not merely companionship. And it is this understanding of marriage that constitutes the facts-on-the-ground for the biblical authors. So we should be careful not to mistakenly use our current existential anxieties as the primary criteria for understanding these biblical narratives. Instead, we should recognize these stories for what they truly are: demonstrations of God's faithfulness in and through the complex realities of our concrete life in the world.

Along similar lines, the second reason that we need to consider these biblical descriptions of marriage is the seeming neutrality of the narratives themselves, especially when it comes to marriages that appear to depart from what we believe to be God's original intent. Some readers may even be wondering whether the takeaway from my reading of these texts is that polygamy, incest, and concubinage are acceptable practices for the people of God. This of course is not the case. My point is that, in contrast to the way that so many modern sermons are crafted, these texts were not written as propositional statements designed to provide readers with "principles" for "godly living." These are stories rather than statements. But they are also more than that. At their core they are about paternity, not ethics (at least not in a narrow sense of the word). And it's vital that we understand them as such. To read these stories as rational arguments for an ideal form of marriage rather than narrative explorations of God's faithfulness is a category mistake.

Finally, and maybe most importantly for our purposes, the many and diverse descriptions of marriage that we find in the biblical witness emphasize time and again that marriage is a function of a prior and far more significant calling. There are undeniably a number of related goods that the marriage relationship provides, such as companionship and sexual intimacy. Nevertheless, these narratives depict marriage as having to do with something larger and far more expansive. Abraham was already married (to his half-sister) when he was called. Isaac had literally no say concerning the woman who would become his wife. And Jacob married two (possibly four) women. But in every case, their marriages were in service of a more fundamental calling. None of the patriarchs was called to marriage "generically." They were called to marry specific people for a specific purpose—to produce a lineage through which God would bless the world.

What these texts do not suggest is that marriage is some sort of generic ideal toward which all people are inevitably moving. Marriage functions significantly in these stories not because it is an abstract, universal principle, but because it is incredibly specific, concrete, and local. It has to do with God working in *this* time and in *this* place and with *these* people. And in the case of the patriarchs, God was working in and through their marriages to produce a dense web of intergenerational alliances that would one day bless the world.

So the question is, how might a recovery of these narratives provide us with a thicker understanding of marriage today, especially if our specific calling does not necessarily depend on being married, or demands that we delay marriage for some indeterminate amount of time? Or what if our unique calling is one that requires us to actively avoid marriage altogether? Or perhaps worse yet, what if we believe we are called to marry a particular person for a particular purpose, but that person does not quite fit the bill for the ideal spouse we have conjured up in our mind? And what do we do when there is no specific person out there, but we nevertheless feel as if God has in fact designed us for marriage? How then should we understand the relationship between these biblical narratives and our own life in the world?

Prescriptions for marriage. Clearly, when it comes to marriage, the biblical text seems to offer more questions than answers. Even in those places where the text *does* offer us concrete answers, it often remains unclear as to how and to what degree they are applicable today. Nevertheless, we can group these texts into the second broad category of prescriptions for marriage. To be clear, though, these prescriptive texts neither require nor even recommend marriage for everyone. Rather, they outline a series of proscriptions (what not to do) for those who either are or should be married. Much like the descriptive narratives we considered above, prescriptive texts start with the assumption that marriage is a cultural given, but they go the additional step of seeking to ensure that the marriage relationship is functioning properly both in its own right and as a part of society as a whole.

For example, in Leviticus 18 instructions are given regarding what seems to be every possible familial relationship imaginable, including a prohibition against marrying a woman and then also marrying her sister as a "rival wife" (Lev 18:18). Deuteronomy 17:17 shifts the focus from commoners to the kings of Israel, who are not to marry "many wives" on account of the people being led astray by foreign gods (although what constitutes "many" is not so clear). Elsewhere in the same book, we read about the various steps one must follow in order to issue a certificate of divorce to a wife who "does not please" her husband, as well as strict instructions regarding who the divorcée can and cannot remarry (Deut 24:1-4). If all this were not enough, we also find in Deuteronomy rules for marrying prisoners of war. After prevailing in battle, if one should see "an attractive woman whom you wish to take as a wife ... you may have sexual relations with her and become her husband and she your wife. If you are not pleased with her, then you must let her go where she pleases. You cannot in any case sell her" (Deut 21:10-14).

To modern ears, these passages sound a bit like fingernails on a chalkboard, and rightly so. It is at least part of the reason why so many Christians disregard them. But it's important to keep in mind the concrete realities that defined the context in which these texts were written. Women in the ancient world were particularly vulnerable. Men had all the power. Beyond marriage, there were virtually no viable options for women who were single or widowed. If they could not marry or remarry, many were forced into prostitution or the like. So in a context where men could purchase women, marry women, have sex with women, and then simply discard these women when they were no longer "pleasing," the biblical prohibitions were designed to guard against ongoing oppression and injustice. Whether a slave, a sister, or a foreigner, God called the people of Israel to treat these women with justice and mercy (Mic 6:8), even if that meant marrying more than one wife, remaining married to a prisoner of war, or refusing to divorce a woman simply because she was "less than pleasing."

As a consequence, some of the texts in the First Testament require that certain people, given certain circumstances, ought to (and in fact must) marry or remain married. The only problem is that in almost every instance these passages present us with a very clear set of rules that modern Christians, for one reason or another, simply ignore.

For instance, as outlined in Exodus 21:7-11, a man who purchases a female slave or concubine must not only marry her and grant her all the privileges of a wife, but remain married to her, even if he decides to "take another wife." Along similar lines, Deuteronomy 25:5-6 lays out the expectations for Levirate marriage, which requires a man to marry his brother's widow in order that she might bear a child to carry on the lineage of her dead husband. The law stipulates that it is the brother's moral obligation to marry his sibling's widow, even if he is already married (contrary to Lev 18:16; 20:21).

One of the most unsettling examples of biblical prescriptions for marriage is found in Deuteronomy 22:28-29. This passage demands that anyone who rapes a female virgin who is not otherwise engaged must pay the victim's father and marry her. That's not a typo. The First Testament's legal code actually stipulates that perpetrators of rape must pursue marriage with the woman whom they sexually assaulted. Not only that, but the rapist "may never divorce her as long as he lives" (Deut 22:29).

These texts are striking for a number of reasons, including how much they diverge from what most Christians have in mind when they speak about the "biblical view" of marriage. At least when it comes to the narrative descriptions of marriage in Scripture, the text is not actively condoning what modern readers might see as clear departures from "God's original design." Yet in these prescriptive texts we encounter what appears to be a vision for marriage that deviates significantly from the "biblical view" as many would articulate it today. What is more, these legal prescriptions are not merely accommodations. They are also mandates. As such, they place God's chosen people in a position that expects (and even demands) that they enter into seemingly ad hoc marriage relationships that might very well consist of more than one spouse, involve a sibling or close relative, or even bring together the perpetrator and victim of sexual violence.

My point here is not that Christians need to start abiding by all these prescriptive texts (and the same goes for the other prescriptive portions of the First Testament). Nor am I suggesting that we reconsider our stance on polygamy or incest. Rather, I simply want us to acknowledge a difficult truth: When it comes to determining either (a) who is or is not meant to be married or (b) what a "godly/Christian/biblical" marriage does or does not entail, members of the Christian community are often guilty of arbitrarily elevating those portions of Scripture that confirm our preconceptions while conveniently ignoring those that do not. These visions of marriage turn out to be quite tidy and internally consistent, just as one might expect. But they are far from "biblical" because they cannot (or simply refuse to) account for the diverse and complex nature of the biblical witness itself. Put differently, the First Testament picture of marriage never quite matches our own because its concerns are far more robust than ours.

Again, this is not to say that the biblical text is incoherent or that it never points us toward a picture of God's intentions for the created order—marriage included. As Jesus frequently reminded the legal experts of his day, these laws were created not as ideal visions for marriage, but because of the hardness of the people's hearts (see Mt 19:8; Mk 10:5). Nevertheless, I do want to suggest that the often flippant and all-too-easy ways the Christian community uses the concept of a "biblical vision" of marriage is not helpful and ultimately not faithful to the whole of the biblical witness. The First Testament rarely presents us with abstract principles or ideals that we can apply in a simple and straightforward way to all people in all times and in all places. But this very indirectness and complexity is what keeps us actively involved. It presses us to consider over and over again what it means to live faithfully in light of the text, its historical context, and our present situation. Scripture invites us not to rework or redefine its vision for marriage, but to continually recontextualize it so that it might be heard anew in such a time as this.

Another prominent feature of these prescriptive texts is their clear focus on justice. Interestingly, the biblical authors are not incredibly worried about setting moral boundaries for marriage (although ethics certainly does play a role here). They are more concerned with urging God's people to enact justice in every sphere of life—including marriage. Given that marriage was primarily an economic exchange in the ancient world, and that women were marginalized to the point of being seen as not-quite-fully-human, legal proscriptions regarding marriage functioned as one of the primary means for ensuring justice for the powerless and the oppressed. Why do the prophets use the language of "hatred" to describe divorce (Mal 2:16)? The answer is not so much about the moral dilemma it presents. It's about justice. Divorce in the First Testament almost always left an otherwise powerless, marginalized human being (or group of human beings) without provision or recourse. And in the words of Malachi, this form of injustice is its own kind of "violence" (Mal 2:16), for it is the tragic undoing of God's covenant promise.

Thinking about marriage and divorce as a matter of justice should cause contemporary readers to pause at least for a moment. Because marriage in the modern world (both inside and outside the church) is primarily if not exclusively about an individual's personal happiness and sense of fulfillment, we rarely consider the various injustices that can and do emerge from our decisions to marry, divorce, or remarry. Single women, widows, and children don't have it as bad as they did in the sixth century BCE, but things are hardly equitable today, even in the modern West. And the situation is even worse in the developing world. So before we too quickly write off the First Testament's emphasis on marriage as a form of justice, we would do well to think about how the decision to be married or remain single does or does not enable us to enact justice in our own time and place.

Finally, it is clear from these prescriptive passages that marriage is indeed a good, both for the individuals involved and for society as a whole. Good marriages are not only life giving but just, which is why so much ink was spilled over what marriage entails and how spouses should treat one another. Indeed, in the words of Proverbs 18:22, "The one who finds a wife finds what is enjoyable, / and receives a pleasurable gift from the LORD." Without any kind of qualification, those who are given the gift of marriage are given a good thing.

But good marriages don't simply happen. They require an incredible amount of hard work and a daily willingness to set aside one's own needs for the sake of the other. Marriage has nothing to do with personal wish fulfillment, at least not from the perspective of the First Testament. This is part of the reason why the biblical authors spend so much time talking about the rigorous demands of marriage—not to dissuade anyone from being married, but to provide a very clear picture of what is required for a marriage to function as the gift that it is.

The inverse also happens to be true. Bad marriages are not just bad. They are terrible. They are not only soul-crushing, but unjust and inequitable. What is more, they affect both the spousal relationship and the community at large. Only a few chapters after espousing the gift of marriage, Proverbs also says: "It is better to live on a corner of the housetop / than in a house in company with a quarrelsome wife" (Prov 21:9). It is also why there are so many legal proscriptions outlining what to do when marriages go bad. For the sake of justice, certain people in certain situations must marry. But for the sake of the community's well-being (not to mention sanity!), some people should never get married. Being single (that is, living on the corner of a rooftop) certainly comes with the very real challenges of loneliness and isolation. Yet according to Proverbs not only are some things far worse than loneliness, but marriage can be the loneliest place in the world.

So the question is, why does the church operate as if this were not actually the case? Why do we so often treat marriage as if it were a relatively pleasure-filled and undemanding relationship designed to provide individuals with personal happiness when we know that bad marriages are downright destructive and that even good marriages require spouses to sacrifice their personal happiness on a daily basis for the sake of the other? Why are we not more cautious when deciding to get married (or remarried), or when counseling others to do the same? Why are local congregations not doing everything in their power to incorporate the single person who is living on the proverbial corner of a rooftop into the larger community rather than prodding him or her into an unlivable situation? And why do we do all of this when the biblical evidence so clearly points in another direction?

If my instincts are right, the problem is not so much our understanding of the "biblical view" of marriage (although this is part of the issue). The problem lies in our understanding of the "biblical view" of the human being.

THE FIRST TESTAMENT ON WHAT
IT MEANS TO BE HUMAN

To debunk the normative view of marriage that has captured the imagination of the church, we need to address what the biblical witness actually says about marriage. This has been the focus of the first part of this chapter. But as odd as it might sound, we also need to consider what it doesn't say. This argument from silence is necessary because, at least in my estimation, a great many Christians have developed their picture of the "biblical view" of marriage on the basis of a disproportionally small number of First Testament texts that are not actually about marriage at all, but are rather about what it means to be a human being. And when we fail to make this distinction in our reading of the biblical text, we (perhaps unknowingly) reinforce the assumption that being married is a necessary condition for being and becoming fully human and is thus a perfectly legitimate norm to uphold.

More so than any other portion of the First Testament, the creation stories of Genesis 1–3 serve as the key texts for those who understand marriage to be a constitutive element of the human person. According to this perspective, because marriage was an integral part of God's original design for humanity, it is the principal (and ultimately the only) avenue through which we are able to fully express what it means to be truly and authentically human. But does this picture of the human person actually follow from the text itself? My basic claim is that it does not.

It is important to note that there is biblical precedent for connecting our understanding of the marriage relationship to the creation accounts in Genesis. Both Jesus (Mt 19:3-9; Mk 10:6-12) and Paul (Eph 5:31) directly reference Genesis 1:27 and Genesis 2:24 as they talk about marriage. We will consider these New Testament passages in more detail in the next chapter, but for now it is enough to point out that in the Gospels Jesus is actually responding to questions about divorce, not about what it means to be human. And Paul references the Genesis account in Ephesians as a way of making his point that "the two" who are becoming "one flesh" are Christ and the church (Eph 5:31-32).

Nevertheless, in Genesis 2:23, just after the man waxes poetic about the newly formed woman ("bone of my bones and flesh of my flesh"), the narrative stops on a dime. We are then told, "That is why a man leaves his father and mother and unites with his wife, and they become a new family [or *one flesh*]" (Gen 2:24). Here the biblical author interrupts the narrative in order to directly address the reader, as if to say, "I need to make something very clear." In the ancient world, men did not leave their family or their family's land. As we discussed above, having a son meant that the family had someone who could provide for them, and this provision was directly connected to the cultivation of the land. So it would make very little sense for a man to leave his place of origin because it would severely jeopardize his family's livelihood. Instead, like the story of Rebekah leaving home to marry Isaac, the common practice was for the woman to leave her father and mother to join the man's family, to worship the man's gods, and to be forever dependent on the man's provisions.

But what Genesis 2:24 describes is exactly the opposite, which makes the narrator's point as clear as it is subversive. In a shocking reversal, it is the man in Genesis who uproots himself and leaves everything behind for the woman. And only by doing so is he able to "cleave" or "unite" to her (Hebrew *davaq*), a word that does not simply denote sex, but rather the personal commitment involved in an ongoing relationship. In the words of biblical scholar John Goldingay, "Men express that commitment in their willingness to leave the family in which they have grown up, to make a new start with a woman from another family."[9]

According to the Genesis account, then, the biblical vision for the right ordering of creation is one in which women are not to be forever subjected to men, nor is their flourishing to be dependent on marriage deals negotiated by and for men. This is a radically countercultural vision because it does away with any sort of a hierarchy between the man and the woman. In contrast to the way that marriage was commonly understood in the ancient world, no one "owns" anyone else and no one is subjected to the other, whether through a marriage transaction or otherwise. This point is further underscored by the fact that the Hebrew word for "wife" (*be'ula*)—a word that has its root in the verb "to own" and presupposes a real estate understanding of marriage—is nowhere to be found in the first three chapters of Genesis.[10]

Instead of the more specific Hebrew words for "husband" and "wife," the creation accounts in Genesis 1 and 2 both begin with the term "humanity" (*'adam*), which is the word used to denote human beings in general. Although there are times when this same word can be translated with the proper name "Adam," this is the rare exception. More often than not, *'adam* is better translated simply as "the human" or "humankind." Significantly, though, the author of Genesis 1 goes one step further and tells us that "humankind" (*'adam*) is intrinsically and essentially composed of both "male" (*zachar*) and "female" (*neqevah*): "Then God said, 'Let us make humankind [*'adam*] in our image, after our likeness.... God created humankind [*ha'adam*] in his own image, in the image of God he created them, male [*zachar*] and female [*neqevah*] he created them" (Gen 1:26-27).

So God creates human beings (*'adam*) in the image of God as "male" and "female" (and not, it should be noted, as "husband" or "wife"), which suggests that humans are not only fundamentally *plural* beings, but also *sexual* beings through and through. "Humanity" is a corporate entity that includes both male and female. Neither males nor females on their own embody what it means to be fully and truly human. It is only when male (*zachar*) and female (*neqevah*) in all their sexed difference are considered together that we begin to understand any talk about a common "humanity" (*'adam*).

This way of reading Genesis raises a number of questions about the "biblical view" of human sexuality to which we will return in the next chapter. But it will be helpful to tease out a few key points here. In the first place, if this male-female distinction lies at the core of what it means to be a human being, then human sexuality is first and foremost about who we are, not simply what we do. It's about our capacity for relationship, our profound desire for connectedness and intimacy, our longing to transcend our isolated individuality by becoming one with the other. It isn't merely about whom we have sex with, or when we get to have sex, or even whether we get to have sex. It is so much deeper than that.

By locating our sexed difference at the center of our humanity, the author of Genesis is radically expanding our vision of both what it means to be a human and what it means to be a sexual being. *Everything* we do as human beings is related to our reality as sexual creatures. At the same time, *every* form of sexual expression issues from and affects the very core of our humanity—no matter how "casual" we would like it to be.

The Genesis account thus challenges various modern notions of the human person that are reductive to the point of being misleading or downright false. It urges us not to collapse the whole of what it means to be human into a single form of sexual expression (or the singular way we desire to express it). Human sexuality is beautifully complex and manifests itself in countless forms, the most significant of which have to do with being in intimate relationship with the other and the Other.

Indeed, as Caroline J. Simon suggests in her insightful book on Christian sexual integrity, there are no less than six different "lenses" through which modern persons understand and evaluate the relationship between our sexuality and our humanity (the "covenant," "procreative," "romantic," "plain-sex," "power," and "expressive" lenses).[11] The central Christian task, says Simon, is not to isolate any one of these views of human sexuality as the "biblical ideal" so that we can discard the others. This would be to treat sexuality in the reductive way that Genesis resists. Instead, she suggests that we take up a more holistic view of human sexuality—one in which clarity and insight come through the convergence of multiple lenses. To treat something as complex and expansive as our sexuality as if it were simple and straight-forward is to narrow it into something unrecognizable and perhaps, even worse, subhuman.

Along similar lines, if we take the Genesis accounts seriously, neither should we reduce sexual expression to something as banal as mere intercourse. As David Allen Hubbard once put it so well, "All sexuality doesn't end in intercourse."[12] And I might add, all coitus isn't sexy. So we would do well to reclaim a view of human sexuality that understands something as seemingly mundane as drinking coffee with a friend as a profoundly sexual act. Following from the Genesis account, every single thing we do embodies and enacts our sexuality—the basic unity-in-diversity that constitutes us as human beings. Which means that Christians need to be asking questions about living with sexual integrity not just in the bedroom but in every domain of life.

Genesis 2 develops this vision of the human person as two-yet-one when God notices that the human (*'adam*) is alone. For the first time in the narrative, God declares something in the created order to be "not good." Specifically, it is "not good for the human to be alone" (Gen 2:18, my translation). Apparently, the entire created order, which was teeming with various kinds of non-human life, was not quite enough for the human. So God makes an *'ezer* for *'adam*, a "companion who corresponds to him" (Gen 2:18). The word-for-word translation for "companion" here is "like-opposite-him." According to most biblical interpreters, Genesis gives us no indication that this counterpart is in any way subordinate to the man (after all, *'ezer* is a word most often used to refer to God, as in Deut 33:29; Ps 27:9; Hos 13:9). If anything, given that her arrival on the scene serves as the climax of the story, the narrator might even see her as the pinnacle of creation. But the point of the text is not to elevate either of these human beings above the other. The point is that God creates a corresponding human who, unlike the animals, is in fact "bone of my bones and flesh of my flesh" (Gen 2:23). It is "not good" for the human to be alone because at its core humankind was created to be in intimate relationship with a distinct-yet-corresponding other.

It is therefore all the more significant that the human calls God's newest creation "woman" (*'ishshah*) because this term clearly expresses the woman's essential relatedness to the "man" (*'ish*, Gen 2:23). Lost in our English translations is the fact that the Hebrew words for "man" and "woman" sound nearly identical. In fact, to pronounce "woman" in Hebrew, all one has to do is say "man" with an audible "ah" at the end of the word. In purely aural terms, this breathy exhale serves as the only real distinction between the two, and it not only evokes the way God breathed life into the man and the woman, but also makes one wonder whether the man was not so much exclaiming at the sight of the woman as he was sighing in contended delight now that he was in her presence.

Thus, in a striking parallel to Genesis 1:27, where "humankind" is composed of the sexually differentiated-yet-corresponding male (*zachar*) and female (*neqevah*), Genesis 2:23 understands "humankind" to be "good" (complete or whole) only insofar as it incorporates both man (*'ish*) and woman (*'ishshah*). Neither of these passages diminishes the man nor the woman, but they acknowledge that on his own the man is simply "not good." In fact, without the woman, the man is not quite fully human. Or, to put it somewhat differently, a human being is not the radically free, autonomous individual we imagine that person to be. We are fundamentally persons in relation, fully realized only in the midst of a community of others who correspond to us, but are not like us.

According to this reading of the Genesis account, "humankind" is made up of male and female, man and woman. It's about being a person in relation. At least that's what I am suggesting these passages say. But what is perhaps even more important in a book about marriage and singleness is what these passages don't say. And what the authors of Genesis 1–3 never say is that this man and this woman are married.

That's correct. As I mentioned above, neither the word *husband* nor the word *wife* is ever used in the creation accounts. Given our modern sensibilities, which rightly find distasteful anything that sounds like one human is "possessing" another, most English translations of Genesis render the genitive construct of "his woman" or "her man" as "his wife" or "her husband." Now, I certainly appreciate the reasoning behind this decision. "His wife" does indeed sound more palatable than "his woman." And it's far less cumbersome than the more accurate "the woman of the man." But in the original languages no mention is made of husbands or wives. This is because these aren't stories about marriage per se, but about how humanity came to be. These stories give us a sense of what makes us tick. They're about our common humanity, which has its origin in our being created in God's image as male and female, man and woman—not as "husband and wife."

Even in the well-known passage of Genesis 2:24 that is so often used in modern wedding ceremonies—the one where a man leaves his father and mother—the language is still *'ish* (man) and *'ishshah* (woman), not husband and wife. This doesn't mean that we can say with certainty that these first humans were not married, or that they did not eventually become or at least function as husband and wife. It just means that the text doesn't give us any indication one way or the other. So to suggest that this "flesh of my flesh" moment between the man and the woman is the institution of a wedding ceremony or that it is clear evidence that marriage is divinely blessed as humanity's highest ideal is to be guilty of overinterpreting the text.

Interestingly, though, what we do know is that they don't consummate their relationship until after they have left the Garden. This too is an argument from silence because the narrative simply does not provide us with many details, but it appears that Adam and Eve do not come to "know" each other (in the "biblical sense") until after they are exiled (Gen 4:1). Does this mean there was no sex in the Garden? If so, this would align well with Jesus' description of resurrection life, which we will address in the next chapter. But even if we decide that sex was the only way that these two humans could have been "fruitful" and "multiplied" (Gen 1:28), we cannot get around the fact that the text implies an intimacy in the Garden between the man, the woman, and most importantly God that precedes and surpasses sexual intimacy. This human-divine-human intimacy, which the narrator evokes with images of God walking about the orchard "at the breezy time of the day" (Gen 3:8), is itself a highly generative and fecund image, so much so that we may very well be jumping to conclusions when we see sex in places where it otherwise goes unspoken.

Nevertheless, whether Adam and Eve were engaged in marital relations in the Garden or not, what the text does tell us is that something goes terribly awry. A metaphysical rupture takes place that transforms what was once a beautifully diverse human community into a reality marked by hard and fast distinctions, distance, and separation. No longer would the man and the woman live in mutual interdependence. Instead, they would now experience radical independence, which would forever set them over and against both one another and the created order. And this is seen perhaps nowhere more clearly than in how their domestic lives would now be organized (Gen 3:16-19).

From this view both marriage and "marital relations" seem to be less about God's original design and more about a response to a broken and disordered creation. They are less-than-perfect, less-than-ideal accommodations that are not unlike the garments of animal skin that God makes for the man and the woman in Genesis 3:21—gracious provisions for surviving in a world that is now broken. In a world marked by sin and death, being fruitful and multiplying has taken on a whole new meaning for the man and the woman. In a post-Eden world, marriage becomes a means for reclaiming what was lost—the kind of intimacy and vulnerability that is necessary for humanity not only to survive ("be fruitful") but also to thrive ("multiply").

All this to say, even though some readers may really want Genesis 1–3 (and more specifically Genesis 2:23-24) to be saying that marriage is an integral component of being fully human, there is very little evidence to support this claim. Again, this doesn't mean that the biblical authors had no concept of marriage or "husbands and wives" when writing about the first parents. It simply means that, from the perspective of the First Testament, marriage is always already rooted in a prior theological understanding of human origins, and not the other way around. In other words, marriage does not encompass the whole of what it means to be a human being, nor is it the pinnacle of human existence. Instead, the biblical vision is one in which humankind is a community of persons living in intimate and mutually interdependent relationship with each other and God. It is through the lens of this particular anthropology that the biblical authors understand the significance of marriage both for the husband and wife and for the larger relational web in which they live.

MARRIAGE AS METAPHOR

If the creation stories in Genesis are indeed providing us with an alternative vision for what it means to be human—one rooted in a mutual, self-giving commitment to the other—then it would seem that human beings were created with a built-in aching for otherness. Even God recognizes this deep longing within the human, going so far as to say, "It is not good for the human to be alone" (Gen 2:18, my translation). Many otherwise well-meaning Christians have taken this portion of Scripture to mean that singleness is not simply a lonely or isolating experience but an actual denial of God's good gift to humanity. Worse yet, some even see it as a failure on the part of the single person. It is for this same reason that so many within the church envision the individual's "life quest" primarily as a journey toward a divinely appointed spouse. And the community's role in this journey is to help the single person find that special someone who alone can fulfill the longing for otherness that resides deep within all of us.

Without discounting the profound longing for wholeness that we all feel, what I have hopefully made clear by now is that this is a misreading of the biblical text. It most certainly is not good for humans to be alone—we can be sure of that much. But the answer to being alone is not marriage. It's community. Better yet, it's communion, primarily with God and also with each other. This is how the biblical narrative understands what it means to be fully human. And yet, as we noted in the previous chapter, the Christian community often operates with a conception of the human person that seems far closer to the "soulmate" view espoused by Aristophanes in Plato's *Symposium* than anything found in the biblical narratives. Aristophanes claimed that we all long to find the other half of our once-unified soul—that one person to whom we can say (along with Jerry Maguire and Dr. Evil), "You complete me." The problem with this way of understanding our collective "aching for otherness" is not that it pictures humanity as being incomplete. We most certainly are. The problem is that we are incomplete in a far more radical way.

The primary human dilemma according to the biblical narrative is not that we desire otherness or even that we seek to express that desire in a variety of concrete ways. It's that time and time again humans attempt to satisfy their basic aching for otherness through some other means than God. In the case of marriage and sex, we seek to fulfill this desire through the security, intimacy, or pleasure that we believe another human being can provide.

It is thus no small wonder that many of the references to marriage in the First Testament are neither descriptive nor prescriptive, but metaphorical. In fact, the marriage relationship serves as one of the primary images that the biblical authors call on to explore both God's covenant faithfulness to Israel and the incredible damage wrought by Israel's lack of faithfulness. Whether it's the prophetic language about God's betrothal to the people of God (Is 54:5), the numerous analogies of Israel acting as an adulterous whore (Jer 3:20; Ezek 16:1-63; Mal 2:10-16), or the actual marriages of the prophets, which serve as living illustrations of Israel's unfaithfulness (see Hosea), the First Testament routinely speaks of the God-Israel relationship in terms of a marriage, emphasizing the relational fallout that occurs when, like an adulterous spouse, the people of Israel look beyond their covenant relationship to address their deep-seated longing for otherness.

Of course, not all the marriage metaphors in the biblical text are negative. For example, Song of Songs is an extended, celebratory love poem that explores the God-human relationship in highly intimate, even sexual terms. It is not clear whether the lovers in this historically scandalous book are in fact married or even betrothed. But what is clear is that this poem—like any poem—is asking readers to entertain a meaning that is more than merely physical or material. We're not just talking about human love here (even though human love and sexuality are certainly a big part of the equation). As Ellen Davis has said (somewhat controversially), it is a mistake to understand the Song in terms of either pure analogy or strict physicality. Instead, "the poet places this love song firmly in the context of God's passionate and troubled relationship with humanity.... The Song is about repairing the damage done by the first disobedience in Eden, what Christian tradition calls 'the Fall.'"[13]

So in an important sense the Song of Songs encapsulates the First Testament's take on what it means to be a human being. We are the ones who are possessed—enraptured even—by the One who loves us. "I am my lover's and my lover is mine," says Song of Songs 6:3. That's what it means to be human. We of course don't want to lose sight of the fact that this is a love poem from one human to another. But according to the First Testament, it is also the case that God is a bridegroom who is infatuated with his bride, inviting her to join him in that most intimate of spaces where they are each fully in the presence of the other. This is a return to the Garden, a return to the place where we were only ever truly human because we were in the presence of our Creator, our husband and lover. Which is another way of saying that in an ultimate sense to be fully human *is* to be married—just not to another human.

ABOUT A CHRISTIAN DIVORCE

By Sarey Martin

I reached my hand across to the other pillow at 3 a.m. many, many times. His head was rarely there, particularly in the last year. I would often get up to look for him and sometimes plead with him—if he was in the house at all and if I was able to wake him. If you've had the experience of having a drug addict or alcoholic in your immediate family, then you can imagine the array of peculiar positions I found his body in, and the surrounding combination of debris that defied explanation.

Having realistic expectations was something I took pride in when going into marriage at age twenty-six. Unlike the rose-colored, "Christian" glasses I was so critical of, I knew that I was about to do something that was going to be very difficult. And as an overachieving eldest child, I was down for a challenge.

My husband was someone I'd known since we were ten years old. He confessed to having a huge, lifelong crush on me, which was a very adorable narrative we often shared when we reunited in our early twenties and fell in love. It felt to me that we became the best of friends very quickly. We were "partying" more than is prudent for people professing Christian faith, but we often talked about our desire for God and getting more serious about our faith and soon found a church to call home.

I eventually surrendered my practices of excess. But my husband transferred his to a terrifying, underground lair of secrecy and lies, where they grew.

I very slowly learned the extent of his problems. At first I spent a good amount of time trying to manage and hide it all. Then I got honest with myself and realized the degree of difficulty we were experiencing in marriage was not the normal kind. Gradually I began looking for help in my church community, trying to articulate a problem that I didn't quite understand myself. It took some time, but I did get help, and I am thankful I received a lot of compassion and grace rather than judgment.

A couple years of theft, lies, and disasters ensued, during which he went to detox, rehab, and sober living facilities multiple times, all the while expressing a lot of remorse. Without fail, though, he would start using drugs within a week or two after release.

Eventually, I made the hard decision to leave. I told him to deliver me a plan for getting and staying sober, and if I saw him living it out, I would be back by his side. I held his hand through hell and high water, and now it was time to try tough love.

But it didn't work. He eventually found another woman to manipulate. He got arrested a few times. And now I don't know where he is.

I highly value marriage and never expected to be put into this corner. I held to the traditional view that the only biblical reason for divorce was infidelity, and even then I believed reconciliation was possible. The redemptive potential in that scenario was inspiring to me. But I never had proof outright that my husband was unfaithful to me, and he so often made such a display of tears over his failures that it was incomprehensible to me that he wouldn't someday change. Instead, he gradually drifted away behind a plethora of smoke and mirrors, until I found myself alone and trying to figure out how one gets unmarried. I considered myself in the 1 Corinthians 7 category of a believing spouse abandoned by an unbeliever.

My closest friends at church showed me a lot of kindness, and when they said, "I can't imagine what you're going through," I knew it was true. I was glad they didn't know what it felt like, but it also compounded the sense of isolation I felt. When I was around single friends who were lamenting their loneliness, I found myself asking if it was really better to have "loved and lost, than to never have loved at all." I knew they wouldn't believe me when I told them that the loneliness I experienced in marriage was far more excruciating than the loneliness I'd felt as a single person. I wanted to ask them to imagine what it was like to meet a person who you felt was perfectly suited for you, experience marriage, sex, and conversations about starting a family, and then helplessly watch it all slip through your fingers. I had stepped into a shadowy version of the ideal they longed for—one that vanished as quickly as it had appeared.

And now I feel like a marked woman. I'm sure when I walk into church on Sunday there are those who have questions they dare not ask me. I'm sure there are people wondering what my marital status is and what happened, but they won't ask. They might ask someone else about me and make their judgments. I run the story of my marriage and divorce through my mind over and over again, ready to explain it to church staff, or a future romantic interest, or a new friend, or a future employer so that it is an air-tight explanation of everything I tried to do to save the *Titanic*.

Divorce is its own kind of hell. Yet I remain thankful that this is how I learned what Paul spoke about when he heard the Lord say, "My grace is enough for you, for my power is made perfect in weakness" (2 Cor 12:9). That's where I find strength now: not in my own wisdom or efforts, but in the power of Christ resting on me.

4

LIKE A VIRGIN

THE NEW TESTAMENT ON SINGLENESS
AND WHAT IT MEANS TO BE SEXUAL

IN A 2015 SPEECH ANNOUNCING his candidacy for president of the United States, Mike Huckabee drew explicitly on the language of his Christian faith in order to make his appeal to voters. A former Southern Baptist pastor himself, Huckabee spoke of the lessons he learned while growing up in his hometown of Hope, Arkansas:

> I learned that God loves me as much as he loves anyone. But he doesn't love some more than others. I learned the Pledge of Allegiance, the Lord's Prayer, and the Preamble of the Constitution. We prayed at the start of each day and we prayed again before lunch. And I learned that this exceptional country could only be explained by the providence of Almighty God.[1]

Building on this increasingly common blend of American nationalism and Christianity, Huckabee went on to suggest that the primary problem that American society faced was its profound sense of moral waywardness rooted in an abandonment of "biblical" principles. And even though all of this might seem a bit out of place in a speech designed to kick off a presidential bid, one of Huckabee's primary concerns was the manner and degree to which the Bible was (or was not) informing our shared understanding of marriage: "We've lost our way morally. . . . And we are now threatening the foundation of religious liberty by criminalizing Christianity and demanding we abandon biblical principles of natural marriage."[2]

The question of how one understands the biblical text and its relationship to our common life is by no means new. But it remains a particularly pressing matter today, especially as it concerns the way the Christian community conceives of marriage, singleness, and sexuality. Complicating matters even further, at least in the American context, is the unique kind of political co-opting of biblical theology that has taken place as we have moved from the late twentieth century into the first two decades of the twenty-first century. In a post–Moral Majority world (that is, since the mid-1970s), it is commonplace to hear candidates running for public office refer to something along the lines of Huckabee's "biblical principles of natural marriage" as a way of framing (and justifying) their political agendas.

The problem here is not that politicians can't be thoughtful interpreters of the biblical witness. Nor is the problem politics itself. No matter what side of the aisle we find most comfortable, all our interpretive efforts are bound up with politics in one way or another. Rather than pretend that we can somehow do away with our political leanings, we instead need to do the hard work of making our various biases explicit so that we can engage them critically and in community.

When it comes to how we understand the "biblical view of marriage" (or even what we mean by that phrase), one of the primary hurdles we face today is the Christian community's tendency to read the biblical text in ways that uncritically privilege certain political commitments over and against the commitments of its own interpretive tradition. In a highly polarized and increasingly partisan political climate, terms like *marriage* and *human sexuality* become identity markers for all-encompassing ideologies that often bear little resemblance to the biblical text itself or the historic Christian faith. So it's important that we acknowledge and ultimately move beyond these purely political readings in order to avoid a kind of ideological heavy-handedness in our engagement with Scripture.

But what is of equal importance in these politically fraught times is our ability to identify what is actually at stake any time we offer a particular take on what the Bible does or does not say. And as chapter three hopefully made clear, one of the things that's at stake is nothing less than our basic understanding of what it means to be human—what theologians like to call our "anthropology."

It would be a mistake, though, to blame contemporary politics for all our problems. When it comes to marriage, the Protestant church in general and evangelicals in particular have been guilty of simply making too much of a good thing. In her insightful book on unrequited love, *Loves Me, Loves Me Not*, Laura Smit makes a similar claim:

> Protestantism has done much to elevate the worth of marriage. . . . However, in asserting the value of marriage . . . Protestantism has consistently ignored the Bible's clear teaching on singleness. In contemporary American Protestantism, we actually see an underlying assumption that "family values" and "Christian values" are synonymous. Protestants have often argued that marriage is necessary for civil order and that Christians are thus obligated to maintain the creation order by preserving marriage as the norm.[3]

If Smit is correct (and I think she is), then the normative picture of marriage that has captured the imagination of the American church is not merely a departure from the biblical vision (although it surely is). In a very real and significant sense, it is idolatrous. Marriage serves as an object that many Christians obsessively pursue (with the encouragement of their community) in the hopes that it might satisfy their deepest desires.

This is exactly why Smit goes on to suggest in the brief appendix to her book that it is a matter of some urgency that the Christian community reconsider and ultimately submit itself anew to the New Testament teaching on marriage and singleness. If it is to ever have a chance of serving as a credible witness in the contemporary cultural context, says Smit, the church needs not only to rethink its handling of Scripture, but also to reorganize its common life accordingly.

In certain respects this chapter (and this book as a whole) picks up where Smit's argument leaves off, focusing on a number of New Testament texts that address the question of marriage, singleness, and sexuality. Much like our discussion of the First Testament, our goal here is to reconsider the distorted picture of marriage and sex that holds the church captive by exploring what the Bible actually has to say.

Of course, as we noted in the previous chapter, doing so is easier said than done, especially given the fact that the Christian community tends to equate being married with what it means to be fully human. After all, if we start with the assumption that humans remain forever incomplete in the absence of "the one" for whom they ultimately long and for whom God has specifically designed them, then it makes perfect sense to conclude that it is not only inhumane but also dehumanizing for anyone to be without one's divinely appointed spouse. Short of marriage and sex, one simply cannot live as a fully flourishing human being.

From this view, the act of coupling—as an expression of our passionate desire for reuniting with our "other half"—is not simply self-justifying, but morally foundational. And it is for this very reason that the Christian community often emphasizes and even elevates biblical texts that reinforce its prior assumptions about marriage and sexuality while disregarding or downplaying those that do not. It's why Adam and Eve are (mis)understood as being spouses first and humans only second. It's why sermons about King David focus rightly on the great tragedy of his marital infidelity, but seem to overlook God's apparent willingness to provide him with even more wives if he had simply asked (2 Sam 12:8). And as the present chapter will make clear, this understanding of marriage and sex as self-justifying is also why the New Testament's vision strikes so many Christians as not only radically counterintuitive, but "unnatural" and irrational—an impossibility even.

We desperately need to reconstruct a more biblically informed vision, which is why we now turn our attention to what the New Testament has to say about these matters. While the New Testament texts are fairly diverse in terms of their form, content, and audience, they nevertheless demonstrate a surprising degree of consistency concerning their approach toward marriage, singleness, and sexuality. I want us to focus on three of these commonalities in particular.

In the first place, the New Testament authors are clear that marriage is not the normative relational model for the Christian individual or for the Christian community. Marriage is simply one possible option for followers of Christ. It is neither the chief aim of human life nor the pinnacle of human existence.

Second, from a New Testament perspective, celibate singleness is an equally legitimate option for the Christian—perhaps even the preferred one. Not only does it offer a more realistic description of our default status over the course of our life, but it also anticipates the subversive dynamics of the coming kingdom.

Finally, the New Testament authors consistently suggest that having sex is not necessary for human flourishing. The genital expression of our sexuality is not a requirement for living a full, complete, and integrated life because all life is in an important sense "sexual"—a notion that amounts to a near absurdity for modern readers, most Christians included.

AND THEN THERE WAS NONE: MARRIAGE AND SEX IN RESURRECTION LIFE

In the previous chapter, I made the somewhat provocative suggestion that sex and marriage might not have been a part of life in the Garden. Not only do the authors of Genesis use the generic language of "man" and "woman" rather than "husband" and "wife" to talk about the first humans, but according to how the story actually unfolds, this man and woman do not come to "know" each other until after their expulsion from paradise. We can speculate all we want about how sex would have surely been necessary for these humans to "be fruitful and multiply" and how consequently marriage would have been implied as well. But the text itself simply does not provide us with any of this information.

Still, the notion of a sexless and marriage-less Eden is not a hill I'm willing to die on. Needless to say, I wasn't in Eden, so I'm not privy to any of the details outside the biblical testimony. But I am pressing the question of marriage and sex here because, as a kind of interpretive thought experiment, it helps to expose the variety of ways we bring assumptions to a text like Genesis 1–3. When we assume that marriage and sex are constitutive elements of our humanity, we have a tendency to uncritically read those assumptions into the gaps that are not filled by the narrative itself. This doesn't mean that the first humans were absolutely not married. They very well may have been. It just means that we need to be clear about what is actually found in the text and what we as modern readers are bringing to it.

The more important point, however, is that the reading of Genesis that I have proposed seems to align much more readily with the New Testament witness, especially the teachings of Jesus and Paul. Of course, the Gospels don't provide us with any greater detail than Genesis does regarding sex in the Garden. Nevertheless, they do give us insight into how Jesus would answer the question of whether marriage and sex are requirements for a fully flourishing human life.

In an account that is found in all three of the synoptic Gospels, a group of Sadducees approach Jesus with a question meant to expose the absurdity of his belief in a physical resurrection (Mt 22:23-32; Mk 12:18-27; Lk 20:27-40). Referencing the legal prescriptions concerning Levirate marriage, these religious leaders present the case of a hypothetical woman who marries seven brothers successively after each has died. In the resurrection, they ask, whose wife will she be? Jesus' answer is as straightforward as it is shocking: "The people of this age marry and are given in marriage. But those who are regarded as worthy to share in that age and in the resurrection from the dead neither marry nor are given in marriage" (Lk 20:34-35).

According to Jesus, marriage is a relationship that is bound up with the present age. However, in the resurrection—that is, in our fully realized human life in the age to come—no one is married. By extension, neither is anyone having sexual intercourse. Some interpreters go the opposite direction and suggest that because no one will be given in marriage in the age to come, we will be free to enjoy total sexual union with anyone (and everyone?) who delights in us. As the argument goes, no one will "own" anyone in the way that the Sadducees assumed this hypothetical woman was owned by her seven husbands, so sex will be freed from the inherently destructive power dynamics of the present age.[4] The problem with this reading is that Jesus seems to be rather clear that both marriage *and* sex are coming to an end. This is what he means when he says that we will become "like angels in heaven" (Mk 12:25). As William Loader has rightly pointed out, it would have been both unprecedented and outrageous on a number of levels if Jesus were advocating an open-sex view of resurrected life. And no outrage of this kind is reflected in the responses that we find in the Gospel narratives.[5]

A similar error would be to understand Jesus' language about becoming equal to angels as an indication that resurrected humanity will be asexual, as if becoming fully human involved the complete casting off of our sexuality. But Jesus never implies that we will be anything less than the fully embodied and sexed beings that we were created to be from the very beginning. Nor will we be anything less than the relational creatures that we are. Even so, according to Jesus, when we are resurrected into the fullness of our true humanity, marriage and sex will not be a part of the equation.

To contemporary ears, the notion of an eternity without sex sounds rather unappealing—repellant even. And this is as true for Christians as it is for anyone else. So we may be tempted to rationalize a fair bit while reading this text, convincing ourselves that Jesus must be talking only about the age to come. At least for now in the "present age" we can rest assured that sex remains an integral part of human life. Surely even Jesus would acknowledge that sex is an essential element of what it means to be human in the here and now, or at least recognize along with Freud that sex is an unstoppable force which when not expressed leads to dysfunction and pathology. And all of this would be especially true for the Christian, for whom marriage is the God-appointed solution to the insoluble problem of sexual desire—right? Well, not quite.

Consider Matthew 19 (and Mk 10:1-12), where a group of Pharisees approach Jesus with a question about the Mosaic laws on divorce. Jesus answers by quoting Genesis 2, taking care to underscore the way a husband and wife have become "one flesh." Jesus concludes by stating, "They are no longer two, but one flesh. Therefore what God has joined together, let no one separate" (Mt 19:6). Much like the author of Genesis 2:24, Jesus is addressing his audience directly here. In this case, it is the Pharisees. His point is that once two humans are married they are united physically, emotionally, spiritually, and socially. And this union should be taken with utter seriousness, not with the kind of flippancy that the Pharisees' question about divorce implied. In fact, according to Jesus, the union between husband and wife is real even when it is not faithful, which divorce legislation is to recognize rather than neutralize.

From Jesus' perspective, to divide "one flesh" into two is far more than a matter of simply divvying up the possessions of a household. It is to undercut God's creative purposes in the world. So Jesus says no, divorce does not in fact align with God's original intentions for marriage. In marriage God unites two people in a covenant bond as equal partners, much like the first humans were inextricably bound to one another.

But—and this is a big "but"—this is not the same thing as suggesting that all human beings were created for marriage or that they are somehow incomplete without it. The emphasis of Jesus' teaching here is on the indissolubility of marriage, not on what it means to be human.

Naturally, the Pharisees press Jesus to explain why then Mosaic law would allow for divorce if in fact it contradicted God's intentions. Jesus responds by saying that Moses permitted divorce only because of the hardness of the human heart. In truth, says Jesus, outside of "immorality" (Greek *porneia*) on the part of a spouse, to divorce and remarry is equivalent to committing adultery (Mt 19:9). Divorce is thus an accommodation for those living in a hard-hearted world.

The disciples are understandably nonplussed in light of what Jesus has said, so much so that they suggest that it might be better to avoid marriage altogether. After all, if a husband has no options for ending a marriage that is obviously not working out in the way he would like, why would anyone take such a risk? Jesus' reply is telling, in part because he doesn't correct the disciples' misgivings. Instead, he says, "Not everyone can accept this statement, except those to whom it has been given. For there are some eunuchs who were that way from birth, and some who were made eunuchs by others, and some who became eunuchs for the sake of the kingdom of heaven. The one who is able to accept this should accept it" (Mt 19:11-12).

If the disciples were already having trouble with Jesus' thoughts on divorce, his comments about eunuchs probably didn't alleviate their concerns. So what exactly do Genesis, Mosaic laws, and eunuchs have in common? According to Jesus, the unifying thread that ties them all together is the kingdom that is already-but-not-yet present. Jesus brings up eunuchs in order to say that, despite how difficult it may be to accept, those who are celibate in the present age (whether by choice or not) are living, breathing previews of life as it is in the kingdom. In other words, resurrection life is a state in which no one is married and everyone is celibate.

At the same time, though, by quoting the Genesis passages about humanity being "male and female" (Mt 19:4), Jesus makes clear that his vision of resurrection life is by no means asexual. It would of course be possible to describe some theoretical, asexual state in a number of ways, but "human" would most certainly not be one of them. Instead, for Jesus the coming kingdom is one in which human sexuality will finally be given full expression. And yet somehow this sexuality will be expressed in a way that involves neither marriage nor sex, not because they are bad or wrong, but because this new reality will render them superfluous.

It is significant that Jesus was able to say all of this without diminishing the value of marriage or its role in God's creative purposes in the world. If anything, Jesus urges his disciples and the religious leaders of his day to take marriage more seriously and not less. His teachings on divorce are evidence that Jesus affirmed marriage as a divinely created good. But Jesus radically reorients the view of marriage and sexuality that was commonly held by his contemporaries—one that also remains prevalent today.

For instance, it does not seem that Jesus would support the claim that "according to Genesis 1 and 2, we were made for marriage, and marriage was made for us."[6] In fact, Jesus' interpretation of Genesis 1 and 2 moves in exactly the opposite direction. Nowhere in Matthew 19 does he suggest that "marriage was made for us." Rather, his point is that marriage was not made for *divorce*. Neither is he saying that humans were "made for marriage." Instead, humans were made for each other, and while some of them will marry in this life, no one will be able to experience the fullness of their humanity until they are resurrected into a reality in which marriage no longer exists.

So for Jesus those who are given in marriage "in this age" should commit to their relationship in a way that reflects God's original intentions *for marriage*—as an indissoluble covenant. But Jesus also makes clear that not everyone is called to marriage. Indeed, in an ultimate sense no one is. For those "to whom it has been given" (Mt 19:11), celibate singleness is an equally legitimate and God-given gift. In other words, according to Jesus, God gives to some the gift of celibate singleness and to others the gift of being married. There is no sense in which one is better or worse because at their core marriage and singleness are reflections of the myriad yet particular ways God invites each of us to be faithfully present in the world. Another way of putting this is to say that for Jesus marriage and singleness are a matter of calling—of vocation.

Still we should not lose sight of the truly scandalous nature of Jesus' words. As he points out in Matthew 19, many people have a hard time believing that a life without sex (and by extension a biological family and offspring) is possible, much less fulfilling. But some of his listeners may have had just as much trouble accepting the notion that marriage also has no place in the age to come.

I must confess that I personally struggle to embrace this part of Jesus' teaching. There are no words for how much I love my wife. And I've been married long enough now that it's hard for me to imagine the world or my place in it as someone who isn't married. Of course, as a (perpetually exhausted) father of three young children, it's not too difficult to imagine a state of existence without sex. But one without marriage is another matter. So while I can speak only for myself, I am sure I am not alone in feeling genuinely unsettled when I think of a reality that doesn't involve my wife still being my wife and me still being her husband.

But this may very well be the point. Even though I am married, in no way does that exempt me from treating marriage as an idol. Just like a single person who longs for nothing more than finding the perfect spouse, I too operate at times as if marriage is something that can actually quell the restlessness of my heart—something that can make me whole. This deep-seated desire is what prompted me to pursue marriage in the first place, so it's certainly something that I want to affirm. But this very same impulse also causes me to clench my fists around it now, doggedly refusing to let it go, regardless of what Jesus says about the age to come. So when it comes to my marriage, I am often guilty of seeking fulfillment in and through something that is ultimately not fulfilling. In other words, because my deeper problems were not born from being single, marriage didn't "solve" anything, and it never will. I am simply treading a well-worn path that leads all the way back to the Garden.

All this to say, whether single or married, sexually active or not, Jesus' words are unsettling precisely because they confront us with a difficult truth about the object of our desires. We actually *do* believe that marriage and sex will make us whole, and we *don't* trust that a world without them would actually be fulfilling. In effect, Jesus' words about life in the kingdom pull the rug out from under us, highlighting just how misdirected we have become. Deep down we simply don't believe that Jesus' vision of resurrection life will ever be enough to truly satisfy us.

"I WISH THAT EVERYONE WAS AS I AM": SINGLENESS AS ICON

In his book *The Divine Magician*, Peter Rollins explores the human tendency to create and pursue idols. Because we make idols out of anything and everything—including marriage and romantic love—Rollins suggests that the Christian faith harbors an event that is structurally similar to a magic act. Much like Adam and Eve, all humans long for some object that lies on the other side of a veil of prohibition (like a magician's curtain). Because this object is inaccessible to us, we invest it with a kind of religious significance, revering it as sacred. As a result, in our daily lives we operate with the assumption that if we could somehow obtain the object of our desire (such as a spouse), it would provide us with the kind of wholeness and well-being that we seek.

But Jesus pulls the magician's curtain back to reveal the truth: Our sacred object is an illusion. And it always has been. There is nothing behind the curtain that will ever fulfill us. In fact, the "lack" that marks our lives—the "emptiness" we obsessively attempt to fill—is actually created by the very object that we seek. So even when it is obtained, our experience of the fulfillment it provides is profoundly *un*fulfilling. Thus for Jesus to say that marriage and sex are not part of resurrection life is not to make a once-substantive reality disappear. Instead, it is to reveal to us that our sacred object never actually existed in the first place.

What I find most interesting about Rollins's book is how often he refers to marriage and romantic relationships to make his point about the idolatry that pervades the Christian community. Indeed, as Rollins points out, the obsessive quest for marriage among single Christians and the elevation of the marriage relationship within our Christian communities seems to be one of the more fitting images for humanity's idolatrous tendencies.

> To understand this, we need only think about the ubiquitous fantasy, propagated across our culture, of a couple who are able to make each other whole, complete, and fulfilled. Not surprisingly, the stories that describe this vision tend to end at the moment when the couple meets, often signaled by the phrase "and they lived happily ever after." What this suggests is that after all the dragons have been fought, the evil stepmothers overcome, and the curses broken, the couple melts into each other's arms and finds satisfaction.[7]

According to Rollins, Jesus does not reveal our idolatry in order to save us from our desires—as if our core longing for intimate human relationship were the problem. Rather, Jesus locates our desire in another register altogether. In other words, Jesus isn't some cruel bully who is taking away our favorite toy and making us feel childish and guilty for enjoying it in the first place. Instead, he is opening up a reality in which our desire is "emboldened, deepened, and robbed of its melancholic yearning."[8] To use Rollins's language, Jesus is signaling the disappearance of the idol and the appearance of the icon: "When we are caught up in idolatry, we focus on some special object that makes everything else in the world mundane. In contrast, the iconic way of being helps us experience the mundane as infused with special significance. In theological terms, this is the idea of God in the midst of life."[9]

As the "image [*eikon*] of the invisible God" (Col 1:15), Jesus is quite literally the "icon" of God in the midst of life. But as it concerns our understanding of marriage and sexuality, the iconic nature of Jesus' ministry is about more than just his teachings. If Jesus is in fact the "new Adam" (Rom 5:12-15; 1 Cor 15:20-28, 42-49) and thus the only true human being, then his lifelong singleness and celibacy undermines the notion that marriage is the only relationship in which a human might flourish in the fullest sense of the word.

The apostle Paul's singleness functions in a similar, albeit qualitatively different, way.[10] In both cases, though, their teachings about marriage and singleness were rooted in a prior and more fundamental way of seeing and thus loving the world. Much like those who were eunuchs "for the sake of the kingdom" (Mt 19:12), both Jesus and Paul literally embodied in their own life and being something of a reality that was still to come.

It is at least in part for this reason that Paul was able to speak credibly to members of the newly forming Christian communities with such a challenging word: "I wish that everyone was as I am [celibate and single]. But each has his own gift from God, one this way, another that" (1 Cor 7:7). Much like Jesus' teaching on celibacy as something that is "given" to people, Paul is suggesting here that God gives to some the gift of celibate singleness and to others the gift of marriage. They are both inherently good gifts, and should be received as such, but neither represents an "ideal" state to which all Christians ought to conform.

Yet, what is perhaps even more important for Paul is that both forms of Christian life—single and married—are not first and foremost about personal fulfillment or self-actualization, but about the right ordering of our desires. Sex has its place, but it isn't ultimate, which means that a Christian's sexual passions need to be directed in ways that will lead to both individual and communal flourishing. In Paul's mind, the best way to cultivate this kind of generative life is through the disciplining and directing of our sexual desires in every relationship. Paul makes this clear when he repeats himself: "To the unmarried and widows I say that it is best for them to remain as I am [celibate and single]. But if they do not have self-control, let them get married. For it is better to marry than to burn with sexual desire" (1 Cor 7:8-9).

This is neither a prudish suppression of sexuality nor an attempt to say that marriage is valuable only insofar as it extinguishes our sexual desire. Instead, much like Jesus, Paul is situating all our passionate longings within the larger framework of Christian community and discipleship. For not only is the genital expression of our sexual desire not ultimate in any sense, but as Christians our sexuality is not finally our own. So even when Paul offers up the possibility of sexual expression within marriage as a "concession" for those who are "burning" with desire (1 Cor 7:6), its primary function is to direct this desire in a way that will allow the community to thrive, and not simply to satiate the lone, sexually frustrated individual.

The Greek word for "burning" here is *pyrousthai*, which invokes a sense of overpowering excess not unlike an uncontrolled forest fire (it's where we get the words *pyrotechnic* and *pyromaniac*). What Paul is addressing here are not the base-level sexual urges that every human being experiences on a daily basis, but rather sexual desire run amok—a kind of chaotic impulse that threatens the livelihood of the surrounding community. In other words, to "burn with desire" is not simply to have one's internal sexual embers stoked. It is to run the risk of burning the entire forest to the ground. It's pyromania gone wild.

Thus for Paul there are two equally legitimate channels for directing one's sexual desire (or desire of any kind) in a way that leads to the community's flourishing. The first option, which Paul personally favored, is to remain single and celibate. However, Paul's letter to the Corinthians suggests that those who are called to marriage—the second option—must also demonstrate the right ordering of sexual desire, not only for the sake of their marriages but also for the sake of the broader community.

Apparently there were some within the church at Corinth who were suggesting that married Christians should remain celibate in order to honor God with their bodies. In response Paul acknowledges that

married couples would do well to mutually agree to a period of abstinence in order to "devote [themselves] to prayer" (1 Cor 7:5). This is a
rather revealing insight in its own right, for it underscores the fact that
even for those who are married or about to marry, the Christian community needs to develop a more robust notion of celibacy within
marriage. As it turns out (and as any married person will readily admit),
real marriages do not involve endless sexual activity, which means that
vast amounts of married life demand that spouses direct their sexual
desires in ways that are strikingly similar to the practices of those who
are single and celibate.

Nevertheless, Paul rejects the notion that a husband and wife should
remain permanently celibate (1 Cor 7:1-3). After all, to say that married
couples should avoid sexual expression altogether would be to deny
that marriage and human sexuality were created goods, designed and
given to us by God. So Paul makes it clear that husbands and wives
should not deny each other sex. But in the midst of offering this
pastoral advice, what he does *not* say is that simply because two people
are married they are free to express their sexuality in whatever way
they desire. In fact, it's quite the opposite. On a very basic level, to be
a Christian spouse is to renounce one's rights over one's body and its
attendant desires, for the bodies of both the husband and the wife now
belong to someone else. "It is not the wife who has the rights to her
own body, but the husband. In the same way, it is not the husband
who has the rights to his own body, but the wife" (1 Cor 7:4).

The idea that neither spouse has any authority over his or her own
body would have been profoundly countercultural in Paul's day, but it
is equally challenging for contemporary readers, even if for different
reasons. Whereas a first-century audience would stumble over Paul's
claim that husbands have no rights over their own bodies and are
subject to their wives, contemporary readers are more likely to object
to the way Paul calls into question the inalienable rights of the autonomous individual. Interestingly, the word for "rights" in this passage
is *exousiazo*, which is perhaps better translated as "power" or "authority."

The basic point remains the same though: As a Christian spouse, my body is no longer my own. It belongs to another. I have no "power" over it, even as it concerns the various ways I desire to express my sexuality in and through my body.

But this doesn't mean that the relationship between a husband and wife is a zero-sum game. It's about the right kind of mutuality. A husband, for example, is giving his body as he is receiving his wife's as his own. In this way, he observes his wife's power over his body so as to enjoy not only his wife's body, but also his own.[11]

From Paul's perspective then, just as it is with celibate Christians, the sexual desires of married people also need to be rightly ordered if they are to be truly life giving, which is to say that they are to be directed toward the other in self-giving love. Whether one is single or married, a fully flourishing human life simply does not come about by acquiring the object of one's sexual desires. Instead, it only ever comes about when we are altogether freed from our obsessive quest for personal wholeness through sexual expression. The lifelong process of directing and disciplining our sexual desires is not about finding an "appropriate" Christian expression for one's sexuality. It's about cultivating a generative space in which we routinely set aside our own desires so that the other might thrive.

This communally grounded, others-oriented approach to marriage, singleness, and sexuality is key to understanding other Pauline passages about marriage. The well-known (or perhaps infamous) statements found in Ephesians 5:21-23 and Colossians 3:18–4:1 about wives submitting to their husbands and husbands loving their wives are prime examples. Neither of these texts can be properly understood without reference to Paul's conception of Christian community as an intimate and organic network of people who lay down their individual passions and desires out of concern for the health of the whole body (1 Cor 12:12-31). It doesn't help that many English translations of Ephesians 5 insert a heading between verses 21 and 22. Because of this editorial addition, which suggests that verse 22 marks the beginning of an entirely new section of Paul's thought, we are led to a rather harsh and disjointed reading of the text—one that would seem to emphasize the wife's submission to the husband (Eph 5:22).

Yet Paul's prior and indeed more basic command comes in the preceding verse. The people of God are to be filled with the Spirit and therefore constantly "submitting to one another" (Eph 5:21). So rather than teaching wives to subject themselves to their husbands, Paul is saying that at every level of the organization and in every one of their relationships, the Christian community is to be actively engaged in mutual, self-giving submission to one another.

What is more, the earliest manuscripts do not even contain the word *submit* in Ephesians 5:22. Because it is implied by the prior verses, scribes began to include the verb for the sake of "clarity," and modern translations have simply followed suit. But this fact only underscores the point that, whatever we make of these editorial additions, Paul's injunction to "submit" is best understood as a mutual form of submission—one that makes a claim on every member of the body of Christ.

This also holds true for Paul's words in Colossians 3:18–4:1, where Paul is once again speaking not to autonomous individuals but to a community. In particular, he is addressing those who make up a Christian household. And just as in Ephesians 5 and 1 Corinthians 7, Paul makes clear that every aspect of our common life together should be marked by mutual submission and self-giving love. As it is with parents and children, servants and masters, fathers with sons, so too should it be with husbands and wives.

The point here is that Paul understands marriage and singleness in the same way that he understands every Christian relationship—as an occasion for directing our desires in life-giving ways. The Christian faith as Paul sees it is one in which all our passions are reoriented and redirected along the lines of self-giving love. It is a life in which we harness our sexual passions in ways that are constructive for God's people in the world.

Paul's view of marriage and singleness is therefore neither anti-body nor anti-sex. To be sure, he is concerned with "sexual immorality" (Greek *porneia*) of every kind, both within marriage and outside of marriage (see 1 Cor 6:9-18; Eph 5:5; Col 3:5; 1 Thess 4:3). But this isn't to denigrate desire, nor is it an attempt to say that our passions are inherently destructive or corrupt. Rather, it is simply to acknowledge that our desires can and often do become misdirected. Regardless of the kind of relationship we are in or the amount of sex we are having, we have a seemingly infinite capacity for creating and pursuing illusions—those sacred objects that lie behind the magician's curtain. For some, the object is marriage. For others, the object is sex. Or maybe it's both. Either way, our obsessive pursuit of something that will never ultimately fulfill our deeper longings places us on a path that is destructive for our individual lives and the life of the community.

Put differently, according to Paul, when it comes to the question of whether sex is a requirement for human flourishing, it doesn't matter if one is gifted with marriage or singleness. For on its own the simple expression of sexual desire always contains within itself a profound lack—an unfathomable emptiness. It will always leave one unfulfilled because, in an ultimate sense, sex is not actually what we desire. Sex is good (great even!). It provides humans with a pleasure unlike any other, and for some it also brings the blessing of children, so it certainly plays an important role in our lives. But it will never make us whole. All our desires (sexual or otherwise) are reflections of a much deeper and more profound longing that can never be fully met by sex.

Although it certainly appears counterintuitive on the surface, Paul suggests that human beings are able to flourish—to truly thrive—not when they are finally able to express their sexuality through the act of sex, but when they abandon their obsessive quest for individualized sexual expression altogether. Put more positively, we embody and enact our humanity in its full breadth and depth only when we direct our passions toward the other in self-giving love.

In other words, like any human pursuit, sex is fully realized when it is about giving not getting. And according to Paul, we already intuit this impulse toward sexual generosity on some level, only without a great deal of clarity. We see it now as if "in a mirror indirectly, but then we will see it face to face. Now I know in part, but then I will know fully, just as I have been fully known" (1 Cor 13:12). Ultimately we desire to know and to be fully known by the only One whose love can actually satisfy those desires. This is the union for which our bodies long. And it's on account of this deeply embodied longing that Paul wishes that all Christians would remain single and celibate. It is not, as some have suggested, because Paul thought the return of Christ was imminent, but rather because celibate singleness is able to function as an icon for those with the eyes to see and ears to hear.[12] It reminds us that no romantic relationship and no amount of sex, no matter how good they are, will ever actually be enough. It also fosters new relational dynamics in the present, producing ways of being we have yet to even imagine. As such, the icon of singleness helps liberate us from our desperate pursuit of the modern world's most sacred of objects and instead creates a space where we might fall headlong into God's loving embrace.

A "CHASTE" COMMUNITY

If I were to summarize what Jesus and Paul have to say about marriage, singleness, and celibacy or sexuality, it would go something like this: Both marriage and singleness are equally viable vocations through which the Christian can flourish, and each provides a unique set of opportunities for the right ordering of our desires. In addition, both involve seasons of abstinence and thus call upon Christians to direct their sexual passions accordingly. So even though marriage names the context in which healthy sex thrives, *every* Christian is called to move toward chastity in their sexual lives, whether they are sexually active and married or celibate and single.

By "chastity" I do not simply mean abstinence from sex (otherwise it would not apply to married people), nor do I mean to imply that we develop this virtue by merely abiding by some abstract moral imperative. Chastity has a much wider application than celibacy. Following Caroline Simon's work on sexual ethics, chastity is a "dynamic principle enabling one to use one's sexual power intelligently in the pursuit of human flourishing and happiness."[13] It's about directing (and in some cases restraining) our erotic energies in ways that contribute to our own flourishing and the flourishing of others.

The primary reason for practicing this kind of sexual restraint (chastity) is because, for both Paul and Jesus, our sexuality is more about who we are than what we do. And as human beings, before we are anything else, we are persons in relation. Every aspect of our life in the world is always already communally grounded. Despite what the modern world would have us believe, we are not radically independent, autonomous sexual agents, but are intimately connected to both God and our fellow human beings. There simply is no such thing as a free-floating and untethered expression of one's sexuality. So if we are to truly flourish as human beings, we must practice a kind of generosity in restraint, a giving of ourselves to the other in ways that shape us into people who can receive love from the Other.

What is more, according to Jesus and Paul, while marriage and singleness are both God-given gifts and should be received as such, only one of them is coming to an end—marriage. This means that marriage is not (and cannot be) the paradigmatic relational model to which all Christians ought to conform, nor is it a requirement for the health and vitality of the Christian community. Instead, it is singleness (understood as a person in relation) that is the default category for Christian life and in many cases is the preferable option.

The same can be said of celibacy. According to Paul and Jesus, sex, like marriage, is finite. Even though humans will remain fully sexual creatures in the age to come, celibate singleness seems to be the destiny of all believers.

If the New Testament texts were in fact presenting a normative relational model that all Christians were called to pursue, an argument could be made that it would actually be singleness and not marriage. At the very least, it seems to affirm what Laura Smit has suggested: "The burden of proof is on the decision to marry, not the decision to remain single. Christians should assume that they will be single unless and until they have a godly reason to marry."[14] But this too runs the risk of a slight overstatement, for when we locate the words of Paul and Jesus within the larger witness of the New Testament, a somewhat more textured picture emerges.

Without question the New Testament authors make clear that marriage was to be honored by the entire community (Heb 13:4-7). Indeed, Christian spouses were recognized and lauded for their ability not only to offer intimacy and support to each other, but also to serve as a compelling witness to an unbelieving husband or wife (1 Cor 7:12-16). But early Christian communities did not consist of married couples alone. Peter and "other apostles" were married, which is to be expected given their particular cultural context (1 Cor 9:5). But many of those who followed Jesus during his life and after his resurrection were single, and they too held a place of honor within the community. Some had not yet married (such as Philip's daughters in Acts 21:8-9), while others were single either because of a divorce or the death of a spouse (such as Anna the prophetess in Lk 2:36-40). And single people like Nympha were held in high regard for hosting gatherings of the Christian community (Col 4:15-16). In other words, both married and single Christians were considered necessary and integral parts of the Christian community. As a consequence, the community itself was understood to be the primary location for cultivating and sustaining the life and practices of both single and married Christians.

In this context, there is no separating out an individual's (or a couple's) vocation from their larger calling as members of the body of Christ. Married life, single life, and sexual activity are always already corporate realities. This is why so many of the New Testament epistles dedicate space to the ways Christians should approach marriage, singleness, and sexuality as a community. In part the emphasis on these intimate relationships had to do with the Christian community's credibility as a witness to Christ in a cultural context pervaded by a confused and confusing sexuality. Indeed, even those passages about women and slaves that are difficult for modern readers to stomach (such as 1 Pet 3:1-5; Titus 2:4-5) are couched in profoundly missional terms. Ultimately, these letters urge the people of God not to wield power over one another, but to be a people who share whatever power they may have with others in order to be "harmonious, sympathetic, affectionate, compassionate, and humble" (1 Pet 3:8). God's people are called to subvert the cultural power dynamics in this way so that "non-Christians ... may see your good deeds and glorify God when he appears" (1 Pet 2:12). So marriage and singleness are about more than who to take out on a Friday night or whether sex will or will not follow. It's about God's mission in the world.

Beyond its missional significance, though, the New Testament authors are concerned with the right ordering of married and single life within the context of community because it is the community of faith that serves as the primary location for the development of Christian virtue. Operating with the assumption that the common life and practices of Christian life are what ultimately shape, discipline, and direct our passionate longings, the apostles often focused their teachings on how the body of Christ might organize itself in ways that would cultivate and support the unique vocational demands of both married and single believers.

Thus older women and men (who were likely married or widowed) were to "communicate the behavior that goes with sound teaching" (Titus 2:1) to younger women and men (who were possibly single or married). They are to be "temperate, dignified, self-controlled, sound in faith, in love, and in endurance" (Titus 2:2). Part of their "sound teaching" about marriage and singleness involved actual teaching—the exchange of information. For example, Paul encouraged Timothy to remind his faith community that those who were forbidding marriage and requiring abstinence from certain foods were false teachers (literally spreading "demonic teachings"—*didaskaliais daimonion*) (1 Tim 4:1-5).

But the primary and more fundamental way the community was to enable its members to be "temperate" and "self-controlled" was by actually practicing these virtues at both the individual and corporate level. Elders were expected to be "blameless, the husband of one wife" (Titus 1:6). Overseers must also be the husband of one wife, but in addition they are to be "above reproach" in temperance and self-control (1 Tim 3:2). Deacons must not be "given to excessive drinking" (1 Tim 3:8). Likewise, older women and widows are to be honored, especially those who have "practiced hospitably, washed the feet of the saints, helped those in distress" (1 Tim 5:10). At the same time, younger widows should not be expected to remain single forever, especially if their passions would best be directed into marriage (1 Tim 5:11). In every case, though, whether married, single, remarried, divorced, or widowed, every individual is called toward a life of chastity that can be sustained only by the very community that makes it possible in the first place.

All told, the New Testament authors speak of marriage, singleness, and sexuality almost exclusively in terms of their communal dimensions because they recognize that virtues like chastity are virtually impossible to cultivate, much less maintain, without social support. So the picture that the New Testament offers us is anything but a pious moralism. Rather, it's an acknowledgment that a healthy and thriving community—a community shaped by Christian virtue—is one that is no longer "enslaved to various passions and desires" (Titus 3:3) but rather engaged in the hard work of cultivating a generous and generative kind of chastity—a shared way of life that is "good and beneficial for all people" (Titus 3:8).

A RESTLESS COMMUNITY

So what does all this mean exactly? At the very least, we've named our idols, and that is surely half the battle. But where do we go from here? Now that we have reconsidered what the First Testament and New Testament have to say about marriage, singleness, and sexuality, is it as simple as acknowledging that the Christian community's normative picture of marriage falls short of the biblical vision? Likewise, is it enough to tell sexually frustrated single people (and married people!) that sex will never fully satisfy them, so they should just exhibit a little more self-control or get help from the community of faith? Furthermore, who among us has any credibility in any of these matters to say any of these things? Whoever is without sin, feel free to throw the first stone.

In certain respects, the answer to these questions is actually quite simple. But it's anything but easy. In the final analysis, the New Testament texts we have been discussing conceive of Christian life and discipleship in terms of the right ordering of embodied desire. And as we listen more closely to what these texts have to say, we begin to hear a few resounding themes that have implications not only for married and single life, but for our basic understanding of what it means to live as sexual creatures in the midst of a sexually charged culture.

First, sexual restraint in the form of celibacy and generosity actually renders love more substantial, not less.[15] In sex, as in all of life, it is far better to give than to receive.

Second, developing the virtue of chastity is about focusing our sexual energies on committed relationships in the context of community, not on the individual suppression or denial of those passions. As such, chastity has as much to do with marriage as it does singleness.

Finally, in light of the resurrection of Jesus and our own resurrection to come, this kind of entirely-chaste-yet-wholly-sexual passion is both deeper than erotic desire and its source. In an ultimate sense, it is the very state into which we will be resurrected in the coming kingdom.

Again, though, none of this makes married life or single life easy, especially in the already-but-not-yet reality in which we find ourselves. In fact, pursuing chastity in a time of sexual overabundance almost by definition implies a kind of perpetual restlessness. So we can agree whole heartedly with Augustine when he says that "our heart is restless until it rests in [God]."[16] But that doesn't eliminate the acute sense of restlessness that we all feel. In some cases, naming it only makes things worse.

It is for this very reason that the New Testament writers focused so much energy on how the newly forming Christian community should approach marriage, singleness, and sexuality. How the people of God organize their shared life together matters. And this remains equally true for us today. Christian virtue depends on a set of sustaining practices, so when the community of faith orients its devotional life according to a distorted picture of marriage, not only do we encourage something other than virtue among those who are married, but we fail to provide a generative or supportive context for anyone whose vocation might lead them toward a lifetime of singleness and celibacy.

Admitting that we have a problem is certainly a good start. But like I said, that's the easy part, or at least the more immediately concrete part. The more difficult task—and likely the more painful one—is what I would call the reshaping of our theological imagination. Once we come to terms with the many ways marriage and sex function as sacred objects, and after we do the hard work of letting go of the very things we believe will make us whole, how exactly do we move forward? What, if anything, *can* we desire? Where, if at all, might we find fulfillment? Again Rollins is helpful:

> There is an experience of desire that is not oppressive, an experience that offers an alternative to pursuing the sacred-object, retreating from desire altogether, or moving from one ultimately empty thing to another. An experience that is felt most keenly in the experience of love. . . . To love is to experience a world come alive, but it also means opening oneself up to a poignant suffering.[17]

It is not insignificant that Jesus, Paul, and other New Testament writers so often draw on the image of marriage to describe this experience of the "world come alive," or to use more biblical language, of the coming kingdom. Jesus himself suggested that our encounter with the kingdom would be something like a wedding banquet, albeit one with a rather unexpected guest list (Mt 22:1-14). He also likened it to a group of virgins waiting expectantly for the bridegroom, whose arrival is expected but unpredictable (Mt 25:1-13). At other times, though, he even invoked marriage as a way of describing himself. When the bridegroom is present and among us, says Jesus, it is not the time to fast, but to feast—to delight in one another's presence through a sensual embrace of material pleasures (Mk 2:18-20; Lk 5:34-35).

Paul develops this metaphor along similar lines, going so far as to suggest that the "two" who become "one flesh" as husband and wife are in fact a sign and a sacrament of Christ and the church (Eph 5:29-32). For Paul it is this "great mystery" that animates the body of Christ. In a way that cannot quite be captured in words, we will one day be presented to Christ as his bride, our body joining his. So we are to remain chaste, not out of obligation to some universal principle or set of rules, but in order to prepare ourselves to receive the all-consuming love of our bridegroom (2 Cor 11:2). Indeed, as the author of Revelation will later suggest, this union between Christ and his beloved is the culmination of God's project in the world (Rev 19:6-10; 21:1-14). For in that moment when the world comes fully alive—when God dwells with humanity—we will finally meet our Soulmate face to face. Only then will we encounter the One for whom our bodies long. Only then will we know and be fully known— body, mind, and soul. Only then will our hearts finally find rest from their restlessness.

If we take these metaphors seriously, then to move forward as a community and as individuals is, most basically, to respond to the bridegroom's call—a summons that recasts our basic awareness of the world and thus transforms how we interact with it. The temptation will be to make either too much of this metaphor or too little of it. For example, we misunderstand the community's call to marriage when we say things like "marriage is God's intention for every adult human"— the opening words at a wedding recently attended by one of my single colleagues. Conversely, we are making too little of it when we conceive of marriage as nothing more than a mechanism by which we are saved *from* the world—as if marriage were simply a "billboard by which

[God] could shout His message," or a means for a husband to ensure his "wife's sanctification."[18]

There is yet another way—a better way. It is to accept the bridegroom's invitation as a call to focus our passionate energies on the other and for the sake of the other. It is not to deify or denigrate the other, but to love them as we are loved. Indeed, as risky as this proposition might sound, Jesus himself relinquished his own passionate desires for the sake of his bride, the church. This picture of willful self-surrender is a far cry from one that sees marriage as an opportunity for Christians to express all their pent-up sexual angst. Instead, it is an invitation to embrace ever more fully the community that is called to faithfully sustain us along the way.

NOT WHOLE

Anonymous

"I have news."

Uh-oh. I was calling my mom for our weekly check-in. Her statement made warning bells go off in me. This couldn't be good.

She proceeded to tell me that my brother had called her the day before to let her know that he had started dating a young woman in the Los Angeles area. There was the immediate sinking feeling of impending doom at what this meant for me. I had already been under a lot of pressure to find a husband due to the fact that I was the eldest child in a Korean American family and in my late thirties. My younger sister had already married and was pregnant with child number two. My brother is the baby of the family and at the time was the only other single sibling besides me. As long as one of us was single, the other didn't get as much heat. Now things were about to hit the fan.

My mother went on to tell me how my brother had already met the parents of his new girlfriend. I could hear the excitement in her voice. Knowing my brother, he is not one to engage frivolously in dating relationships, so I knew this was serious. I tried to sound interested as my mom rambled on, but really I was just bracing myself for the statement I knew was coming: "I wanted to be happy for him, but I kept thinking . . ." My mom paused and addressed me: "What about you?" Of course. Why can't her oldest daughter find a man and settle down already? She's almost forty!

However, the next thing my mom said took me down with such force it felt like she knifed me.

"I'm afraid to tell Daddy because he'll get really upset. Did you know that we've been fighting because of you? He says it's my fault that you're not married and that I raised you wrong."

My worst fear was confirmed. As a young child and well into my young adulthood, I was subject to the constant and brutal verbal and physical violence my father would inflict on my mother and then later on me and sometimes my siblings. I recall as far back as when I was a toddler the horrible ways my dad would scream at and pummel my mother in front of me. I would block out and dissociate from the noise and pain by focusing on the doll in my lap or the toy piano as I tried to plunk out some melodies. I would go numb and try not to feel anything. I learned early on that my father hated crying, so I trained myself not to emote in front of him.

Tears meant weakness, and my dad wouldn't tolerate it. I would rather my father punish me than my mother, but I was a girl and too small to do anything. Any time he thought one of us kids did something wrong or despicable in his sight, he blamed my mother. Nothing was ever his fault. We were all afraid because we didn't know what would set him off. I tried my hardest to be the perfect, good girl. But I constantly struggled. I worried that I wasn't good enough because of the punishment I endured. I started to think everything I did was wrong. Why else would my dad hit me and yell at me?

My mom continued to yammer on the phone about how one of her close friends at church couldn't understand why I couldn't find a man. "She is so pretty now, why can't she get married?" As a teenager, I had been considered chubby and was constantly told by people in my Korean church community and family to go on a diet. "No one will marry you if you're fat!" my parents would always say. Because to them, fat meant ugly and unacceptable. Now that I was slimmer and supposedly more attractive, it was confounding to people as to why

I was single still. What's wrong with her? She's almost forty! She must not be normal. My mom also stated that she was embarrassed to tell people at church that I was single so she would lie and tell them I had a boyfriend back in Los Angeles.

I remained silent as my mom continued to talk. She said my family was praying for me. Even my dad was praying every morning now that he had become a Christian. "Grandpa, Grandma, Daddy, and me are all praying every day that you find a husband." Great, no pressure.

Finally I quietly said, "Mom, I'm going to hang up now. I'm starting to get upset."

She breezily chirped, "Okay, bye!" and hung up the phone.

Hot tears started to stream down my face and my body was wracked with anger and shame. I was horrified that my father would threaten my mom, which triggered my latent fear that I would be the reason my mom would get hurt. Then the intense rage I felt toward my mother for telling me that my dad flipped out on her left me feeling betrayed. Why would a mother tell her own daughter that her husband was threatening her? Shouldn't the instinct of a mother be to protect her child? I felt betrayed by my mother's desire for self-preservation and her need for external approval. Her oldest daughter was making her look bad among her family and her tight-knit Korean community.

I had heard all of this before. But for some reason, this particular instance felt more painful. Even as a child, I remember my father saying to me, "I don't care if you are smart or do well in school. All you have to worry about is cooking and taking care of the house. That's all you need to be a good wife." I was probably in junior high at the time. The fact that my dad didn't care that I had brains or ideas, or that I may want more in life than to be someone's wife, didn't exactly make me jump at the thought of getting married. And if the model for marriage was my parents, then I sure didn't want to have anything to do with that.

So why is it that my family still sees me as having no value just because I'm not married? Why is it so crazy that I should be single at the age of thirty-eight? It's one thing to be a stain on the seemingly perfect image my parents want to portray to the world. I can live with that. It's quite another to walk through life knowing you're simply not whole.

PART THREE

DEVELOPING
A THEOLOGICAL
FRAMEWORK

COLD FEET

By Claire Crisp

In the months leading up to our wedding, I had such a serious case of cold feet that if it hadn't been for one fundamental realization, I would have called it off.

There was no doubt that I wanted to spend the rest of my life with this man. We were young, devoted to one another, had weathered years of studying and living at opposite ends of the United Kingdom, shared ideals and dreams. Dreams that would eventually see us moving a dozen times over the following decade, supporting each other in three different careers each, and surviving the devastating impact of a chronically sick child.

Despite the fact that neither of us was raised in a conservative church, we did tie the knot in one. Its entrance served as the backdrop to our fresh-faced newlywed pictures. But it was also the place that precipitated my premarital crisis and my sense of being devalued as a young Christian woman.

By way of balance, a great many of Christ's teachings were lived out in both the collective and individual lives of the church's members. These dear people did much good in their neighborhoods, were quick to serve and support one another, and provided us with such rich community that it is no exaggeration to say these fellow believers had become a sort of extended family.

I saw all this clearly and was deeply drawn to it. Yet as a young Christian woman in a church that was populated by traditional families who had been there for decades, and where there were only a handful of "new" couples, I had neither the insight nor the experience to know how better to deal with what I came to understand as rigid parochialism. This kind of dogmatism had little to do with theological doctrine, mind you. It had rather to do with the church's views of marriage.

Looking back, the congregation and pastor didn't know what to do with me. I didn't fit into their view of a young Christian woman who was living "biblically." That is regrettable, because I was driven by a desire to do my utmost before God in every aspect of my life by serving others.

Already I was a qualified professional holding down a full-time job and on-call hours in London hospitals. My work was seen as acceptable, so long as I never missed the two Sunday services, midweek prayer meeting, and Saturday door-to-door evangelism. In short, I was not to take my job too seriously. As a woman, my career (a vocation I had felt called to since my teens) was a productive use of time while I waited for my wedding day to arrive. Or so I was told.

But even if I had wanted to ditch the vocation I had spent years training for, this wasn't an option since my soon-to-be husband was only half way through the first of four academic degrees. And anyway, I didn't want to discard my work. I loved my job rehabilitating patients, and neither of us felt this created any sense of imbalance in our relationship—after all, one of us had to pay the bills, and at that stage, I was that person.

This practical detail was lost on the congregation just as my fiancé was frequently informed he should "step up" and "take his financial responsibilities seriously." In other words, he should find a way to "provide" for me, the one who should be "kept."

My request to the pastor to keep my maiden name and have it documented on the marriage certificate fell on deaf ears, and unfortunately it was regarded as a sign that I was not in the right frame of mind to take the vow of obedience. The idea of submitting to my husband dominated our premarital counseling session with him just a week before the wedding, which made me doubt whether I was in any way up to being a good Christian wife.

Not only that, but coming from a very large non-Christian family, it was intensely important to me that the Christian message of grace and forgiveness be heard from the front during the service. And so I took the opportunity to request such an invitation, assuming our pastor would jump at the opportunity.

The church was more packed that day than I had ever seen it, largely due to the presence of my family—most of whom only ever frequented churches on hatch, match, and dispatch occasions. I'm not sure I will ever get over the shock I felt, standing in my wedding gown under the pulpit, only to hear a public lecture on submitting to my husband. Hardly the gospel message I had hoped would be proclaimed!

Unsurprisingly, my father took this theme up during the speeches at our wedding reception, ditching his previously rehearsed monologue in order to make a point. It was now abundantly clear that his Christian daughter's new role in life was to "obey her husband." This, he said, should start in the morning by her making him breakfast. There was much laughter from our guests, but I was left with a deepening sense of disappointment in both the church and myself.

Twenty-three years later, I have never regretted marrying the love of my life, since he is someone who values people whatever the color, creed, background, or struggles they face. But I do regret having to endure the subtle chauvinism and outright sexism that was dressed up in a spiritual language and code that our church followed. The insidious nature of the discrimination directed my way left me struggling for years to find my true value both as a married woman and as a child of God.

5

THE CALL OF MARRIAGE

(OR, WHY CHRISTIANS *SHOULD* GET MARRIED)

MY WIFE AND I still chuckle when we think about the most common piece of advice that married couples at our church gave us after we announced our engagement: "You have to watch *The Story of Us*. It's *exactly* what the first year of marriage is like."

The Story of Us is a movie from the late '90s about a husband and wife (played by Bruce Willis and Michelle Pfeiffer) who, after fifteen years of marriage, are considering a divorce. To put it mildly, it's awful, but not because of the quality of the filmmaking. It's awful because the two main characters seem to do little more than scream at each other for one hundred straight minutes. There are a few lighthearted moments, but on the whole it's pretty much one petty argument after another, each of which involves the rehashing of old slights, failed expectations, and perceived infidelities.

Unfortunately, we took everyone's advice and watched the movie. When it was over, my wife (my fiancée at the time) turned to me with a bewildered look in her eyes. I returned her gaze with an equal sense of confusion. Is that really what marriage is like—especially the first year? We knew there would be a period of adjustment, but we had already been dating for over two years and had never once treated each other with so much vitriol and such a profound lack of kindness. What exactly was going to take place on the other side of "I do" that would change us so dramatically? More importantly, how could we prevent it from happening?

The members of our church who offered us this unsolicited premarital counseling in the form of a film recommendation meant well, of course, but thankfully they were wrong. As it turns out, *The Story of Us* is not the story of us. Sure, we've had our spats over the years like anyone else, but on the whole, we have done more than merely survive the various ups and downs of married life. We have truly enjoyed the journey. Still, the people in our community of faith who cared enough about our impending nuptials were right to warn us about the challenges of marriage. They weren't trying to be discouraging or cynical. Theirs was a sincere attempt to open our eyes to the rigorous demands of marriage—to help us see what marriage was really like. The only problem was that it left us feeling a bit like Jesus' disciples after they heard his teachings on marriage: "If this is the case of a husband with a wife, it is better not to marry!" (Mt 19:10).

Needless to say, as we walked out of the theater that night, we were fairly convinced that not everyone should get married. But as a young, newly engaged couple, what we needed were a few reasons why we should.

WARNING: CONTENTS UNDER PRESSURE

Given what I have said so far, some readers may be convinced that I have taken up a position similar to the one Jesus' disciples held—that it is better not to marry. But drawing such a conclusion would be either to misunderstand or to intentionally misrepresent my central argument. To be sure, I have been pressing us to reconsider (and when necessary repent from) the ways the community of faith understands, privileges, and prioritizes marriage. But at no point have I suggested that marriage is unimportant, or that it would be better for Christians not to marry. I have simply said that marriage should not be the norm, meaning that it is not for everyone and that various distortions occur when the Christian community operates as if it were—distortions that affect how we understand not only marriage, but also singleness and human sexuality. In other words, what I have called into question is the normative picture of marriage that holds the contemporary church's imagination captive, not marriage itself. In doing so, my goal has not been to devalue or denigrate marriage, but actually to elevate and expand our view of marriage by recalibrating and reframing it.

I realize, however, that I have made some fairly countercultural (and thus potentially unsettling) claims about marriage along the way, which is at least in part why early reviewers would occasionally stop and ask me what my wife thought about the book. How did it make her feel, they wondered, to know that her husband was challenging the church's ideal of marriage? For any readers who have similar questions percolating in the back of their minds, it might be comforting to know that my wife is actually in full support of the book. But it's not because we see eye-to-eye on every detail (we don't), nor because of some kind of spousal obligation on her part. Rather, it's because even a marginally careful reading of the previous chapters would yield a positive and affirming conception of marriage—one that I believe resonates not only with the biblical witness but also with the historic Christian tradition.

Nevertheless, a discussion focused on why some Christians should in fact consider marriage (or, as I will put it shortly, how Christians might respond to the call of marriage) is now in order. I want to stress the word *some* here because at no point should anything that follows be understood as applying to all or even most Christians. To make a case for Christian marriage is not to suggest that it is somehow a higher or more arduous calling than singleness. Rather, it is simply to identify the unique set of challenges and opportunities that marriage presents for those who are called to this particular way of life.

My point all along has been that Christians need to take marriage more seriously, not less. Indeed, one of the primary themes we discovered among the marriage texts in the First Testament is the demand for God's people to treat marriage with a greater sense of gravity. A similar refrain echoes throughout the life and writings of the apostle Paul and, perhaps most importantly, in Jesus' teachings on marriage.

It is Jesus' message in particular that should stand out to us today, for in those handful of instances when Jesus directly addresses marriage, what he does *not* say is that his followers need to do a better job of coercing members of the broader society to live according to their religious preferences. Nor does he say that they simply need to stop getting divorced so frequently, nor that the world around them would fall into order if they merely lived more sexually pure lives—whether as single or married people. No, it is both more and different than that. Jesus does something that is completely unexpected (and equally shocking). He radically redescribes marriage by suggesting that in and through this all-too-human arrangement, the kingdom of God is actually laying a claim on our lives and the world.

Yet, much like the disciples before us, we have misconstrued Jesus' vision of the coming kingdom and its relationship to marriage, and thus we pursue this relationship for the wrong reasons. Especially within evangelical circles, we tend to see marriage as an ideal solution to an unrelated problem (such as the problem of feeling incomplete without one's soulmate or the problem of sexual angst), or a reward for those who are able to maintain some semblance of (sexual) integrity while single, or a mutually beneficial agreement between two parties that generates a sense of individual satisfaction and personal fulfillment. But from Jesus' perspective (not to mention the rest of the biblical witness), marriage isn't a contract. It is first and foremost a calling. Rather than an institution, it's an invitation. As such, marriage isn't a means for self-actualization or self-gratification. Neither is it a reward for religious fervor or the culmination of one's life journey. Instead, marriage is a kingdom event—one in which we are routinely summoned to surrender our self for the sake of the other.

That all might sound well and good, but what exactly does it mean to say that marriage is an "event"? To answer this question, I want us to engage in a theological thought experiment. Taking our previous discussion of the biblical text as our starting point, I want us to think about what might happen if we reconceive of *marriage* as the name we have given to a particular kind of Spirit-breathed happening. This happening can go by other names as well, a few of which we will explore below (justice, generosity, forgiveness, hospitality, love). But however we choose to define or classify it, I want us to spend some time interpreting the event that the word *marriage* harbors. I want us to consider what it means to say that something is calling to us in marriage—something dynamic and transformative and in-Spirit-ed— and that this something is nothing less than what Jesus refers to as the kingdom of God.

It is important to note that the kingdom also calls to us in singleness, which is why the entirety of the next chapter is dedicated to an exploration of what this looks like. But in this chapter, my aim is to identify and describe some of the ways the Spirit of God might be stirring within this thing we call marriage, and then to ask both why and how we might respond to the Spirit's call. In fact, if it is true that marriage is better understood as an "event of the Spirit's call," then we need to deconstruct altogether the reasons for Christian marriage that are currently on offer. We also need to imagine new possibilities for what marriage demands of us—our "respond-ability" in light of this call. So as I outline a few of the reasons why a Christian would respond to the call of marriage, I will also be asking how they might do so.

I have been greatly helped in conceiving of marriage in this way by the Christian philosopher John Caputo.[1] Although Caputo doesn't address marriage specifically, I'm going to follow his lead by "crossing wires" so to speak, taking two concepts that are not normally brought together (marriage and kingdom of God) and placing them into fruitful tension to see what might result. As we watch the sparks fly from this imaginary short-circuiting, we will discover that marriage is not ultimately about romantic love at all, but rather the right ordering of our desires. To respond to the call of marriage is to allow the kingdom that Jesus inaugurated to orient all our loves and affections, directing them toward their true end.

I must reiterate, however, that I am not attempting to identify a set of principles for how to have a "successful" or "more fulfilling" marriage. This isn't a how-to manual for marriage, nor is it a self-help book, although responding faithfully to God's call would work wonders for all our relationships. And while this may seem like a bit of an unexpected turn, I want us to approach marriage in this way for a very intentional reason. If the church has any chance of serving as a *credible* witness in the world, then we need to develop new ways of being the church that more readily address the contemporary situation. And this is especially true when it comes to how we understand and articulate the significance of marriage.

MARRIAGE AS A CALL TO JUSTICE

To spark our collective imagination, I am suggesting that we think of *marriage* as the name we give to a rather peculiar event that allows for the kingdom of God to happen to us. I realize this may sound a bit odd because it's different than how we usually speak of marriage, but it's not meant to be overly convoluted. It's simply a way of talking about a unique encounter in which the Spirit of God stirs, inviting us to live in light of the Spirit's call. But it's also a way of identifying what the Spirit is actually saying in and through marriage so that we might discern how best to respond.

However, if this thought experiment of ours is to be anything more than a projection of our overly active imaginations—that is, if it is to be theologically faithful—then it is important that it develop in conversation with the biblical witness. This means that we need to revisit some of our previous discussions. For instance, as chapter three made clear, many if not most of the descriptive and prescriptive texts in the First Testament that address marriage share a common concern: justice. In fact, a few of the most difficult passages for modern Christians to stomach—especially those that don't seem to align with what is commonly understood as the "biblical vision" of marriage (such as Ex 21:7-11; Lev 18:18; Deut 21:10-14; 22:29)—exist for the express purpose of generating a more just and equitable life for those who were oppressed, marginalized, and otherwise rendered powerless by a decidedly unjust sociocultural environment. Women, children, foreigners, and resident aliens were among the many who were uniquely at risk. Things were even less equitable for widows, orphans, slaves, prisoners of war, and victims of sexual abuse.

If we give these passages a fair hearing, then we have to acknowledge that one of the ways God calls the community of faith to respond to systemic injustice and radical socioeconomic inequality is not only by getting married, but also by remaining married. As anachronistic as it might sound, marriage can be a mechanism by which the people of God are able to embody and enact God's justice in an unjust world.

Let me be clear though. By bringing these texts up, I am not suggesting that there is a one-to-one correspondence between the prescriptive biblical passages in the First Testament and the situation in which we currently find ourselves. Context matters, and this is especially the case when it has to do with victims of sexual assault, war, and domestic violence. However, what I am suggesting is that in the terms established by the biblical witness, the call to marriage, before it is anything else, is a call to "promote justice, to be faithful, / and to live obediently before your God" (Mic 6:8).

What I find personally refreshing about this way of framing marriage in relation to the kingdom of God is that it allows us to reclaim these "Old" Testament texts in a way that actually informs our lived experience today. When we look at modern marriage (both marriage in general and Christian marriage in particular) through the lens of justice, marriage suddenly becomes a tangible means by which we are able to participate in the *shalom*—the holistic reintegration of all that has become disintegrated and disjointed—of the coming kingdom.

Importantly, to say that God is prodding us toward justice and bringing about *shalom* in and through this thing we call marriage is to say absolutely nothing of romantic love, or one's "soulmate," or sexual gratification. Indeed, when the Spirit of God calls to us in the event of marriage, the divine summons that we hear and to which we are ultimately respond-able has almost nothing to do with romantic love. And that's because the call to marriage is not an invitation to play the part of the hero or heroine in a romance novel. Rather, it's a call to be an agent of divine justice.

On a concrete level, this means that the Christian call to marriage demands a response from God's people that is consonant with God's project in the world—even and perhaps especially in the process of identifying our prospective spouses. For example, what might it look like for single Christians to abandon their "ideal spouse" checklists and instead seek out only those partners who would enable them to respond to the call of justice in ways that would otherwise remain inaccessible? Or, to put it differently, what if the chief criteria for a future spouse were not sexual chemistry, a common set of personal interests and hobbies, or even emotional compatibility, but rather a capacity (and willingness) to collaborate in a lifelong project of caring for the outsider, the marginalized, and the oppressed?

This way of thinking about marriage should not sound nearly as radical as it probably does, especially given its direct connections to the biblical narrative. Boaz and Ruth, for instance, married each other not because of romance or compatibility (they hardly knew each other!) but because Boaz was dutifully following the code of Levirate marriage and Ruth was seeking basic provisions for herself and her mother-in-law, Naomi. According to the text, Boaz's decision to marry Ruth was first and foremost about his desire to bring about a more just and equitable reality for this widow and her widowed mother-in-law—members of one of the most disadvantaged groups in the ancient world (Ruth 4:9-12). Likewise, Ruth's desire to marry Boaz had to do with her concern not only for her personal well-being but also for Naomi's well-being. Thus, rather than being compelled by some sense of romantic love (Boaz even praises Ruth for *not* pursuing one of the "young men, whether rich or poor" in Ruth 3:10), it was their shared passion for justice that served as the primary motivation for Ruth and Boaz to marry. And what is perhaps even more striking is that this jointly held calling to enact justice in and through their marriage also effected a change in the concrete, socioeconomic circumstances of those around them, most notably Naomi. For Ruth and Boaz, then, justice begat justice.

Motivated as it was by their collaborative response to the call of justice, Ruth and Boaz's marriage was never just about the two of them. In fact, from the very start their relationship was always overflowing with an excess of compassion and concern for others. It wasn't simply that they were two married people who cared about justice. It was rather that their marriage itself was an enactment of justice through and through.

This should not strike us as all that surprising, especially when we recall our previous discussion of Ephesians 5, which focused on the mutual submission of both husbands and wives to each another and by extension the married couple's submission to the broader Christian community. In fact, if we think about Paul's epistle to the Ephesians in terms of justice, then it becomes clear that he is not simply advocating egalitarianism by some other name. It is far more radical than that. If the call to Christian marriage is indeed a call to justice, and if the justice that flows between two spouses is also meant to spill out into a shared concern for others, then marriage is actually the complete undoing of any desire to be regarded as an equal to anyone, whether as a husband or a wife.

Let me be clear. I am an egalitarian. My interpretation of the biblical witness (as laid out in chapters three and four) leads me to the conclusion that wives and husbands are equal partners in every aspect of married life. There is no hierarchy between the two, as no individual's role can be elevated above the other, whether they are a male or a female (or for that matter a Jew or a Gentile, or a slave or a free person). However, whereas egalitarianism is concerned exclusively with the equanimity that ought to exist between Christian spouses, the call that stirs within marriage operates in an entirely different register. In fact, when Paul urges husbands and wives to submit to one another, going so far as to suggest that husbands are to love their wives as "Christ loved the church and gave himself for her" (Eph 5:25), he is making a far more revolutionary claim than simply that spouses should be "equals." He is explicitly inviting husbands and wives to assume the posture of Jesus, which turns out to be the inverse of equality:

> Each of you should be concerned not only about your own interests, but about the interests of others as well. You should have the same attitude toward one another that Christ Jesus had,
>
> > who though he existed in the form of God
> > did not regard equality with God
> > as something to be grasped,
> > but emptied himself
> > by taking on the form of a slave,
> > by looking like other men,
> > and by sharing in human nature.
> > He humbled himself,
> > by becoming obedient to the point of death
> > —even death on a cross! (Phil 2:4-8)

From Paul's perspective, then, the call to marriage is one that moves us beyond mere egalitarianism. It isn't about equality in some straightforward or superficial sense, although it includes and assumes equality. Nor is it simply a matter of fairness between two spouses, as if Christian marriage were primarily about both parties getting their fair share of dessert each night or having the exact same budget for personal expenditures. Rather, marriage is about justice. As such, it ushers us into a life that is far deeper and more demanding than any simple notion of "fairness" could ever allow. It calls us to adopt the attitude of Jesus in and through our relationship with our spouse and in turn with our community. In an ultimate sense, marriage is about emptying ourselves entirely—both as individuals and as married couples—so that the other might flourish, so that they might experience God's *shalom*.

So are we willing to allow this same basic concern—one that stands at the heart of the Christian faith—to shape how we understand marriage today? I ask because what I am not talking about here is applauding those marriages that just so happen to bring about some sort of justice in the world (although we can and should do this). I'm talking about actively pursuing marriages that bear witness to the *shalom* of the coming kingdom as a part of our Christian convictions. What is more, I am suggesting that as a community of faith we proactively encourage and support this practice when appropriate.

Of course, none of this is to say that *all* Christians should pursue marriage as a way of caring for the outsider, the poor, and the dispossessed in our midst. Rather, the point is that, much like the marriages of Abraham, Isaac, and Jacob that we discussed earlier, contemporary Christian marriage is best understood not as a calling in and of itself, but as a means for actualizing a prior and more fundamental calling. None of us is called to marriage generically, no matter how long we have been dreaming that "someday my prince will come." Instead, as with Ruth and Boaz (and Isaac and Rebekah before them), the Spirit of God only ever calls us to marry *this* person, in *this* time, in *this* place, and for *this* reason. And in some instances, this incredibly concrete, always particular calling will demand that certain of us set aside our own self-interested quest for personal "happiness" or finding our "soulmate" in order to provide for the needs of those who are living on the margins of society.

I have no doubt that some will object to what I am saying here. One objection will likely come from those who simply cannot abide the thought that a "divinely sanctioned" or "biblically faithful" marriage could be based on anything other than romantic love. Surely, they will argue, marriage is principally about being in love and consummating that love. Isn't it?

Truth be told, I wish I could answer this question with a resounding "yes!" But the hard reality we all need to face is that romantic love simply has no sustaining power on its own, and every person who has ever been in a long-term relationship knows this to be the case. So it strikes me as not only hopelessly misguided but also contrary to the biblical testimony to continue operating as if something as fickle and fleeting as romance is capable of supporting a relationship as demanding as marriage. Equally problematic is that our blind allegiance to the myth of romantic love also prevents us from seeing what is actually before us—the very people whom the world has forgotten, overlooked, and disregarded, but whom God has called us to love.

The marriage of C. S. Lewis to Joy Davidman offers an illuminating case study in this regard. Within evangelical circles, Lewis's writings have reached near-canonical status. As a person of Christian faith, he is as close to a modern-day (Protestant) saint as one could imagine. But many of the same evangelicals who otherwise lionize him remain uncomfortable with the circumstances surrounding Lewis's marriage. It's true that at the time the Church of England would not allow divorcées like Davidman to remarry, regardless of which party was responsible for the dissolution of the prior marriage. But what strikes so many today as disconcerting is not that Lewis married a divorced woman without the approval of church authorities, but rather that he married her for the sake of justice and not romance.[2]

Indeed, Lewis was fairly open about the fact that they married each other for no other reason than to keep Davidman and her sons from being sent back to the United States. Her visa already having been denied, it was only by her marrying a United Kingdom citizen that she and her sons could remain in the country. In Lewis's own words, theirs was a "marriage" only in the legal sense, because "the 'reality' would be, from my point of view, adultery and therefore mustn't happen. (An easy resolution when one doesn't in the least want it!)"[3] All of this suggests that Lewis and Davidman's decision to marry was an ad hoc response to a concrete set of circumstances. It wasn't the result of a "savior" mentality on the part of Lewis, as if he had been looking for someone to rescue and Davidman just so happened to fit the bill. Rather, it was a joint effort to keep *this* woman and *these* children at *this* time from once again becoming victims of an abusive and philandering ex-husband.[4]

Setting aside for a moment the question of whether they actually had ulterior motives for the marriage (which is quite possible according to some historians), I am simply offering up for our consideration a modern-day example of the approach to marriage that I have been describing. In Lewis we find a prominent Christian thinker—a man respected for his commitment to theological orthodoxy and celebrated for his imaginative writings—who was apparently willing to enter into the covenantal bond of marriage with a recently divorced woman for the sole purpose of bringing about a more just and equitable reality for her and her children.

Thus, if nothing else, the marriage between Lewis and Davidman offers us a real-world example of how our response to the call of marriage is never the straightforward endeavor that the Christian community often believes it to be. Nor does it look the same for everyone. We aren't dealing here with marriage in the abstract. Instead, much like Boaz and Ruth, Lewis and Davidman had been called to marriage not in some generic sense but for the sake of the specific "widows and orphans" in their midst. And for some Christians, the call to marriage might look quite similar. But even when the details differ from one person to the next, insofar as the Spirit of God stirs within marriage, this divine summons is always laying a claim on our lives. It invites us to translate this call into existence, to find a concrete way to let it happen to us and thus be transformed by the event it harbors. So the question for us as individuals and as a community of faith is twofold. First, are we willing to commit ourselves to the messy and arduous process of discernment in order to help each other know whether we are simply falling victim to a misguided savior complex or whether we are truly responding to a divine summons? Second, do we have the courage to respond accordingly— to allow ourselves (and our marriages) to be transformed by this call to justice?

MARRIAGE AS A CALL TO GENEROSITY

If something does in fact stir within the event of marriage, we have so far identified only one of its dimensions—the Spirit's call to enact and embody justice. This summons reaches into every domain of our lives, including our decisions about whether or not to get married and to whom. But there are other dimensions to this call as well. The kingdom that is breaking in on us also invites us to assume a posture of generosity, a way of being in the world that urges us to approach marriage in terms of "the gift."

Anyone who has ever received a gift knows that gift giving generally operates according to an economy of exchange and reciprocity. It is simply assumed that the receiver of a gift will respond in kind, which leads to all manner of concern and anxiety over the relative value of the original gift and what might take place if the gift in return is of lesser, equal, or greater worth. So a gift—something that we supposedly share freely—is never actually free, but is rather a burden. It obligates the receiver to enter into a contract to which they did not consent.

But the gift of the kingdom that calls to us from the event of marriage is not about debts and repayments, nor the balancing of some gift ledger. It's about generosity. Indeed, as John Caputo puts it, "The idea behind a gift ideally ought to be to give a gift without return, to make an expenditure without the expectation of reciprocation, in a kind of 'mad' generosity."[5]

A "mad generosity." That's a beautiful way of talking not only about marriage, but also about how the concept of the gift reshapes our understanding of why and how a Christian might respond to the call of marriage. It's a notion that fundamentally reimagines marriage as a kind of kingdom madness—something that is utter folly when compared to the wisdom of the world (see 1 Cor 1:25, 27). In the terms established by the economies of the present age, it simply makes no sense to give of oneself without getting anything in return—or to give without at least the possibility of repayment. But the summons we encounter in the event of marriage is, at its core, a call toward generosity pure and simple. It has nothing to do with meeting one's psychological, social, sexual, or spiritual needs. Rather, it's about giving something of ourselves away—up to and including all of ourselves.

I said earlier that this is not a book about how to have a good marriage, and I meant it. But in certain respects I am simply laying out one of the core principles that any professional therapist or counselor would affirm when it comes to building a healthy and thriving marriage. As a good friend reminded me recently (who also happens to be married to a licensed marriage and family therapist), marriage isn't 50/50. It's 100/100. Both parties have to give one hundred percent—all the time.[6] In fact, the same could be said for any kind of robust human relationship. Interestingly, though, this is the exact opposite of how we as a community of faith (and as Christian individuals) most often speak about the significance of marriage and the reasons why a Christian would (and indeed should!) get married.

I return to Martin Luther again here because his teachings offer some clarity concerning the theological tradition that has most discernibly shaped the Protestant imagination. Luther regarded celibacy and virginity with a great deal of suspicion, going so far as to say that "a vow of chastity . . . is diametrically opposed to the gospel."[7] In a post-fall world, says Luther, human sexuality is driven primarily by lust, which is inherently selfish and thus contrary to the love that not only constitutes marriage but also serves as humanity's ultimate goal and purpose. So both celibacy and fornication are equally inadequate responses to the problem of the disordered, self-oriented sexual desire that consumes the human heart. Thus, "the proper Christian solution to the problem of disordered desire, Luther reiterates, is marriage."[8] It's like a medicine that allows humans and human sexuality to flourish properly in an imperfect world.

Now it's important to note again that Luther, along with other Reformers, was seeking to undo the ways singleness in general (and the priestly sacrament in particular) had become an idealized marker of spirituality within medieval Catholicism. Similar to my intent in this book, Luther was trying to right the ship. He sought to correct an overemphasis on singleness that had been in operation within the church for the first fifteen hundred years of its existence. But in arguing for the good of marriage, he went too far. And we need to be careful not to make the same mistake in the opposite direction. Luther was right to say that we all suffer from a basic self-interestedness, and this disordered state finds acute expression in our sexual desires. But he was wrong to imply that the simple act of having sex within the context of marriage "solves" the problem of our disordered desire. As I mentioned before, it is sometimes the case that marriage actually magnifies the problem.

It is not incidental that Luther himself did eventually marry, and for reasons that could never be mistaken as self-interested. In fact, his marriage to Katharina serves as another helpful example of two prominent Christians who married each other as a response to the call of justice.[9] So the issue is neither with Luther's assessment of humanity's selfish condition, nor with his willingness to act courageously and creatively in light of complex, on-the-ground realities. The issue is with the unintended consequences of his prescription. Even though his advocacy for married sex was meant to free Christians to be less self-directed and less driven by selfish lust, his basic vision of marriage (and sex within marriage) lends itself, somewhat ironically, to an almost exclusive focus on the (sexual) needs, (sexual) anxieties, and disordered (sexual) desires of the individual.

But if we think of marriage in terms of a call to generosity, then the last thing a Christian should do is pursue marriage as a way of having one's sexual "needs" met, even if it is a more religiously acceptable way of doing so. That's a recipe for disappointment or disaster. Is it a better option than sexual promiscuity? The answer must be yes, especially if we are to take Paul's pastoral advice seriously (1 Cor 7:9). But given the way that sex actually functions within a healthy, real-world marriage, the marriage-as-a-means-for-addressing-lust rationale can never rise above the level of a pastoral accommodation to imperfect circumstances (just as Paul understood it). It simply cannot be the norm for the Christian individual or community, for it fundamentally misunderstands the "madness" that constitutes the kingdom. Indeed, the call to marriage embodies a topsy-turvy wisdom that appears as utter foolishness to the world (and to many in the church) because it suggests that the only way for us to find true fulfillment (sexually or otherwise) is to give up our vain pursuit of satisfaction altogether and instead devote ourselves to satisfying others. It is a call to be generous—to give without the expectation of getting anything in return.

This kind of generosity—of gift giving—rarely makes its way into conversations about Christian marriage or sexuality. Indeed, as Christian ethicist Erin Dufault-Hunter puts it:

> Sex usually isn't considered in this vein. But it is about generosity, the odd interplay of giving oneself to another in peculiar ways while being taken and then forgetting oneself (in orgasm, for e.g.). . . . It is about recalling that we have given our bodies to Christ and are "no longer our own" in the sense we often speak of marriage. Thus we restrain our sexual lives out of fidelity to this God; the restraint is a giving to God, not merely a "not getting some" on our end. And it must then form us for receiving the love of God, or such restraints . . . have not met their truest end.[10]

Just as Dufault-Hunter suggests, marriage demands that spouses give of themselves sexually, but this kind of generosity in restraint has to do with far more than sex. Sexual generosity and gift giving are about something deeper and more profound than simply "getting some" (or not getting any), and we can say the same thing about marriage. The call to marriage is indeed an invitation to give up oneself and thus to "lose" or "forget" oneself in a certain respect, but this should not be taken to mean that some essential dimension of who we are will go forever unrealized. Rather, to enter into marriage is to willingly curtail our own needs, desires, and wants for the sake of giving ourselves to the other. And when we respond to the call of marriage in this way, we become conduits of the Spirit's generosity. Indeed, to use Jesus' words, it is only when we "lose" our lives by giving them up unconditionally that we ever truly find life (Mt 10:39).

For instance, as our discussion of the Genesis accounts made clear, the marriages of Israel's patriarchs were not primarily—if even at all— about romantic love or finding the other half of one's primordial soul. Instead, they were about God being faithful in bringing about God's promise to Abraham. In a radical and incredibly risky demonstration of divine generosity, God gifted to Abraham and Sarah a son in their old age, a child who served as both a reminder and a literal embodiment of God's promise. So before they were anything else, the marriages of Abraham, Isaac, and Jacob were first and foremost an avenue by which God unleashed and unveiled the gratuitous nature of God's project in the world. God's generosity knows no bounds, and these marriages served as a primary means for translating that abundance into existence. What if we approached marriage in this way today? What if, rather than pursuing marriage as a means for satisfying our own self-interested desires or as a therapy for our various dysfunctions, Christians pursued marriage in order to be conduits of God's gratuitous generosity? Following the pattern set forth by the mothers and fathers of our faith, this might very well entail a concrete commitment to baby making and child raising—a calling that demands nothing less than a lifetime of dying to one's own wants and needs for the sake of another's wellbeing. It could also mean that certain Christians pursue marriage for the express purpose of adopting children into their family or serving as foster parents—ways of responding to the call of marriage that create the necessary conditions for both justice and generosity.

Indeed, outside of parenting, I can think of very few projects in life that require so much of us without any promise of reciprocation. It's not that parenting is unrewarding or unfulfilling. It's rather that, at least for Westerners, the entire relationship depends on one human being giving generously to another human being without any expectation of a return on that investment. In fact, the economy of parenting knows nothing of "repayment" of "debts" because it functions according to the same kind of mad generosity that is indicative of God's kingdom. So even if a child wanted to balance the gift ledger, it would simply not be possible for her to do so. It would actually be absurd because the moment-by-moment sacrifices that her parents make can only ever be gifts, pure and simple. And this is exactly what the call to marriage demands of us—a willingness to enter a space where we're not simply setting aside our self-interested desires for a brief moment in time, but where the very notion of being repaid for the gifts we give is a downright absurdity.

This is of course not to say that every Christian can or even should assume the responsibility (that is, the "respond-ability") of bearing, adopting, fostering, or raising children. The obsessive desire for children can be as idolatrous and misdirected as the desire to get married. But it is to say that Christians who accept an invitation to marriage ought to do so with a sense of openness and even expectancy that they are being called into this indissoluble bond not to have their personal needs met, but in order to serve as a conduit of God's generosity. The particular form that this response takes will vary from one person to the next. Procreation, adoption, and fostering are simply a few of the possibilities. Giving oneself sexually to a spouse is another. But whatever concrete form it takes, the underlying reason why a Christian would pursue marriage remains the same: to give rather than to get, and thus to translate God's generosity into a tangible blessing for others.

MARRIAGE AS A CALL TO FORGIVENESS

If it seems like I am more concerned here with the rigorous demands of marriage than with the joys and wonders this relationship might produce, that's because I am. My reasoning is fairly simple, and it has everything to do with what it means to live as a Christian disciple.

Jesus never claimed that taking up our cross or giving all our possessions away or losing our life in order to gain it would be easy. But just
because the life of discipleship is costly and difficult doesn't mean that
it isn't well worth it. Christian marriage is no different. We don't need
to sugarcoat it, and we definitely don't need to romanticize it. There
are already plenty of voices doing exactly that. As a community of faith,
what we need to do is establish more realistic and sobering expectations
for our brothers and sisters in Christ who are considering marriage as
their vocation. At the same time, we need to develop a more compelling
vision for Christian marriage that foregrounds rather than conveniently
overlooks just how demanding this calling truly is. Some will respond
by pursuing marriage with even more enthusiasm. Others will simply
ignore the community's counsel. Still others, somewhat like the rich
young ruler, will turn away, disappointed that marriage demands so
much (Mt 19:16-30; Mk 10:17-31; Lk 18:18-30). But all of this is to
be expected, for such is the calling to Christian discipleship.

Let me make something abundantly clear: Getting married is the
easy part. Actually being married requires a great deal of hard work.
Having a *good* marriage? That's an even more challenging endeavor. I
would of course be remiss if I did not point out that marriage can also
be incredibly rewarding. It has a breathtaking beauty about it, a mystery
that is often difficult to articulate. Still, it isn't for the faint of heart.

For instance, what is often lost amid all our talk about soulmates
and princesses and sexual chemistry is that the call to marriage is, at
its most basic level, a call to forgive. But in a relationship between two
soulmates, forgiveness is virtually impossible. A soulmate is, almost by
definition, an ideal(ized) spouse, which means that when we discover
our soul's other half, we have met our de facto "perfect match," and
thus a spouse who is never in need of forgiveness. Sure, two soulmates
might experience a few minor quibbles along the way, but it's nothing
that can't be solved by a quick roll in the hay.

In direct contrast to this way of framing things, the call to forgiveness
that we encounter in the event of marriage is not about finding a

spouse who never needs forgiveness, nor is it about forgiving what is forgivable—minor slights or trivial indiscretions. Instead, the call to marriage is about forgiving the (seemingly) *un*forgivable. There is a parallel here to the concept of the gift. Like giving a gift, to forgive someone is not a matter of simple accounting, as when a bank "forgives" our debt once we have made all the payments on our mortgage. No, forgiveness is quite literally a grace—it is a gift that is beyond our ability to understand because it operates according to an entirely different economic model.

Consider God's call to the prophet Hosea. His marriage to Gomer was of course symbolic of something larger than the singular relationship between this man and woman. But the fact that the prophet's marriage served as a metaphor for the fractured relationship between God and God's people doesn't make Hosea's call to marry Gomer any less real, nor does it exclude their marriage from serving as a potential model for how we might understand the call to marriage today.

I want us to think long and hard about this notion because my sense is that it is far more scandalous than it might appear at first blush. If the call to marriage is in fact a call to forgive, then it has nothing to do with becoming our best self or helping someone else become a better version of himself or herself.[11] It is instead an invitation to love someone who neither now nor ever will deserve our love. Which means that one of the reasons why Christians should get married is that in and through marriage they are provided an opportunity to forgive not seven times, but seventy times seven times (Mt 18:22). What is more, when this radical commitment to forgive takes shape in the context of a relationship as intimate and vulnerable as marriage, it's also a commitment to be wounded, perhaps even repeatedly. And the reason is that marriage is a calling to bear burdens, not just to be relieved of them. It's to take on the pains of others, not just to be healed from them.

Does this mean that, like Hosea, all Christians should seek to marry prostitutes? Of course not. Does it mean that Christians must always endure marital unfaithfulness or abuse from their spouse, regardless of frequency or duration? Again, no. There are definitely legitimate reasons why a Christian spouse needs to walk away from his or her marriage. The call to dissolve a marriage (just like the call to marriage) is always concrete and particular. There is no such thing as marriage in the abstract, just as there is no such thing as marital infidelity in the abstract. So what I am most decidedly *not* suggesting here is that Christians are to endure violence or abuse from their spouses. Instead, I'm advocating an approach toward Christian marriage that not only takes seriously the call to forgive (even if in perpetuity), but also acknowledges how incredibly difficult it is to locate this kind of forgiveness at the center of married life. Indeed, this is precisely what it means to understand marriage as an event in which the kingdom of God happens to us. It is an occasion in which the Spirit breathes a radical, deeply unsettling, gratuitous, "mad" kind of love into the world.

The point here is not to suggest that every marriage, if it is to be truly Christian, will involve the forgiving of some kind of sexual infidelity, although tragically many will. The point is rather to establish clear and realistic expectations regarding what marriage actually demands and thus why someone would pursue it as a vocation. While not every Christian will be called to marry a Gomer, every Christian marriage does require spouses to extend forgiveness on a near daily basis—in ways both big and small. Indeed, even the worst ruptures in marriage may begin as small ones, such that unimaginably radical forgiveness may become necessary at some point, at least in part because forgiveness hasn't been given in smaller ways all along. So from the very start, responding to the call of marriage as a Christian should involve a basic recognition that there are no such things as "perfect mates." There are only flawed and unfaithful people who are exactly like us—people who need forgiveness for failures that seem impossible to forgive.

MARRIAGE AS A CALL TO HOSPITALITY

Just as with forgiveness, the call toward hospitality also turns on a kind of kingdom inversion. We often think of hospitality as the act of welcoming others into our private spaces, usually our homes. This is fine and well as far as it goes, but in actual practice we generally invite only friends and special guests into these spaces—"those whose company we enjoy and from whom we can expect reciprocity . . . or else people whose favor we are currying."[12] But the kind of hospitality that calls to us from the event of marriage is not about opening our home only to those who are always already welcome. It's about welcoming into our most intimate of spaces those who are unwelcome and unexpected—even hostile.[13]

When seen in this light, hospitality (much like forgiveness) seems to be a rather risky endeavor. And that's because it is. Whether we are hosting the invited or the unwelcome, the peaceful guest or the hostile stranger, hospitality always involves an element of risk. To eliminate this risk completely would be to do away with hospitality itself. Indeed, the only way to ensure that no guest will ever wound us, or take advantage of us, or simply overstay their welcome is to permanently lock our doors.

In certain respects, it is somewhat easy to see how this notion of hospitality plays itself out in a marriage. In fact, newly married couples will often talk about their first year of wedded "bliss" as being uniquely and unexpectedly challenging. The reasons they offer for this struggle are generally related to the fact that they are sharing the same domestic space for the first time. Various negotiations take place between the newlyweds (some of them highly contested) as these two individuals learn how to be hospitable toward the other who is now constantly in their midst. But even as the marriage matures and the couple manages to find some sort of equilibrium, the call toward hospitality never diminishes. If anything, it is a demand that both deepens and becomes more expansive over time.

Of course, being the risk-averse creatures that we are, we are often drawn to visions of marriage that would have us believe that the ideal spouse is the one who fits into our lives in the most comfortable, un-complicated, and nonthreatening way. It's why we find shows like *The Bachelor* and *The Bachelorette* so compelling. They offer us a picture of what we truly desire—namely, a process for determining who the most compatible mate is among a seemingly infinite collection of potential suitors. The same kind of impulse can be seen in the way online dating sites identify prospective "matches," including those sites that are intended primarily for Christians. Here algorithms assess a laundry list of personal details contained in a user's profile in order to eliminate from consid-eration those individuals who run the greatest risk of being incompatible with the person seeking marriage. In other words, as Alain Badiou notes in his book *In Praise of Love*, these websites are not actually designed to help users identify a suitable mate; they are designed to assuage risk.[14]

But the call that stirs within the event of marriage moves us in the opposite direction—toward and not away from risk. In fact, because hospitality is so integral to the marriage relationship, any Christian hoping to mitigate risk in their lives should seriously reconsider pursuing it as a vocation. The call to marriage is not about our personal comfort or pleasure. And as I have mentioned before, it isn't meant to make us "happy." It is rather an invitation to open up our most vulnerable spaces, making room in our lives for the unwelcome and uninvited other (who is usually our spouse).

But the Christian call to hospitality extends beyond the individual commitments that spouses make to each other. As a call to welcome those who are unwelcome, Christian marriage is a call to create the kind of generative space that can accommodate unexpected visitors. And in our present age of radical individualism, the most unexpected and indeed most unwelcome visitor that I can imagine showing up at a couple's doorstep unannounced is the community of faith otherwise known as the church.

To be sure, many of us give lip service to the community's role in our marriages during the wedding ceremony. Informed as they often are by the Book of Common Prayer, most liturgies simply assume that the community is involved in the establishment of the marriage ("Dearly beloved, we are gathered here today, in the sight of God and this company . . ."). There is even a moment in the liturgy (which is often the first thing to hit the cutting-room floor in nonliturgical ceremonies) when the community is invited to voice either their support for or their objection to the vows being made ("If anyone has any reason why these two should not be married, speak now or forever hold your peace"). But as James K. A. Smith rightly points out, too many contemporary wedding ceremonies, including those that take place within the church, "are spectacles in which we celebrate *your* dyadic bliss. We're there more as spectators than partners. And in that sense, [weddings] are often preludes to the sorts of marriages that follow. When lovers are staring into one another's eyes, their backs are to the world."[15]

If Smith is right (and I believe he is), then one of the ways that Christians can and should respond to the call of marriage is to turn around, both figuratively and literally, and face the community that is now tasked with upholding their union. In light of the call toward hospitality, to be married is not simply to welcome another body into one's domestic space, but to invite the entire body of Christ into our bedrooms. Just as we discussed in chapter four, it is exactly this kind of risky and unsettling hospitality that the apostle Paul had in mind when, time and again, he located the sexual practices of spouses, which we usually imagine to be an entirely private matter, within the larger context of the Christian community.

The Christian call to marriage is not about a dyad blissfully disconnecting from their community or achieving relational independence. Neither is it about the creation of an exclusively "nuclear" family—a household closed off to the rest of the world. It is rather a dive into the deep end of hospitality. It is to swing wide the doors of our life and our homes to the community on whom we are profoundly dependent, whether we realize it or not. Such marriages, says Smith, "take 'the risk of interdependence.' [They] make room for others—including the 'singles' among us who are equal members of the household of God. Such households are incubators of concern for the common good because they welcome the community into their midst."[16]

Such is the call to marriage. I am not sure I can think of a more terrifying or risk-filled proposition. But for anyone who has the courage to respond, it is nothing less than an invitation to collaborate with the seemingly mad, but always life-giving Spirit of God.

MARRIAGE AS A CALL TO LOVE

We have identified justice, generosity, forgiveness, and hospitality as ways of naming this thing that stirs within the event of marriage—the "something" that calls to us anytime we encounter the Spirit of God in our midst. All along, though, what we have really been talking about is love. The kingdom that Jesus announced—the one that he and so many of the biblical authors pictured as a marriage between God and God's people (Mt 22:1-14; 25:1-13; Eph 5:29-32; Rev 19:6-10; 21:1-14)— is nothing if not a radical in-breaking of God's gratuitous love. But this is not just any kind of love. The love that calls to us in marriage is both the source and the ultimate end of all our loves and all our passionate desires. It should therefore not be confused or conflated with desire (erotic or otherwise). Rather, this love precedes and indeed is more profound than sexual desire, which means that its call issues from every inch of existence, inviting us to direct our loves and our lives accordingly.

The church has a unique opportunity here that extends beyond our own internal operations, if only we would recognize it as such. For whether we are talking about it in terms of love, justice, gift, generosity, or hospitality, the Christian tradition understands the call to marriage not as a call to satisfy our own self-interests, but as a commitment to have all our passionate desires redirected and rightly ordered. Which means that marriage is not about the aimless expression of our desires, but is most basically a summons to self-emptying, a pouring out of ourselves for the sake of the other.

Significantly, while broad segments of both pop culture and the church have swallowed the myth of romantic love hook, line, and sinker, a growing number of voices are calling for a renewed vision of love and desire in the modern world. What is interesting about this collection of voices is that many of them are ardently nonreligious and explicitly nontheistic. But what is perhaps even more interesting is that they openly acknowledge the value of the Christian tradition's conception of love and marriage, especially as it concerns the right ordering of human desire.

For example, in his *Religion for Atheists*, Alain de Botton suggests that for all the talk of "freedom" that citizens of modern liberal democracies use, our freedom is never really free unless it is properly directed.[17] In fact, because untethered freedom can only ever be self-interested, we need practices—religious practices—in order to direct this freedom rightly and, ultimately, to cultivate a capacity to actually love the other. In this way, true freedom is always a freedom in restraint. What is more, says de Botton, we need an active and engaged audience if we have any hope of sustaining these kinds of freedom-restraining, others-oriented virtues. Members of religious communities are not simply the spectators who happen to be filling the empty seats at a couple's wedding. Instead, by their very presence they are creating the conditions for the cultivation of virtue. The "dearly beloved" gather together "in the sight of God and this company" because that is how love is both activated and sustained—in and through community.

Along strikingly similar lines, Alain Badiou claims that the contemporary notion of love is in need of reinvention.[18] Rather than something safe and comfortable, love is a risky and adventurous pursuit of truth. It is an event—a real encounter with an other who awakens us from our self-centered stupor. From Badiou's perspective, though, love is currently under threat. It is all too often (mis)understood as a variant of sexual desire and hedonism—a manifestation of the modern obsession with self. In a somewhat provocative turn for an atheist philosopher, Badiou's response to this distorted view of love is not to deny the genuine pleasures that sex and erotic desire provide, but rather to acknowledge that sexual pleasure on its own is ultimately empty. It hints at where love is taking us, but it can never get us there, for genuine love is the beginning of "a two," not the mere (sexual) satisfaction of its constituent parts. Thus for Badiou marriage is integral to the project of reinventing love because it is one of the few mechanisms capable of channeling love toward its ultimate destination, which is to see the world from the point of view of two rather than one.

The call to which both these thinkers are responding is the call to love—not as the unchecked expression of erotic desire, but as the right ordering of all our passionate desires. And in the final analysis, this is precisely the argument I have been trying to make in this chapter. Christians should not seek out marriage if they are simply hoping to have their desires for romance or companionship satisfied or if they are looking for ways to unleash their repressed sexual energies. Why? Not because these things are inherently bad or wrong, but rather, as Badiou and de Botton remind us, because they are ultimately empty.

Instead, Christians should pursue marriage for the sake of having every one of their desires rightly ordered and thus transformed. Whether the right ordering of our passions takes the form of justice, generosity, forgiveness, hospitality, or all of the above, the call to marriage is most basically an invitation to redirect our desires toward the other in self-giving love.

This emphasis on rightly ordered desire is deeply imbedded in the Christian tradition. As far back as Augustine and Gregory of Nyssa, Christian theologians have conceived of marriage as a site for bringing one's desires into alignment with the desires of God. And even though these two Christian thinkers held rather divergent views on the role and value of erotic desire, marriage for both of them wasn't about self-fulfillment or self-actualization, but absolute self-surrender and self-sacrifice—a sign and sacrament of self-giving love.[19] As a consequence, these church fathers believed that marriage was meant only for those who are not only specifically called to this kind of life, but also fully aware of its rigorous demands.

So the Christian theological tradition, both modern and historic, already has the necessary resources for reinventing love and marriage along the very lines that de Botton and Badiou are suggesting. But I am calling attention to the deep affinity that exists between these nontheistic projects and our own because, in the first place, it underscores how an understanding of marriage as an in-Spirit-ed kingdom event helps to reveal all sorts of unexpected allies who share a number of our own sensibilities regarding the meaning and value of love and marriage in the modern world. It also serves to remind us that how we talk about marriage as a community of faith can either undermine or lend credibility to our public witness. For it is no longer a question of if or when the church's views on marriage go public. They always already are. The more important question is how. *How* might the church tell a more faithful and compelling story about marriage?

It is far from certain whether or not we live in a wholly "post-secular" or "post-religious" society. What is a bit less debatable is that modern persons have become increasingly disconnected from the life and devotional practices of the Christian community. But one of the few remaining places where the church and its rituals continue to play a prominent role in public life is in the context of the wedding ceremony. So the wedding ritual is a matter of some significance for the church's mission in the world because it is our public performance of the kingdom—one that has already happened but has yet to come. It thus has the potential for serving as a kind of icon through which people might perceive (perhaps for the first time) the Spirit who is always already stirring in the midst of life.

It is for this very reason that we need to be more thoughtful about why a Christian would or would not participate in this iconic way of life (marriage) rather than simply assume that everyone will or should. It is also why it is vital that the church continue to provide realistic descriptions of what married life actually entails for those who believe they are being called to such a rigorous and demanding vocation. Indeed, the flippancy with which Christians often enter marriage, along with the rate at which these marriages dissolve, undermines the credibility of our witness and calls into question our (often very public) claims regarding the significance of marriage itself.

But if we are truly responding to the call of love that emerges from the event of marriage, our focus must eventually shift away from these largely internal, self-directed concerns. As a community of faith, we need to ask what is taking place when we perform our narratives about marriage in the public sphere. Do we have the courage to enact and embody a different, even countercultural narrative—one that offers an alternative to the prevailing cultural scripts that reduce love to romance, spouses to soulmates, and sexuality to sex?

In other words, what would take place if we saw the wedding ceremony for what it really is—an opportunity to bring the Christian vision to bear on public life? Would we continue to enact a picture of marriage that succumbs to the same illusions or delusions expressed by the myth of romantic love? Or would we attempt to bear witness to a much deeper story—one that invites us to direct our desires away from our own self-serving ends and to discover both the original source and the ultimate end of all our passionate longings? What might it look like to enact this radical vision of others-oriented, self-giving love in a wedding ceremony? What might it sound like? What might it feel like?

If I were to venture a guess, I would imagine that it would look, sound, and feel a lot like the homily delivered at a recent wedding by my colleague at Fuller Seminary Tommy Givens. I offer an excerpt of his sermon here as a way of bringing this chapter to a close and summarizing my thoughts on why Christians should get married and also why it might be best for marriages to come with a warning label. May we have the ears to hear what the Spirit of God—the One who stirs in the midst of this beautifully risky thing we call marriage—is saying.

I think the Christian faith came traditionally to call marriage a sacrament partly because we don't know what we're talking about. We know that this kind of immersion in the power of life is more than we understand or can control, that we are playing with fire, that this kind of intimacy with the power of life is dangerous. We call it a mystery so that we will treat it with reverence and due care. So much are you giving yourselves to one another in marriage that you will hurt each other. Your lives are becoming too exquisitely tangled with one another to be safe from each other, and if you are blessed with children they will be the product not only of your virtues but of your sins as well, as will the countless other lives touched by your shared life. Despite what we might think, these perils are a part of the deep beauty, the glory, of this form of friendship called marriage.

You're getting married in front of all these people because you haven't gotten to this point without help, and you can't go on as married without help. You really don't know what you're doing today, and we're here as witnesses so that in the future we can remind you what you did and help you figure out what it is. Your friendship can be life-giving only as it is nurtured by other friendships, and the rest of us are here today to say that we are those friends to you. You can only imagine all the ways in which you are going to need others. Neither of you can be all that the other needs. But because of what others give you, you can be more for one another than you can even imagine, so much that it will spill out from your life together as more life for others. The friendships of others can give you the perseverance that will make the bond between you a joy too profound for words.

The sage of Ecclesiastes ends the passage [of Ecclesiastes 4:7-12] by writing that a cord of three is not quickly broken. Not a cord of two, but a cord of three. Marriage is an intense form of friendship, but it is not the whole of friendship. Something even deeper than marriage binds human beings to one another, and it is that something of which the sacrament of marriage is a sign, that something that is the soil of life that feeds a life-giving marriage and is its hope. As Christians we say that this something is a someone, that the reality of love that binds human beings together by the strong cords of friendship became a human being, Jesus, walking among us, enduring all the forces that tear us apart from one another: one who so gave himself to others that the immense power of life gushed from his body, to bring healing, forgiveness, life through death. He was himself a person born out of wedlock, let us remember, and, as far as we can tell, one who never married. Perhaps that is because he came not to be an example of marriage but to be the love of which marriage is a sign.

SINGLE NOT SOLITARY

By Colton Simmons

I am twenty-six years old. I live in Los Angeles. I have a great community of friends. I just finished my master's degree. I have a great job working for a thriving nonprofit. And I'm single.

Doesn't adding that last descriptor sound like I'm trying to sell you on my eligibility as a bachelor? Maybe it's because I placed the "single" part at the very end, but I think no matter what, singleness is lacking. Or so we're told . . .

I once heard a stand-up comedian say, "Being single is a mixture of loneliness and euphoria. It's lonely right before you go to bed at night, and euphoria the whole rest of the day."

My mother started grooming me to become a hopeless romantic from a very young age. Her preferred method of influence was anything starring Meg Ryan and Tom Hanks.

Perfection.

Is there any other word for their on-screen chemistry? I'm secure enough in my masculinity to admit I can quote nearly every word of *You've Got Mail*.

Thanks to changing tides in pop culture and advancements in technology, for their story to be culturally relevant today, Tom and Meg would have to meet on Tinder, hook up once, then never talk again.

So I've had to adjust my view of the "perfect relationship" and "true love."

My mentor and all-purpose father figure is a man I call Pritch. He's amazing. He is seventy years old and has an empire of healthy relationships with everyone from devout ministers to famous, atheist actors. He loves people, and they love him back because they know he will never stop seeing the best in them. Pritch makes you believe that the top five percent of yourself, where all your character and talents are operating at peak capacity, is who you always are and always can be. He holds no judgments, looks past all your indiscretion and sharp edges, and loves you Into becoming your best self.

Did I say he's amazing?

Pritch is also single. He has never been married. He has no kids. Nothing but that empire of healthy relationships I just mentioned. Oh, and an incredibly successful career as a professor and pastor for over four decades.

See, I never saw Pritch's life in the movies. I never saw Tom Hanks give it an honest shot, realize both he and Meg were better off as friends, and live happily ever after pouring into his friends, peers, employees, and family.

Yes, family. It is possible to have an abundance of family without being married or having kids (sorry, Mom). Pritch has basically adopted a couple with whom I went to college and become so close with them that Pritch was the first person they told when they found out they were having their first child. As it turned out, that child was born on Pritch's birthday.

So Pritch now celebrates every birthday with his grandson—and the rest of his family.

I could go on for days about Pritch and the collage of photos hanging on the wall in his office taken with friends from all over the world who have been lucky enough to encounter the tsunami of love that is Pritch. Truth be told, Pritch has a photo of me on that wall that could certainly be used as blackmail down the road.

I give you this portrait of Pritch's life because it's quite possible that you've never met a Pritch nor seen anything as beautiful as his life depicted in art or the media. Pritch is single and whole, and quite frankly that scares me to death.

Even though I am filled with respect and admiration for Pritch, I worry that God put him in my life in order to strip me of my hope for marriage, romance, and even sex. Many people find mentors who are married, but alas, I did not.

The idea of lying down beside the woman I love and who loves me unconditionally sounds incredible. To be understood and intimate with one other human being in such a profoundly unique way as this has driven me to do crazy things, unhealthy things to fill a void created by idolatrous desire.

I don't know how to let go. Maybe you don't know how to either. But I promise you this, over the past five years I've journeyed with one of the healthiest, most joy-filled people I've ever met, and he lets go every day.

And you know what? He still has two burial plots in his family's gravesite. One for him, and one for . . . maybe.

That to me is the epitome of a balanced hope. "Dying to yourself" does not mean pretending you don't have desires. It's holding your desires in an open hand waiting patiently for God to fill it with exactly what you need.

Take your hope to the grave. Become a hopeful romantic, and know that single never means solitary.

6

DESIRE IN SINGLENESS

ASCETICS AND ETERNITY (OR, WHY CHRISTIANS *DON'T NEED* TO GET MARRIED)

By Joshua Beckett

"REMEMBER THAT YOU HAVE A CALLING—to serve Christ! Focus on the inheritance and not the deprivation. And find ways to open yourself up to beauty." I heard this wise counsel a few years ago, while I was volunteering at the ecumenical monastery in Taizé, France. I was in the middle of a week of silence and had been reflecting on the existential, vocational, and theological questions revolving around my long-term relational future. At twenty-eight years of age, with both persistent same-sex attractions and a traditional Christian sexual ethic that rules out a same-sex partner, marriage appeared to me to be an increasingly unlikely prospect. Thus I wanted to know what made celibacy a life-giving vocation for the monks, rather than a bleak exercise in ascetic abstinence. Brother Emile, a Canadian monk in his late fifties who had lived in the community since the age of twenty, was my accompanying mentor.[1] He shared with me the wisdom born of decades of a faithful life, and in the quiet hills and vineyards of Burgundy, supported by a warm community and stirring music, "opening myself up to beauty" was not a difficult endeavor.

This was a very different take on celibacy than what I had heard throughout most of my years growing up in conservative evangelical churches and networks. Among my peers, celibacy was treated like a terrible joke—something simultaneously to be laughed about and cringed at. We understood that God might call someone to a life of celibacy. We had, after all, read 1 Corinthians 7, so we knew it was a fringe possibility. But it was like the call to a remote mission field—a life of hard work and isolation reserved for the spiritual elite, but most certainly not for regular Christians.

Additionally, I experienced the ambivalent pressures of evangelical purity culture, pledges of abstinence until marriage while at the same time being *Wild at Heart*. In their better forms, these messages taught me that bodily holiness is a way to honor God. At other times, however, I experienced a bizarre combination of fear-mongering religion (premarital sex's utterly devastating consequences) and prosperity gospel (amazing sex in marriage promised as God's reward for obedience). Also, the prohibition against looking lustfully at women was drilled into me early on, and I became very skilled at refraining from that sin. Yet as a teenager coming to grips with my sexual orientation, there was a gap in my discipleship: I was never trained to avoid lusting after male friends, peers, and celebrities, which was the more urgent need. I slowly began to realize that these messages kept the broader culture's idolatrous obsession with sex intact, but simply placed it in a more legalistic frame.[2]

Although there is much from my evangelical upbringing that I remain grateful for, as I look back on the messages about sex and marriage that I received, I am disappointed by their misleading visions and false promises (for example, I still have not received my "reward" of married sex). And I am angry at the ways that they hurt my female peers, who were often made responsible for both their own sexual purity and that of their guy friends—an impossible double standard.

Ultimately, it was neither promises of wedded bliss nor fears of dire consequences that sustained my pursuit of holiness in the midst of temptations while I attended college at one of the nation's top party schools. Rather, in the words of the psalmist, I had already tasted and seen the Lord's goodness (Ps 34:8), and an abiding vision of Christ's fierce love for me provoked a deep response of loyalty to him. This same dynamic of love and loyalty remained a guiding light in my mid-twenties as I experienced a crisis of friendship, community, and ministry that resulted from my falling in love with another guy.

Things became even more challenging when I moved to Southern California for further study after my sojourn in France. Although I was blessed to find a hospitable church and an intentional residential community, I experienced cognitive dissonance about the topic of celibacy. Through participation in a student group and a film festival dedicated to dialogue around the intersection of faith, gender, and sexuality, I met and befriended several other gay Christians whose perspective on (and practice of) sexual ethics differed markedly from my own. Hearing their experiences of celibacy (as repressive, painful, and body denying) provoked intense soul and Scripture searching: Did I really have to make a choice between finding a boyfriend and honoring the Bridegroom, or could I somehow have both?

These existential and theological reflections unfolded within the context of the contentious national debate on the legality of gay marriage, which was only recently legally decided via the *Windsor* and *Obergefell* Supreme Court verdicts. Seeing LGBT (my own) sexuality being reduced to a political football, with Christians themselves often exhibiting the most offensive insensitivity, was profoundly discouraging. Ultimately, I find the revisionist theological arguments (sanctioning same-sex unions) unconvincing, and I have reaffirmed my commitment to follow Jesus in a state of chaste celibacy.[3] But the process of discernment often felt draining and devoid of the beauty to which Brother Emile testified.

I share this personal introduction to say that I resonate with Kutter's description of both the promise and the pitfalls of the Christian community's understanding and behavior in the realms of marriage, singleness, and sexuality. Although my perspective is certainly shaped by my own experiences as a celibate gay Christian, my hope is that these thoughts will be relevant to many other Christians who experience singleness for a protracted time.[4]

In the post-*Obergefell* United States, sexual ethics have risen to the fore in public and Christian discourse, and certainly important ethical conversations still lie before us. However, a comprehensive Christian theology and ethic of marriage and sexuality will remain incomplete without a corresponding reformation of church practice (expanding the space for unmarried people to participate in Christian community and leadership) and a renewal of theological imagination (connecting the vocation of celibacy to desire, beauty, and love).

It is to this latter task that I set my attention and constructive energy. This brief proposal is far from comprehensive, but my hope is that sketching some connections between a theology of desire and the practices that make celibacy beautiful and life giving will propel further creative conversation. At its core, my argument is that beauty opens up a space for the unfulfilled desires inherent in celibacy to be placed in a larger, ultimately God-directed frame. But before addressing a theology of desire and the practice of celibacy, we first need to return to the biblical writings to hear their witness.

SINGLENESS IN THE BIBLE

Earlier chapters already looked in-depth at how the Scriptures deal with marriage. With that background in mind, we also need to consider the ways that the Bible attends to single people in their unique life circumstances. Of course, "singleness" itself is not a biblical idea at all! The notion of autonomous individuals existing in isolation (rather than embedded in community) makes sense only in the aftermath of the intellectual and cultural changes of the Enlightenment. The Bible talks of the unmarried, the eunuchs, the widows, and the virgins—but never the singles. At times in this chapter I still use the language of singleness because it is so deeply a part of our social imagination. But I want to emphasize that the Bible both presupposes and prescribes a far richer understanding of humanity.

It is true that the First Testament, from the creation accounts onward, highlights marriage, sex, and children as divine gifts, and often as the context for divine promises. For instance, God promises Eve that victory over the serpent will come through her seed (Gen 3:15). God promises Abram that all the nations of the earth will be blessed through his descendants (Gen 12:3). God promises Sarah a son within a year to extend their covenant relationship (Gen 21:1-2). And God gives the distraught Hannah a son, whom she dedicates back to the Lord as a temple servant and eventually a prophet (1 Sam 1:10-20).

This pattern of marriage, sex, and children being an expression of God's gifts and promises remains the major accent for most of the First Testament. Yet even though the First Testament generally assumes that marriage is functionally normative for most people—part of "the facts on the ground" for human society—it never prescribes it for everybody. Additionally, the Bible's frame of reference is not our contemporary notions of "the happy couple" or the post–World War II nuclear family, but rather the complex, deeply interdependent relational systems of the clan, the tribe, and ultimately the covenant people of God.[5] In remembrance of the Lord's deliverance of Israel from Egypt, God's people were expected to fulfill their covenantal obligations to one another and to show special care for the most vulnerable and marginalized populations: the widow, the orphan, the resident alien, and the poor.

By the end of the prophetic period, these vulnerable peoples themselves had gained new prominence, and there were hints that the marriage trajectory was about to be transcended (though not, of course, rejected). The book of Isaiah is especially vocal in highlighting the place of the unmarried in the purposes of God. It makes the startling claim that, contrary to popular opinion, barrenness is a sign of blessedness: "Shout for joy, O barren one who has not given birth! / Give a joyful shout and cry out, you who have not been in labor!" (Is 54:1). Soon after, Isaiah creates a remarkable new space for male eunuchs, who had traditionally been excluded from Israel's worship life:

The eunuch should not say,

"Look, I am like a dried-up tree."

For this is what the LORD says:

"For the eunuchs who observe my Sabbaths

and choose what pleases me

and are faithful to my covenant,

I will set up within my temple and my walls a monument

that will be better than sons and daughters.

I will set up a permanent monument for them that will remain."

   (Is 56:3-5)

These surprising developments create a connection between the present lived realities of unmarried people and the hopeful visions of God's future promises.

The New Testament extends and accelerates this shift, transfiguring the First Testament's assumptions without dishonoring the Scriptures that went before. Although marriage continues to be honored and celebrated as holy and good (Heb 13:4), its place within God's purposes becomes increasingly relativized. This is especially true in the life and ministry of Jesus. Born as the result of the virginal conception of Mary, the Savior himself never married. In his teaching he denied the ultimacy of marriage and sexuality (Mt 22:30). And when his mother and brothers sought to leverage their ties to him, he publicly redefined family and relativized biological relationships (Mt 12:50).

Following Jesus' ascension, the early church sought to strike a careful balance between affirming the goodness of the created order (including marriage and sexuality) and reorienting their whole lives in light of the new covenant and the kingdom ushered in by Jesus' death and resurrection (see particularly 1 Cor 7:29-31). In the church marriage and family certainly have their honored place, but the priority of focus is reserved for the entire family of believers, the "household of faith" (Gal 6:10 ESV) living communally in light of the gospel of God and together offering worship to God (1 Pet 2:9-10). Rather than occupying a space at the margins, unmarried persons attain new dignity and an eternally oriented calling. For them the gift of celibacy means not loneliness but liberation from stifling social expectations and the freedom to devote themselves wholeheartedly to loving God and other people (1 Cor 7:32-35).

THE REMARGINALIZATION OF CELIBACY

Unfortunately, the early church's careful balance proved difficult to sustain. The marginalization of celibacy in general, and of unmarried people in particular, is a complicated story, reaching back to the medieval and Reformation periods (recall, for example, Martin Luther's over-correction). Nevertheless, this longstanding eclipse of celibacy as a viable vocation has been accelerated more recently due to secularism.[6] Canadian philosopher Charles Taylor speaks of the rise of an "immanent frame" in which people "come to understand our lives as taking place within a self-sufficient immanent order; or better, a constellation of orders, cosmic, social and moral . . . understood as impersonal."[7] As a result, (post)modern people are much less likely to experience their lives as "porous" (vulnerable to supernatural forces) but exist as "buffered" selves (invulnerable and in charge).[8]

There is a deep connection between the rise of the immanent frame and the further eclipse of celibacy as a viable human (and Christian) vocation.[9] As God recedes from the day-to-day consciousness of our societies and communities, earthly relationships (especially erotic ones) become freighted with much greater significance. But they cannot sustain the weight that is thrust on them. As a consequence, people without a sexual partner come to be seen as deficient and pitiable. We are considered incomplete human beings until we find that "special someone," rather than distinct and potentially fruitful in our own unique way.

Unfortunately, over the last several decades Protestant churches in North America have often capitulated to the prevailing narratives that find ultimacy in sexual relationships. They have done so even while admittedly setting tighter limits around licit sexual expression—usually in covenanted, monogamous heterosexual relationships. Yet even though churches do not pressure unmarried people to embrace all the contemporary sexual scripts (especially those oriented toward hedonism and promiscuity), our culture's idealization and idolatry of sex is also rampant in contemporary churches.

Thus marriage becomes the normative pattern of human (even Christian) life, notwithstanding the strong biblical warrant for celibacy. This painful, lamentable reality not only means that churches are squandering a priceless opportunity to bear prophetic witness to the resurrection. It also ensures that life in Christian communities remains continually difficult for unmarried persons, whether never married, divorced, or widowed, even as members of each of these groups experience their own unique challenges. These are the facts on the ground for celibate persons in church and society.

TOWARD A THEOLOGY OF DESIRE

Charles Taylor has clarified much of the nature and contours of our cultural moment and in doing so has thrown down a gauntlet that demands a theological response. Thankfully, Christians have not been silent, so it is not necessary to develop a meaningful theology of desire and life practice for celibacy from scratch. I have found particular assistance from three contemporary writers, each of whom operates in light of Taylor's concerns. All three reflect on desire theologically, and this common thread makes several contributions toward a holistic celibacy. My goal here is to uncover the distinct (though often hidden and unexpected) beauty of an unmarried life in God, while helping celibates follow Brother Emile's counsel—opening ourselves up further to beauty.

Philosopher James K. A. Smith, in his *Desiring the Kingdom* and *Imagining the Kingdom*, draws on the thought of Augustine to develop a theological anthropology of desire. According to Smith, we are imaginative, narrative, liturgical animals—shaped both by the stories we tell ourselves and by the practices in which we engage. Put more simply, "we are what we love," and we love what we imagine.[10] Thus, recasting celibacy in a positive light means taking into account the reality that "human beings are—fundamentally and primordially—lovers."[11] We can only love celibacy if we conceive of celibacy as lovely, rather than the body-denying, pleasure-repressing, immanent prison that many of my friends dreaded.

This is a tall order, requiring a significant reorientation of our imagination about sexuality. Smith is helpful here as well, locating sexuality as "a realm of meaning *between* instinct and intellect."[12] Thus "Christian 'perception' of the world is also a kind of erotic comprehension—a visceral 'between' way of meaning the world that constitutes our environment as God's good-but-broken creation that, in turn, calls to us and beckons for a response."[13] Part of this response, which any adequate practice of celibacy must address, includes the specter of unfulfilled sexual desire that continues to lurk in the shadows. But for now we simply need to hear Smith's claims: that the erotic both includes and transcends sex, and that desire in itself is not the problem (rather, the real challenge that we face is misdirected and disordered desire). Indeed, "agape is rightly ordered eros."[14]

Reformed theologian William A. Dyrness adds further depth to this frame with his *The Earth Is God's* and *Poetic Theology*. His starting point is "the presence and work of God in the contemporary situation and, especially, in the passions that move people to act, build, and create."[15] Dyrness assumes that "God is already deeply involved in [modern persons'] lives, and is already in conversation with them."[16] In fact, people's desires, as expressed in their cultural projects, are humanity's response to creation and its Creator:

Culture [is] the continuing human response to God's ongoing project of reconciliation and renewal. It is the communal, active, embodied engagement with God's purposes as these are both distorted by human rebellion and reflected in human institutions.

> Both in its pain and its glimpses of greatness human practices necessarily embody the human response to God's presence and the call of the Holy Spirit.[17]

For Dyrness, the experience of beauty is fundamental to human life, and concrete aesthetic practices are the theological sites where God is present and active—in and through people's desires. Relatedly, Dyrness displays the strong link between aesthetics and transformation, between beauty and justice. Beauty calls us out of ourselves (the opposite of idolatry, which is self-centered) and evokes two responses of justice—protection and extension (the opposite of injustice, which is ugly and defaces beauty). Thus "any project of human betterment will seek to appreciate and celebrate the aesthetic impulse that is already present in the community."[18] Since the Holy Spirit is already present in the realm of human desires, we should expect exciting, creative possibilities for social and communal transformation when celibate persons reorient their lives—which are already charged with desire—toward the interface between beauty and justice.

Anglican priest and theologian Sarah Coakley gives an even more comprehensive account of the Spirit's activity in *God, Sexuality, and the Self*. She begins by helpfully locating desire as more fundamental than sex or gender. Desire is a "category belonging primarily to God, and only secondarily to humans as a token of their createdness 'in the image.'"[19] This has profound implications for how we understand human desire: "Desire, I now suggest again—even fallen desire—is the precious clue woven into the crooked human heart that ever reminds it of its relatedness and its source."[20]

This framework hits the ground for celibacy particularly in two places. First, rather than the lack that celibates customarily associate with desire in our own experience, in God desire "connotes that plenitude of longing love that God has for God's own creation and for its full and ecstatic participation in the divine, Trinitarian, life."[21] Second, the Holy Spirit both ignites and constrains desire in people, fostering human participation in divine desire (especially through practices of contemplation).[22] The "Spirit is the vibrant point of contact and entry into the flow of this divine desire, the irreplaceable mode of invitation for the cracking open of the crooked human heart. The Spirit is the constant overflow of the life of God into creation: alluring, delighting, inflaming, in its propulsion of divine desire."[23] Erotic desire is innately powerful; it has incredibly potent force, linking the animal and spiritual realities of our being and possessing the capacity to draw us out of ourselves. Depending on how it is directed, erotic desire can be either life giving (and therefore innately creative) or life destroying (and therefore innately dangerous). Yet because of the activity of the Holy Spirit, human desire—even potentially dangerous erotic desire in celibate persons—is not something to be shunned or suppressed. Rather, we can honestly acknowledge our powerful desires and yield them to the even more powerful Spirit of God, to be refined according to God's will and harnessed in new, creative, life-giving, community-building, and society-transforming directions.

TOWARD A PRACTICE OF CELIBACY

Oriented by these helpful insights, it is now time for the task of discerning and constructing a celibate way of life that is fruitful and beautiful. Three questions guide our search, one from each of the writers surveyed above: (1) How might the Holy Spirit be igniting and constraining desire in people who find themselves in a state of celibacy, whether temporary or lifelong (Coakley)? (2) How can we foster the connection between aesthetics and transformation for single people and their communities (Dyrness)? And (3) How does a renewed celibate imagination shape our loves (Smith)? In conversation with Coakley, Dyrness, and Smith, as well as other theologians who have given more direct attention to the topic, I would like to propose six interrelated elements for a meaningful life practice of celibacy.

Acknowledgment of the ache. Life without a sexual partner is often a lonely experience. While no Christian theology worth its salt can claim that sex is essential to human flourishing—since Jesus' own celibate life instantly defeats that line of thinking—the Bible does unambiguously identify sex as a wonderful gift from God. Within the marriage covenant, sexual activity serves several wholesome purposes, including the promotion of unity between spouses (Gen 2:24), the procreation of children (Gen 1:28), the fostering of a sense of belonging and intimacy (Song 2:4, 16), the release of emotional joy and physical pleasure (Prov 5:15-19), and the establishment of a safeguard for chastity (1 Cor 7:2, 9).

Although none of these goods should be idolized as ultimate, the powerful ways that they can come together in covenantal sexuality should be celebrated. Similarly, their palpable absence in the lives of single people is often an occasion for lament. It is certainly important not to overemphasize this point, as if the essence of celibacy were sexual abstinence.[24] Still, an honest look at celibacy—even as it rejects the narrative that human beings can find completion only through a spouse—must also include a deep sense of pathos. The human condition is painful for everyone, but especially when it is unmitigated by the comforting, delightful presence of a sexual partner.

Yet anguish and longing do not have to be borne alone. Sarah Coakley reminds us to be open to the Holy Spirit working powerfully to direct human desire in a Godward direction. Musical worship, embodied prayer, and uttering groanings too deep for words (Rom 8:26) can yield cathartic release of the celibate ache for emotional and erotic union, even as they together remind all of us (married or not) of our radical incompleteness on this side of the resurrection.

And once loneliness has been acknowledged, it can be transcended. As Brother Roger, the founder of the Taizé monastery, movingly wrote:

Only let the flame that never dies away keep burning. And the yes blazes up within. The yes of celibacy is lived out in the giving of one's life ... and it becomes possible again and again to go beyond oneself. The heart, the affections, the times of aloneness are all still there, but someone Other than oneself is transfiguring them. And your soul can sing: I belong to Christ. I am Christ's.[25]

Openness to beauty that consoles and transforms. As Brother Emile wisely counseled, opening oneself up to beauty—cultivating a posture of openness to God's good, true, and lovely gifts in creation, community, and culture—is a crucial practice for celibates (and, for that matter, married people as well) to live flourishing lives. In many ways, this is not so much a practice of Christian celibacy, but rather its core, animating vision. Yet it is useful to attend more precisely to the roles of consolation and transformation that beauty—whether experienced in music, art, poetry, story, service, advocacy, or time in creation—plays. This is not to instrumentalize beauty, as if God's created order and human cultural projects are valuable only when they fulfill these roles. Rather, my hope is that we will learn to uncover the power of beauty more concretely.

Indeed, the ways that beauty works "on the ground" are stunningly diverse. For example, Eve Tushnet, a celibate lesbian Catholic, discusses the associations between Catholicism and gay people in nineteenth-century Britain:

> Same-sex attracted seekers . . . responded strongly to Catholicism's physicality. The incense smoke and flaking paint, the hint of cannibalism that recalled the Church to Her disrespectable origins, the kneeling, and the statues called to gay men and women. If you're persecuted for your reaction to gender and physicality, you may become intensely aware of bodily realities; and Catholicism, alone in the mainstream Western religious landscape, kept insisting that bodies were both important and bizarre.[26]

Protestant Christians have noted these connections as well. William Dyrness encourages us to cultivate the practices of play, celebration, and ritual as significant for our communal life and for broader society. Corporate worship is especially important in this regard: "Liturgy schools us in justice, but it also anticipates shalom and the rest and joy of the Sabbath."[27] And as Protestants, we would do well to recover the aesthetic and embodied dimensions of our worship if we hope to cultivate a transformative space in which all of us—single and married—might be able to open ourselves to beauty.

Orientation toward the other. This timely reminder leads into the next component of our theologically informed life practice of celibacy—moving beyond oneself to turn toward others in self-giving love, nonsexual intimacy, and practical service. Put simply, the biblical vision of celibacy entails neither lonely isolation nor autonomous independence, but a life freely lived to God, for others, and in joyful interdependence (recall 1 Cor 7:32-35). It is true that abiding love within and beyond the Christian community is costly—both in the sense that it is precious and that it requires sacrifice. But it is possible because the self-giving love of Jesus both enables our adoption into God's family and provides the example we are to emulate in our relationships. We belong first to God, who is both the ground and goal of all our self-giving love for one another. James K. A. Smith expresses this reality well: "Our ultimate love moves and motivates us because we are lured by this picture of human flourishing; rather than being pushed by beliefs, we are pulled by a telos that we desire."[28]

Celibate people are often well aware of the fragility of human love. Indeed, in the presence of unmet erotic desire, it can be all too easy to transfer one's perceived and felt needs to another mortal human who is unable to meet them, causing damage. Yet this clear and present danger should not be an occasion for fearful withdrawal, but rather for imaginative redirection toward beauty. Wesley Hill, another celibate gay Christian, offers a fruitful example:

> Being gay is, for me, as much a sensibility as anything else: a heightened sensitivity to and passion for same-sex beauty.... I don't imagine I would have invested half as much effort in loving my male friends, and making sacrifices of time, energy, and even

money on their behalf, if I weren't gay. My sexuality, my basic erotic orientation to the world, is inescapably intertwined with how I go about finding and keeping friends.[29]

A space for God alone to fill. Again, our turning toward others in love is possible only because God has first loved us, and because God sustains us even when human relationships fray and fracture. Just as the previous chapter noted that the call to know and belong to God is prior to, and more fundamental than, the vocation of marriage, so also the preservation of a space for God alone to fill is central to a flourishing celibate life. Henri Nouwen elaborates: "And so, every relationship carries within its center a holy vacancy, a space that is for the first Love, God alone. Without that holy center, partnership and friendship become like a city without domes to remind it of its center, a city without meaning or direction for all its activities."[30]

The practice of contemplation—a solitude that is focused on actively attending to God—is crucial here. This may come as a bit of a surprise. After all, isn't one of the obvious difficulties of the single life the reality that much of it is spent alone? Perhaps. Yet there is a vast difference between loneliness (defined negatively by lack and characterized by the absence of other people) and solitude (defined positively by fullness and characterized by the presence of God). Solitude usually includes physical aloneness, but more deeply it involves yielding our distractions, affections, fears, and hopes to God, the source and goal of our life. Loneliness, on the other hand, can strike even in a room filled with other people, and it tempts us to focus inward on our own insufficiency and deprivation. Loneliness is an affliction that all human beings experience, but solitude is a gift that requires contemplative discipline. Sarah Coakley explains how contemplation refines human desire: in "its naked longing for God, it lays out all its other desires—conscious and unconscious—and places them, over time, into the crucible of divine desire."[31] Such inner space is quite germane to celibates, even as it also indicates a focal point of interdependence with married people.

Solidarity with married people. Such interdependence constitutes the next component. Solidarity between married people and celibates springs forth as we come to recognize our mutual state of incompleteness and need, both for communion with God and for community with other people. Building off his earlier theme, Nouwen expounds on the ways that celibate and married persons help one another in Christ:

> The celibate person is a support to married people in their commitment to each other, because they are reminded by the celibate of their own "empty" center. Seeing the life of a celibate person, they know that they need to protect and nurture their sacred center and thus live a life that does not depend simply upon the stability of emotions and affections. Their lives as husband and wife are also to be rooted in their individual and common love for the One who called them together. And, married people witness to those who have chosen the celibate life, demonstrating how the love of God creates a family and an intimate community from rich and creative human relationships. Married people gift celibate people with a vision of how their love leads them to become fruitful, generous, affectionate, and faithful to their children and to others in need. Married people are a living reminder of the covenant that celibates live with God. Thus celibacy and marriage need each other.[32]

This vision of families and singles mutually acknowledging their needs and mutually fulfilling them in generosity is a winsome one. It is marked by holistic hospitality that recognizes the diversity of gifts that the Spirit of God has distributed throughout the Body of Christ, with no discrimination according to relational status. In many churches that fail to reflect this vision, the problem is not only that single people are kept at the margins of the congregation's leadership and social life, but that even when we are included, it is only as guests. The hospitality only flows one way. As a result, the unmarried are neither respected as capable of offering any significant hospitality of our own nor challenged to step outside of ourselves to do so.

In many congregations a major course correction is needed to re-balance the blessings and burdens of hospitality between married couples and celibates. A proper place to start is at the Lord's Table, a sacred space where all of us are invited to remember our gaping needs and God's abundant provision. William Dyrness comments that the sacraments "connect us with each other, especially with the poor and marginalized, with the created order, and with God. They . . . represent reconciliation, hospitality, and nourishment—both physical and spiritual—which are to influence all of life."[33]

Locating life and vocation in eternity. If we rightly attend to it, we find that the Lord's Supper pierces the immanent frame and reorients us—as individuals, families, and communities—to the broader context of God's eternity. One of the most appropriate responses we can offer is silent reverence, remembering God as both the source of our life in the world and the goal toward whose eternity we yearn. Silence is a multifaceted phenomenon. It is not the antithesis of speech, song, and laugher, but rather their launching pad and their safe harbor. And the correlation between silence and eternity does not come at the expense of the goodness of the created order or the messiness of fallen humanity. Instead, silence serves as a reminder of the distinctness of God's transcendence, even as God is also immanently engaged among us.

Silence can also be another means of fostering solidarity between celibates and married persons as we reflect together on our common source and goal. In light of God's eternity, our differences in relational status are not nearly as significant as how we orient them. As British Baptist theologian Steve Holmes recently argued,

> Marriage can be discipleship, not just concession, and it can be discipleship in just the way celibacy can. Celibacy is of course the Christian norm—to assert otherwise is to deny the resurrection—but both marriage and celibacy, well practiced, are modes of asceticism, thick clusters of practices that serve to reorder our sinful and wayward desires and make us fit for the Kingdom.

> Marriage, Christianly practiced, is not a way of indulging our desires, but a way of redirecting them. The only way we can make Christian sense of marriage as anything more than a pastoral accommodation to human weakness is to see it as a mode of practice for living in the Kingdom, although in the Kingdom we will neither marry nor be given in marriage.[34]

This astute account reframes our common categories. Instead of married people on one side and single people on the other, there are two paths that remain open to all people. Both singles and spouses can embrace the disciplined exercise of self-giving love, which can flourish in either celibate or married form. And both the unmarried and the married can choose the way of selfishness, which can take a variety of distorted forms, such as autonomous independent singleness or unhealthy co-dependent partnership.

The choice between these paths is an old one. Augustine, the church father to whom James K. A. Smith frequently looks for inspiration, gave voice to the painful condition that occurs when "the delight of eternity draws us upwards and the pleasure of temporal goods holds us down."[35] His solution, to throw himself on God's empowerment for proper love, remains apropos today: "Bring to me a sweetness surpassing all the seductive delights which I pursued. Enable me to love you with all my strength that I may clasp your hand with all my heart."[36] This zeal is both nurtured and assuaged in holy silence.

FINAL THOUGHTS

The celibate life is costly, yet deeply rewarding. In Christ the unmarried can open themselves up to beauty through a reoriented imagination, a connection to community and justice, and above all the mighty, mysterious work of the Holy Spirit, who both ignites and constrains desire. In these and other ways, we discover afresh that the same God who established the goodness of creation (while the Spirit was hovering over the deep) continues to be at work among us in the midst of our desires, bringing order to our chaos, light to our darkness, and fullness to our emptiness. Facing social crises and an immanent frame, at a time when married and celibate Christians are in desperate need of meaningful partnership for mutual transformation, this eternal God remains our hope.

DECEMBER

By Joshua Beckett

As mile follows upon mile

Past hills of flint and rivers of mud

With snowflakes that fall but do not hinder

And a sun that rises but does not warm

Shared intimacies emerge

As out of hibernation

Born of trust once tattered

Now tested

The release of laughter delights

While sober concern is saturated with affection

And the eyes understand

Without needing words

Greetings are momentary—

Arms that invite and enfold

The temporary interlocking of the ears

Chests bearing heartbeats briefly aligned—

But the embrace endures

7

SEX, SAINTS,
AND SINGLENESS

PRACTICAL (RE)CONSIDERATIONS

EACH YEAR, I teach a class for Fuller Seminary that takes place at the Sundance Film Festival. At the 2016 festival, a number of us watched a film called *The Lobster*. Starring Colin Farrell as David and Rachel Weisz as The Shortsighted Woman, the movie is cynically bizarre even by Sundance standards. But it succeeds in offering a darkly humorous and, at times, scathing parody of modern notions about marriage, singleness, and romance.

The basic premise of the film is that according to the laws of its dystopian world, single people (whether they are divorced, widowed, or simply unmarried) are required to move into a hotel filled only with other single people. While residents at The Hotel, they have exactly forty-five days to find a romantic partner. More often than not, it is a shared "distinguishing characteristic" like speaking with a lisp or frequent nosebleeds that identifies two individuals as a prospective match. Once they have found each other, they are given larger rooms (and sometimes children!) to test their compatibility. If all goes well, they are sent back to The City as a ready-made nuclear family.

In stark contrast, those who fail to find a mate in forty-five days are turned into an animal of their choosing. Most decide to become dogs or some other domesticated beast. David, the protagonist, wants to become a lobster. Lobsters, after all, can live to be one hundred years old.

The only downside is the slight risk of being captured by humans and boiled alive.

In the forest just beyond the property of The Hotel lives a group called The Loners. They are not only militantly single, but they also strictly prohibit sexual activity among their members. To help each other avoid becoming romantically involved, they listen to techno music on personal media devices while dancing alone in the woods. It is no small coincidence that David and The Shortsighted Woman first meet when David flees The Hotel and joins up with this group of rebels. The two soon discover they are both shortsighted, and, given this immediate connection, their love blossoms.

Somewhat ironically, David and The Shortsighted Woman suddenly find themselves caught between a dominant culture that literally dehumanizes those who are not married and a fringe group that has rejected these societal norms so fully that there is no longer any space for relational intimacy whatsoever. To be sure, the residents of The Hotel have given themselves over to a wholly romanticized picture of marriage as the only viable option for human flourishing. And they are willing (or forced) to pursue this vision at almost any cost. But The Loners, even in their rejection of this relational paradigm, seem to be no better off. They may have found freedom from The City's oppressive marriage norms, but they have also lost the capacity to enter into intimate relationships of any kind.

Like so many other Sundance films, *The Lobster* isn't trying to be much more than a darkly satirical take on the romantic comedy, so we need to be careful not to treat it as a straightforward social commentary. Still, given the ways it so closely reflects the current state of things both in society at large and within the church, the film does present us with a biting, not-so-thinly-veiled critique of the contemporary cultural imagination. It dares to suggest (with frighteningly accurate precision) that we are all caught between two approaches to marriage, singleness, and sexuality that, while seemingly antithetical, operate according to the same basic logic and make nearly identical assumptions about the world and our life in it. On the one hand, we have The Hotel's idealized picture of marriage, romantic love, and what it means to be a human being. On the other, we have The Loners' exacting vision of singleness, relational intimacy, and what it means to live as a person in community.

It's all of course highly fantastical and at times even shocking, but that's exactly the point. By shifting the marriage norm into the foreground of the film's narrative, *The Lobster* simply makes it explicit, daring us not to look away. It not only calls attention to the dire consequences of embracing such a distorted vision of life and human flourishing, but also invites us to respond to the very angst we feel when we see such horrors laid bare.

In certain respects, I have attempted to make a parallel move in this book. I have been asking us all to take a long and hard look at the current state of marriage and singleness within the church (especially within Protestant evangelicalism) and to have the courage not to avert our gaze. But I have also suggested that we find some new ways of responding to the world we have created. Historically speaking, the Christian community has tended to respond to a great many of its theological distortions by swinging the pendulum too far in one direction or another. And a very real danger in writing this book is that I make a similar mistake. Taking a cue from *The Lobster*, my argument could easily devolve into little more than an appeal for residents of The Hotel to reject marriage altogether and flee to the surrounding woods, as if to suggest that it is only among The Loners that any of us will be able to find true contentment.

But anyone who's been paying attention knows by now that I have no intention of drawing these kinds of distinctions. In fact, it would strike me as a complete waste of time to come all this way only to suggest that all Christians should remain single or, conversely, that more should be married (or stay married). No, my intentions are far more radical. My sincere hope is that together the Christian community might adopt a different relational paradigm altogether—one rooted in our common vocation and our shared identity as the bride of Christ.

But how exactly do we bring about this kind of paradigm shift? And how might it take root where it really matters—at the local church level? Well, the simple (but not at all easy) answer is that we need to develop new norms. And if, as I have suggested all along, norms are woven into the fabric of a community's imagination not only by (1) the various ways we explicitly talk about them but also through (2) our embodied practices and (3) our organizational structures and systems, then it stands to reason that our first step toward developing new norms would be to reconsider each of these three aspects of our shared life together.

So in an effort not only to bring the book to a close but also to identify a few places where we need to develop this conversation further, I want to name a handful of practical ways the Christian community might do away with its idolatrous picture of marriage and focus its attention more fully on cultivating and supporting the unique vocational demands of *both* single *and* married people.

TELLING A NEW STORY

The most direct and immediate thing we can do, especially as church leaders, is to start telling a new story about marriage and singleness—in public and as often as possible. Whether for a senior pastor, a Sunday school teacher, a small group facilitator, or an enthusiastic layperson, Christian leadership is nothing if not a storytelling endeavor. It's about telling and retelling the story of God and God's people in ways that allow us all to make sense of our concrete, lived experiences. In certain respects, this is what I have been attempting to do in this book—to talk about our norms in ways that are not only more in tune with the biblical witness, but also more capable of helping both single and married people respond faithfully to the world as it has been handed to them.

I am of course not alone in this regard, nor am I the first to raise these specific concerns. While my approach is distinctive in that I am coming at the topic from the perspective of a theology of culture, I am really just joining a growing chorus of voices challenging the church to reconsider its understanding of marriage and singleness. For example, Wesley Hill, Debra Hirsch, and Laura Smit have all recently written important books that critically engage the church's normative picture of marriage. And while they each contribute something unique to the conversation, their efforts are united in telling new stories about married life, single life, and sexuality that are as compelling as they are faithful.[1] Numerous conferences and web-based resources are also articulating the need for us all—single and married alike—to be freed from distorted theological frameworks that elevate one of these callings over another.[2]

These authors' narratives have proven helpful for numerous married and single Christians not only because of *what* they communicate but also because of *who* is doing the communicating. This is an important point to keep in mind as we consider three specific ways the church might instill new norms through its storytelling and storytellers: sermons, sex education, and saints.

Sermons. The various books, conferences, and blogs that I just mentioned represent some of the more prominent avenues through which evangelicals communicate their internal narratives and by extension express their most powerful norms. But given the distinctly Protestant origins of evangelicalism, it is preaching that remains the primary (and sometimes only) vehicle for articulating Christian norms at the local church level. So one very practical way that we can begin to bring about a paradigm shift as individuals and as a church community is for our preachers to be more intentional about addressing both single life and married life with consistency and in equal measure.

This means that, in the first place, sermons need to emphasize (maybe even overemphasize) the rigorous demands of marriage for those who are called to enter this covenant relationship. If, as I have claimed, the myth of romantic love is ultimately misdirected, then both professional and lay church leaders who serve in preaching roles need to be willing not only to critique this myth at every turn in their sermons, but also to have the courage to cover difficult passages about marriages in the

Bible that don't so easily align with our preconceived (romantic) ideas about "biblical marriage." These passages are integral parts of the biblical witness, so they need to be treated as such. And this is especially true when it comes to our handling of the First Testament texts. It does no one any good to expect our preachers to function as modern-day Marcionites who cherry pick passages that support what we already believe while simply ignoring or outright rejecting anything that might make us uneasy. In fact, when this approach to preaching becomes standard operating procedure, not only do we internalize a distorted view of Scripture as a whole, but our sermons are no longer able to function in any kind of critical capacity. Instead, they simply perpetuate an already existing feedback loop—one that works to reinforce the marriage norm all the more.

In addition to telling a different kind of story about marriage and drawing from a different set of biblical texts when we do, we need to completely discontinue the all-too-common practice of preaching marriage-centric sermons that alienate or otherwise marginalize those who are single. Instead, we need sermons that explore and expound on the structures, commitments, and obligations of other kinds of intimate relationships—those that may have nothing to do with marriage but are nevertheless integral to the health and well-being of our communal life. This of course doesn't mean that preachers should stop talking about marriage altogether. But if we know full well that a significant portion of the (adult) worshiping community is single, we need to ask why any of us who preach would craft individual sermons, much less entire series, around a topic that has no bearing on the lives of so many people.

This question has to do with more than the simple fact that some individuals might not always be able to "apply" a sermon directly to their lives. Instead, as Christena Cleveland has pointed out, "when a sermon is primarily (if not wholly) devoted to marital love and the most oft-repeated human relational metaphor for God's love is a marital one ... it communicates to single people that the human relational experience of God's love is limited to the institution of marriage."[3] In other words, when the normative picture of marriage is allowed to orient all the stories that preachers tell, it not only serves to alienate single people from the community of faith but radically truncates our understanding of who God is.

So while there are numerous biblical and theological reasons for why I think it would be helpful for us to reconsider how we preach about marriage and singleness, there's also a sense in which I am simply calling for preachers to become better communicators. One of the basic principles of communication is called "decentering." As the person who is responsible for delivering a message, my first task is not to figure out what *I* want to say or how *I* want to say it. My first task is to find a way to place myself in the position of those to whom I would like to communicate—to take an others-oriented approach. But in the context of Christian worship, there are at least two significant challenges that work against this decentering process. First, given how the marriage norm presently functions within the evangelical subculture, many preachers simply assume (on quasi-theological grounds) that everyone within earshot either is married, wants to be married, or should be married. So it naturally follows from this line of thought that sermons on marriage really *do* relate to everyone. When everyone in the worshiping community falls neatly into one of two categories, married and yet-to-be married, there is no need for the married preacher to be others-oriented at all because the "other" (who in this case is single) doesn't exist. The marriage norm has rendered them quite literally invisible.

A second difficulty is that even when decentering does happen, it is almost always moving in only one direction—from the married preacher to the single person. This is because the overwhelming majority of our preaching pastors are married. The same can be said for many if not most of those who lead evangelical parachurch ministries and nonprofit organizations, as well as those who are invited to speak at any of the various ministry conferences that take place every year throughout the United States. At the risk of pointing out the obvious, we need to create more opportunities for single people to preach, teach, and lead. Period. Whether we are married or single, we all have a great deal to learn from the wisdom and insight of our single brothers and sisters, and to organize ourselves in such a way that single people are precluded from leading us corporately is to be a body without its vital organs—incomplete, unhealthy, and inadequate for the task at hand.

So while it's true that my suggestions regarding who should be preaching and what they should be preaching about are concerned with basic communication strategies, I'm getting at something deeper as well. We need single people to be preaching equally as often as married people because we as a community of faith—a community composed of both single and married persons—need to be constantly decentered. This of course is not to say that just because someone is single they should automatically have access to the pulpit. There still needs to be a process of communal discernment to determine whether a person has received a call to ministry and whether they have been adequately trained and equipped to effectively and faithfully fulfill this calling. This process will look different from one community to the next depending on denominational structures and church polity, but the larger point I am making is that, from the very start, we need to be more intentional about identifying, equipping, and empowering single persons who are called to preach. And even more importantly, we need to create space for them to do so.

This approach is one of the essential elements of engaging with the world empathetically—of loving our neighbor as ourselves (Mk 12:31). It's about seeing the world through the eyes of those who don't quite fit into our "normative" categories. And one of the ways the church can cultivate a space where this kind of others-directed love becomes possible is by telling new stories about marriage and singleness in and through our preaching.

Sex education. If our sermons routinely addressed the concerns of single Christians in equal measure to those of married Christians, and if we had more single people preaching and teaching, then we would already be well on our way toward developing a new set of guiding narratives—those commonly held stories that articulate our norms and thus orient and organize our shared life together. But to tell a new story about marriage and singleness is also to tell a new story about sex and sexuality.

As we noted before (especially in chapters three and four), human sexuality is more than its genital expression. It is a holistic reality that touches on every aspect of our lived experience. As Christians, we need to develop the capacity to demonstrate sexual integrity not just in our bedrooms, but in every domain of life. So the church needs to start telling a story about sex that both broadens our notions of human sexuality and allows us to imagine more constructive and life-giving ways to direct and guide our sexual desires.

Put differently, the Christian community (evangelicals in particular) needs to rethink its approach toward sex education from the ground up. The story we tell about sex (to young people and adults, single people and married) needs to do more than simply make a case for abstinence, not because abstinence is bad or wrong, but because living with sexual integrity is a far more complex matter than just saying no. It's about all of us—single and married alike—being and becoming a chaste community. It's about harnessing our erotic energies for the sake of the other. It's also about demonstrating a "generosity in restraint" (as we put it chapter five) that provides human beings with the only form of sexual expression that is truly fulfilling in any ultimate sense. This is a far cry from the approach taken up by most purity campaigns in that it recognizes the need to direct our erotic energy toward its proper end, putting it to use even (and perhaps especially) during seasons of celibacy. Rather than an outright denial of our sexual impulses, it's an attempt to create a space in which these impulses might produce something constructive.

Approaching sex education in this way does require us to relativize the glories of sex to a certain degree. Sex may be "great," as the Silver

Ring Thing chant suggests. But as it turns out, there really is more to life than orgasms. And as shocking as that might sound to (post) modern, neo-Romantic ears, our ability to make this claim is really just a reflection of spiritual (not to mention emotional and psychological) maturity. Or at the very least it demonstrates a more measured realism. Indeed, for the church to tell a story that emphasizes chastity rather than mere abstinence, we have to embrace a much deeper understanding of all our intimate relationships—especially those that are not principally erotic. As Christians we acknowledge an intimacy that both precedes and surpasses the kind that derives from genital expression, which means that part of our task as the church is to create the necessary conditions for this sort of intimacy to emerge and to flourish—an intimacy rooted in our mutual interdependence with God and each other.

Once again married people have a great deal to learn from our single brothers and sisters in this regard. Given the way that marriage is so often elevated and idealized, it is a bit too easy for married Christians to withdraw into their blissful dyad and forget how vital the broader community of faith is for their life and well-being. As Ecclesiastes 4:12 reminds us, though, it is a chord of *three* strands that is not easily broken—not two. A husband and wife on their own are not enough for each other. Instead, we are only ever whole when we are living in mutual interdependence both with God and with the people of God, which means that single Christians are uniquely situated to help married Christians learn how to live as persons in relation with those who are not their husband or wife. In this way the example of faithful single Christians can serve as both a reminder of our call toward community and a demonstration of how to live in such a way that our own lives (and bodies) become intimately bound up with the entire body of Christ.

Saints. Finally, while it's certainly important for us to think about how we might tell new stories through our sermons and sex education, if we really want to bring about a paradigm shift in the way we understand singleness and marriage, we need to do so on the level of our imaginations. And for this to occur, the Christian community needs to develop stories that tap into the mythic underpinnings of life as a whole. In many cases these would be stories that we actually tell our children—shared narratives akin to fairytales. They would be tales of women and men navigating a complex world filled with darkness, monsters, and evil, but at the same time replete with beauty, wonder, and joy. As such, these "fairytales" would do what all good stories do. They would offer all of us (children and adults) paradigms for what it means to be human. They would paint a picture of the world not as it is, but as it could be—as it should be.

There's just one catch. Given our understanding of both marriage and singleness as equally legitimate vocations, it would be a failure on our part if the fairytales we created were to follow the same pattern established by Disney's princess films or stories like "Is This the House of Mistress Mouse?"—quintessential expressions of the modern myth of romantic love. We don't need any more stories that feature two lonely people (or mice for that matter!) pursuing marriage for the sake of warding off loneliness. Instead, what we need are stories that elevate and celebrate characters who flourish as single people—stories that culminate not in their marriage but in their being and becoming persons in relation. We of course also need to tell a new story about marriage and all that it entails. But my sense is that if we can first develop a series of fairytales that offer up a more robust vision of singleness, the stories about marriage will follow shortly thereafter.

The good news on this front is that the Christian tradition already has a treasure trove of these kinds of narratives. As we think about creating fairytales that picture singleness as the God-given gift that it is, we don't even have to make anything up. We simply need to tell and retell the stories of the actual Christian women and men who have come before us—those who have lived full and flourishing lives not in spite of their singleness, but in and through their singleness.

I am intentionally using the term *fairytales* to describe these stories about exemplary models of Christian faith. But the unsettling truth (at least for Protestants like me anyway) is that this would be better described as telling the stories of our saints. I realize that the word *saints* might make some a bit uneasy, so rest assured, what I don't mean is that we need to start praying to other human beings, no matter how pious they might have been (although even this way of framing things is to misunderstand sainthood). What I mean is that Protestant traditions in particular would do well to create some kind of collective practice whereby we routinely acknowledge, reflect on, and tell stories about our spiritual exemplars—models of Christian virtue who were also real, flesh-and-blood human beings struggling to integrate their deepest longings with the unique demands of their vocation.

One thinks immediately of people like Dietrich Bonhoeffer or the late Henri Nouwen. But it is also the case that we need to tell the stories of lesser-known saints who are in our midst. Colton Simmons's story about his mentor Pritch is a great example.[4] And just so we don't miss the point of his vignette entirely, it is not insignificant that, like Nouwen, Pritch is also a single and celibate man of faith.

As Simmons points out, there is nothing "easy" about having Pritch as a personal mentor or a model for what his life might one day look like. Indeed, his lifelong story of discipleship is incredibly challenging—terrifying even. Nevertheless, Pritch's life presents us with a paradigm for what is truly possible, which is why the church needs the stories of women and men like him—our modern-day saints—now more than ever. We need constant reminders of the "impossible possibility" of single celibacy. And we need these stories to take root deep within the church's imagination, because once they do, they become something more than mere fairytales. They become icons. When we allow the stories of single celibate Christians to take hold of our collective imagination, we begin to see the world in and through their lives. By doing so, we aren't diminishing the significance of sex or romance. If anything, it's the opposite. Just like these faithful disciples who have gone before us, we're embracing a deeper reality (perhaps for the very first time) in which every mundane element of our life is charged with a special significance all its own.

SINGING NEW SONGS

If Protestants in general and evangelicals in particular fail to tell the stories of their saints, it is all but certain that someone else will. For example, in 2012 HBO released a mini-documentary called *God Is the Bigger Elvis*, which tells the true story of Dolores Hart. Once a rising star in Hollywood, Hart worked with the likes of Elvis, Marlon Brando, and Warren Beatty. Yet, just as her career was taking off, she walked away from it all. In 1963 she left behind her life of fame and celebrity to join the Regina Laudis Benedictine Abbey. And just as every other member of this religious community was required to do, she took a vow of celibacy upon entering the cloister.

It is evident that the filmmakers are fascinated not only with Sister Dolores's vow of celibacy (especially given her past life), but also with the means by which she is able to find sexual fulfillment while remaining celibate. And why wouldn't they be? Hart's story is equal parts captivating and compelling—one well worth telling. And one of the more interesting elements of the story is the way Dolores and her fellow nuns understand and talk about their vows of celibacy. On numerous occasions the sisters suggest that their relationships prior to entering the abbey (romantic or otherwise) were simply not enough to satisfy their deep desire for either human community or communion with God. As a result, many of them speak of their vows of celibacy as a "spousal commitment to Jesus." And it is this spousal commitment that constitutes their relationship both with God and with their community.

When the filmmakers press the nuns to expound on what it means to be married to Jesus, the question of sexual desire is never far behind. Tellingly, the sisters never respond with any kind of thin or underdeveloped notion of human sexuality. In fact, echoing our discussion in chapters three and four, they routinely remind their interviewers that "sexuality isn't limited in the way we think of it. . . . It's getting beyond the very narrow dimension of sex that's the physical, genital-based sex."[5]

What is perhaps even more interesting is that many if not most of the nuns identify the practice of corporate singing as the primary means by which they experience and express their sexuality: "To sing is a physical act. [In singing] I get a great amount of pleasure. And I want to bring pleasure to other people. . . . My voice goes out, my acolyte partner's voice goes out, and they blend together. It's really an act of physical union. And it transcends into something that is much higher and deeper."[6] For these single, celibate, Christian women, corporate singing isn't a pale reflection or poor imitation of the genital expression they have renounced. It is rather a more profound and infinitely more fulfilling expression of their sexuality—one that the simple act of copulation could never even begin to touch.

Needless to say, one of the reasons that HBO found Sister Dolores's story compelling enough to produce a documentary about her life is that in our contemporary cultural context, this kind of lifetime commitment to single celibacy is absolutely countercultural (and it most certainly runs against the grain of celebrity culture). But what is even more culturally transgressive is Sister Dolores's suggestion that there are forms of erotic expression that are far deeper and far more satisfying than the act of sex. In other words, when it comes to sex appeal, Elvis can't hold a candle to God.

It should not be lost on us that these stories emerge from a Benedictine community—a Roman Catholic religious order with a centuries-long history. I point out this fact only to say that evangelicals might do well to take a cue here from our Catholic brothers and sisters. We need to do more than simply tell the stories of Christian women and men who live faithful (and fulfilling) lives of single celibacy. We also need to develop devotional practices that take everything we *say* about marriage and singleness and actually connect it *to our bodies*. After all, this is where norms exert their power most fully—in the way we embody them and enact them bodily. So we need to develop new practices that habituate our bodies in different ways. We've already addressed a few of the ways this might take place as it concerns the devotional practice of preaching, but rather than stop at simply revising or adapting already existing practices, I want to name a few new practices we might implement.

The arts as (sexual) expression. It is not incidental that the nuns of the Regina Laudis Abbey point to corporate singing as the devotional practice that not only directs their erotic energies but helps sustain them in their common vocation. Indeed, because of its aesthetic shape, music making in particular allows for a kind of embodied expression and communal intimacy that simply cannot be realized through any other means. In other words, music (like so many other forms of art) opens up a space for individuals to commune with one another in ways that would otherwise remain inaccessible. But it's more than that too. Because Christian worship is always already corporate, the devotional practice of singing also generates the very audience that, to borrow again from Alain de Botton, is necessary for sustaining our virtue.[7] In this way music has the capacity not only to provide us with a profoundly sexual experience in the context of Christian community, but also to sustain us in our efforts to be and become chaste.

In contrast, a great majority of the evangelical initiatives that focus on directing the sexual desires of Christians (like those discussed in chapter two) are not only highly individualistic but also largely preventative in nature (such as purity balls, chastity pledges, and online accountability programs). In other words, they are concerned primarily with curbing or suppressing sexual desire rather than harnessing its energies for good. But the paradigm shift I am proposing requires us to move from preventative measures to sustaining practices. It's not enough to simply keep people from having sex, whether it's keeping single people from having sex with anyone or married people from having sex with the wrong someone (though this can and should be part of our communal vision). Instead, what we need is to develop

communal practices that provide us with a deeper, broader, and ultimately more fulfilling engagement with the whole scope of our sexuality. So this isn't a call for us to use art in worship as a way of distracting
us all from our desires. It's rather a call to see art as the very means
by which we might experience an intimacy with God and each other
that overwhelms all our desires.

While corporate singing is perhaps one of the more obvious forms
of artistic expression that involves both our physical bodies and the
community as a whole (in large part because most of our churches
already practice the art of singing together), music is not the only art
form we might pursue. Dance, theater, visual art, poetry—we can and
should incorporate any or all of these into our ritual lives in ways that
not only open up avenues for individuals to share their gifts with the
larger body of Christ, but also provide all of us—married and single—
with a tangible means for experiencing sexual fulfillment even in the
midst of seasons of celibacy.

So the question the Christian community needs to ask is how we
might turn toward the arts in this way. How might we think about
engaging the arts in worship not as a precursor to the "real" substance
(the sermon), but as a form of embodied, sensual, and even corporate
sexual expression? And what would it mean for us both as individuals
and as a community if we pointed toward these acts of aesthetic de-
votion not as cheap replacements for sex, but as an actual form of
unparalleled sexual fulfillment with real sustaining power?

Public rituals and rites of passage. To say that we might bring about
a paradigm shift in the church's understanding of marriage and singleness
by "singing new songs" is not to suggest that we just start singing
together and then call it a day. To be sure, as the sisters of Regina
Laudis would remind us, corporate singing is one important means by
which the community of faith can sustain and support its members—
whether single or married. But in addition to the more routinized
rituals that comprise the bulk of our worship practices (like singing,
praying, and preaching), it would also be helpful to rethink our approach

to periodic rituals and rites of passage. In particular I'm thinking of practices that we could develop that would function as analogues to the wedding ceremony.

It is fairly interesting that outside of baptism (for children or adults), the only rites of passage we publicly observe (at least with any consistency) are wedding ceremonies and funerals (and confirmation in some traditions). We don't really have any other practices designed to bring the community of faith together in order to celebrate an individual's passage into a new stage of life or to bless any other kinds of committed relationships. This notable absence is unfortunate because it not only places adult single people in a perpetual state of limbo that will only come to an end when they die, but also implies that the only kind of covenant relationship that either matters or is truly binding for Christians is marriage.

But if, as we have already noted, the marriage relationship alone really isn't enough to meet the needs of either spouse, and if, to use Jesus' words, the greatest demonstration of our love is to lay down our life not for a spouse but for a friend (Jn 15:13), then it stands to reason that we would do well to develop public rites that affirm, celebrate, and bless what we might call "covenant friendships." Wesley Hill explores this idea in *Spiritual Friendship*, so rather than attempt to say something he hasn't already said, I will simply point anyone interested in a more elaborate discussion of covenant friendship to Hill's helpful volume.

However, whereas Hill is primarily concerned with the kind of love that celibate, gay Christians might be called to pursue, I want to extend the category of friendship to include the entire community of faith.[8] The Christian community needs to take friendship more seriously. As Hill points out, friendship is understood to be a relatively weak bond in the modern West: it is "the freest, the least constrained, the least fixed and determined, of all human loves."[9] But this is a far cry from Jesus' vision of friendship. For Jesus, friendship was an extension of the relationship he shared with God the Father (Jn 15:15). Much like marriage, it was as intimate as it was indissoluble.

This is exactly why Hill suggests that friendship, at least for the Christian, should perhaps not be so free and unconstrained:

> Should we consider friendship as always freshly chosen but never incurring any substantial obligations or entailing any unbreakable bonds? Or should we instead—pursuing a rather different line of thought—consider friendship more along the lines of how we think of marriage? Should we begin to imagine friendship as more stable, permanent, and binding than we often do? Should we, in short, think of friends more like the siblings we're stuck with, like it or not, than like our acquaintances? Should we begin to consider at least some of our friends as, in large measure, tantamount to family? And if so, what needs to change about the way we approach it and seek to maintain it?[10]

If the Christian community were to afford friendship the level of significance Hill is describing here (and I for one think we should), we would need to create some mechanism by which to sustain it, because nothing along these lines presently exists. We should consider developing some public rituals that not only symbolize the commitment that two friends are making to one another when they enter into a covenant bond, but also call the community to support these friends throughout the course of their journey.

These rituals could take on a number of forms depending on the given context, but whatever form they assume, they would serve as a tangible means for making public a commitment that is stronger and more substantial than one based simply on mutual interests or sympathies. The commitment might be between two Christian friends (whether male or female, gay or straight) who are both called to a life of celibacy. Or it might be that a married couple befriends a single person (whether that person has never married, is widowed, or is divorced), along with his or her children. Or it may even be something that two entire families embark on together—a shared commitment to care for, love, and walk through life with one another as a kind of extended family.

The reality is that these types of relationships already exist in the church on various levels, albeit informally. My immediate family, for example, "adopted" a single friend a number of years ago. Although there is no legal paperwork identifying him as such, he is no longer simply a family acquaintance. He is now a "brother" who has the very same rights and privileges as the children born into our family. My children call him "uncle," not merely as a term of endearment but because that's who he is. As a family, we have made our vows of fidelity to him explicit, which is to say that my biological kin and I are now bound to him in a covenant relationship. I realize this might strike some as a bit unorthodox, but that is exactly my point. As it stands, there simply are no public rites by which the community of faith might formally recognize, celebrate, or bless my family's commitment to our adopted brother in Christ. As a result, it's difficult for many Christians to even imagine what it might look like for some people (whether married or single, with children or without) to dedicate themselves to this kind of nonspousal covenant relationship.

Yet beyond helping us imagine a deeper and more enduring bond between brothers and sisters in Christ, public rituals also have practical import. They help formalize covenant bonds in such a way that all parties involved (both the individual friends and the broader community) can and should expect something more of each other. The process of going through a public ritual serves as a way for each of these friends to enact the claims they are making on the life of the other. It's an act of both assuming the other's burdens as one's own and at the same time obligating the other—spiritually, psychologically, and even economically.

One of the most immediate outcomes of this kind of commitment would be that, rather than leave single Christians at risk socially, emotionally, and financially every time their network of ad hoc relationships dissolves, these public declarations would help create more stable and life-giving conditions for everyone involved. It may be that covenant friendship is not always strictly "till death do us part," but neither is it the kind of relationship that can be abandoned on a whim. This form of friendship is far more demanding and thus more stable than that, in large part because the community has formally recognized it as such.

What is more, because of how rituals work, over time these rites would make their way into our bodies, which is the whole point really. For our ability to imagine a world where both married and single Christians share in the unbreakable bond of friendship depends largely on the degree to which this idea gets deep into our bones. Until then, it will only ever be a nice idea.

Seasons of celibacy. We of course don't need to restrict these rites to the public enactment of covenant friendships. They can also function as a means by which we ritualize and affirm other types of vows related to single and married life. For single Christians, this ritualization might take the form of a ceremony where one formally and publicly commits to a vow of celibacy or pledges to live as an interdependent member of a particular community or family. It may even be something like the entrance ceremony of a religious order, complete with a ritual act that makes one's commitments tangible, like the cutting of Sister Dolores's hair when she joined the abbey.

For married Christians this process of ritualization might look something more like a public pronouncement whereby each spouse enters into a period of sexual abstinence for the sake of prayer and at the same time calls on the witnessing community for their support. If this were to take place, married Christians would not only be taking seriously Paul's advice regarding the ways spouses can practice the right ordering of desire within marriage, but they would also be standing in solidarity with their single sisters and brothers who have committed themselves to a life of celibacy. Like any spiritual fast, these periods of intentional, prayerful abstinence would serve to ground and reorient participants' lives, whether they are sexually active or not.

These suggestions are by no means novel, nor are they incredibly earthshattering. Nevertheless, the kind of solidarity that rituals of this sort might help to generate between and among single and married Christians is exactly what the church needs right now. Quoting Hill again: "What we need now isn't disinterested, disembodied companionship. We need stronger bonds between brothers and sisters in Christ. We need ways to voluntarily surrender our freedom and independence and link ourselves, spiritually and tangibly, to those we've come to love."[11] Amen and amen.

FORGING A NEW FAMILY

> Then Jesus' mother and his brothers came. Standing outside, they sent word to him, to summon him. A crowd was sitting around him and they said to him, "Look, your mother and your brothers are outside looking for you." He answered them and said, "Who are my mother and my brothers?" And looking at those who were sitting around him in a circle, he said, "Here are my mother and my brothers! For whoever does the will of God is my brother and sister and mother." (Mk 3:31-35)

Jesus was nothing if not a provocateur. Much like his comments regarding marriage no longer existing in the coming kingdom, his thoughts on familial relationships were equally shocking (especially to his family, no doubt!). In both cases, though, Jesus is shaking up our religious sensibilities so that we can imagine a new kind of kinship altogether. He presents a new vision for how we might organize our shared life together that hinges not on biology but rather on a shared commitment to God's kingdom. And in the final analysis, this is where our entire discussion has been leading—to the forging of an altogether new kind of family.

The task before us as a church is not so much to determine the ideal number of single and married people (as if there were such a thing), but rather to organize our systems and structures in ways that provide a more supportive and life-giving context for both single and married persons to live faithfully in the modern world. It is a call not only to orient our communal life in the direction of God's coming kingdom, but also to recognize that, even if we never join a religious order like Sister Dolores and the nuns of Regina Laudis, we all share a spousal commitment to Jesus. Regardless of whether we as individuals ever marry, we, the church, are the bride of Christ.

So there truly is an urgent need for Christians (especially evangelicals) to start telling new stories about marriage and singleness. It is also vital that we develop new practices whereby these stories become embodied—taken up as daily habits. But these efforts will only go so far if we don't also address the many ways the marriage norm exerts its influence (often invisibly) on the organizational structures of the Christian community. Let's briefly consider three possibilities for how we might address these on-the-ground concerns.

Hospitality. In chapter five, we talked about hospitality as a way of life in which we open up our most intimate spaces to the uninvited and unexpected stranger. To be hospitable is to create room in our life not for those who are already like us—those who share our preferences and predilections—but for those who are unlike us, whose very presence runs against the grain of our most basic sensibilities. Yet, in a strange sort of irony, the attempt by many churches to be more hospitable by creating ministries devoted entirely to single Christians (complete with dedicated worship services, small groups, and social activities) often results in the very opposite. Rather than bringing together the like and the unlike, these targeted ministries often simply segregate the body of Christ into various affinity groups.

So my simple suggestion is this: let's desegregate. Rather than organize the church's various happenings along the lines of who's married and who's not, let's consider every one of our gatherings as an opportunity to wrestle through the difficulties that inevitably arise when we engage in hospitality—when we really do open our lives to the other who is not like us.

Whether we are married or single, each member of the body of Christ is called to worship, pray, eat, and live life together. And more times than not (at least in my experience), what emerges from this process is nothing less than a beautiful mess—emphasis on mess. Even though we may be called to this communal way of life, that doesn't make it any easier. Hospitality is a lot of things, but easy isn't one of them. There is very little risk involved in committing time and energy to people who fit comfortably within our preexisting patterns of life, which means that genuine Christian hospitality doesn't start until we feel uncomfortable.

For anyone who doesn't believe me, just try scheduling a prayer time or Bible study for a small group composed of both single and married people. Then, for a real challenge, add children of various ages to the mix. It won't take long to discover that what I am suggesting here is far easier said than done. There simply is no way around it: hospitality is difficult. It requires so much of us. But our ability to grow and mature (as individuals and as a community) depends on our willingness to be pressed to the point of personal discomfort—to be stretched in ways that we would likely not choose for ourselves.

Unfortunately, our current church structures aren't designed to stretch us much, if at all. In fact, in many cases they not only make it possible but actively encourage individuals to engage exclusively with a small segment of the broader Christian community who happen to look and act and talk just as they do. What is more, once people become embedded in one of these clearly defined subgroups (such as a "singles" ministry, or a "young marrieds" group, or a "twenty- and thirtysomethings" ministry), there are virtually no mechanisms or established structures by which individuals might commune with the broader community. Even corporate worship, which has as one of its chief goals the coming together of the entire body of Christ, often becomes secondary or "optional" in light of these demographically focused associations. It's a self-perpetuating system built on like-minded groups organized around common life stages.

As with most of life, though, very few things that are worthwhile come easily, and this is especially true when we are attempting to orient our shared life toward the kingdom that is already here and yet to come. For now, let's just take an initial step in this direction by asking the what-if question. What if, rather than organize our ministries in ways that minimize the kind of risk and discomfort we all need but would rather avoid, we restructured in ways that pressed us further toward hospitality—toward being a people who were practiced in the art of being uncomfortable? What kind of family would we be then?

Generosity. The question that I most often hear from church leaders when I recommend doing away with some of our more niche ministries is: What then do we do? If we have no formal singles ministry, what do we do with singles? If we have no young marrieds group, how do we meet their unique needs? And what about families with children or teenagers? Setting aside for now the problematic assumptions that stand behind these questions (most of which have to do with what I would call a "marketplace" approach to church life), my response is typically that the best thing we can do is to cultivate generosity—to develop a culture of giving gifts without any expectation of receiving something in return. And the most effective and practical way I know how to do this is to provide people with ministry opportunities that require them to collaborate with a group of others who are not like them.

Indeed, as anyone who participated in group assignments during high school or college will likely attest, nothing else brings out so much the best and the worst in us. The success of any shared endeavor depends not only on our ability to be hospitable to the other members of our group—however different from us they might be—but also on the degree to which we can set aside our own interests for the sake of the group's larger goal. Indeed, the very act of collaboration places us in a situation where we have no other choice but to give something of ourselves without the expectation that there will be an equal return on that personal investment. To collaborate, to co-labor, with others is to be generous. It is to give the gift of our time and energy knowing full well there can be no recompense that would ever "equal" what we've given.

This posture of generosity is only amplified when the project itself assumes the form of meaningful and ongoing service to the broader community. If we really want to develop a new kind of kinship—a family constituted by its generosity—we need to structure the organizational life of the church in ways that spin outward in a collaborative, missional engagement with the world, rather than inward toward ourselves.

This kind of missional collaboration is of course difficult to bring about when the system itself is designed to cater to people's individual needs and wants (whether those be spiritual, psychological, or social). And this is exactly the point. When the church's organizational structure doesn't allow single and married Christians to collaborate as equal partners in a common mission, it not only magnifies the differences between these brothers and sisters in Christ, but it also fails to provide avenues for people (single people in particular) to give of themselves in meaningful ways as full-fledged members of the community. So one simple way we can work against the systemic reinforcement and perpetuation of the marriage norm at the local church level is to reorganize our ministries in ways that bring single, married, divorced, widowed, engaged, and dating Christians together to pursue generosity—to pour themselves out for the sake of the world.

Justice. Finally, the radical kind of familial bonds that Jesus imagines are those that move us toward justice. And one of the more obvious ways that churches can pursue this kind of familial justice for both single and married Christians is related to their hiring practices. Because I have already raised this concern, all I will say here is that the pervasive and systematic marginalization of single people who are seeking pastoral positions in our congregations is not only an unhealthy but also an unjust practice—profoundly so. It's also "unbiblical" and "unorthodox" in the sense that it disregards the model established by the vast number of single church leaders we find both in the New Testament and throughout the first fifteen hundred years of the church's history.

Again, it is one thing to preach and teach that singleness is a legitimate vocation for the Christian and that it is equal to marriage in every way. But if all the people who are actually doing the preaching and teaching happen to be married, in large part because our system overwhelmingly favors pastors who are married and disregards those who are single, then our words mean very little. To shift the paradigm at the local church level, we need to change the system itself. And one of the ways this might take place is through a concerted effort to seek out and hire single people whom God has called to serve in pastoral ministry.

Needless to say, along with this proposal to address issues of systematic (in)justice, the ideas I have outlined in this chapter for cultivating and supporting the unique vocational demands of *both* single *and* married people do not amount to an exhaustive list, nor are they meant to be final in any way. Rather, they are simply starting points—imaginative possibilities that we might consider as we attempt to be and become more fully the people of God in the world.

CONCLUSION

I COULD OF COURSE SAY MORE, but rather than trying to name every possible way that we might develop new paradigms and practices for understanding the significance of marriage, singleness, and sexuality, I hope that the suggestions I have discussed above might serve as starting points for a much-needed conversation. We all need to think through the various implications of the de-norming project I have laid out in these pages. Some of what I have said may already go without saying. Other suggestions are very likely in need of development and refinement. And some ideas may need to be abandoned altogether. But whatever we make of it all, the point is that we need each other's wisdom—now more than ever.

I mention the need for communal discernment here because I want to conclude with a question for us all to consider together. Just as I did in chapter five when I talked about the call that stirs within marriage, I have named justice, generosity, and hospitality as markers of the new kind of family that Jesus envisioned for his followers. But I intentionally left the concept of forgiveness untouched, in part to emphasize its importance. No matter how we as individuals or as a community ultimately understand marriage, singleness, and sexuality— no matter how well our own views resonate or conflict with the biblical witness, the theological tradition, and our local worshiping community—none of us is innocent. Whether we are married or single, sexually active or celibate, we are all failed and flawed people. Throughout the church's long and convoluted history, we have always been willing to respond *pastorally* to our Christian brothers and sisters in ways that not only reflect but assume the brokenness of God's good creation.

And so, in pursuit of loving restoration, we have chosen to accommodate, to make ad hoc provisions, and to demonstrate a radical kind of ethical patience—at least on our best days. And this is just as it should be. After all, to use the words of Jesus, we are a community called to forgive our brothers and sisters not seven times, but seventy times seven (Mt 18:22).

So if nothing else, the Christian community should at the very least be a family who forgives each other. Of that much I am sure. But as it concerns the many conflicting notions of marriage, singleness, and sexuality that are presently alive and well within the Christian community, my question is simply this: What are we willing to forgive? And how far are we willing to allow our forgiveness to reach? Are certain sins actually more forgivable than others, as our current practices of accommodation and restoration seem to suggest? Or are we willing to demonstrate equal measures of ethical patience with every one of our brothers and sisters in Christ? If so, what would this look like in the church today?

I don't ask these questions rhetorically. I have no ready-made answers in mind. I ask them because despite our many flaws, this dysfunctional little family of ours also happens to be the bride of Christ. But in this fairytale romance, our spouse's love has nothing to do with us being "the fairest of them all." Far from it. We are the recalcitrant, unfaithful wife in this story. And yet, he forgives us—unconditionally and unrelentingly. Jesus doesn't love the church—his bride—because we are lovely. No, the church is lovely because we are loved.

I wonder what it would look like for us to love each other in this way—to be "imitators of God" (Eph 5:1)? What if we were a family known not first and foremost for the various stances we take on sex, spouses, and singleness, but for our undying willingness to forgive the unforgivable—to love the unlovable? Anybody can forgive what is forgivable. But that's not the route Jesus chose. Instead, he forgave us when we were beyond forgiveness in order to "present the church to himself as glorious—not having a stain or wrinkle, or any such blemish, but holy and blameless" (Eph 5:27). May we be a family who demonstrates this same kind of love to one another—not only today, but from this day forward, for better, for worse, for richer, for poorer, in sickness and in health. And may we do so not merely until "death do us part," but until death is overcome.

ACKNOWLEDGMENTS

IF PRESSED, I'll admit that I wrote most of the words that appear on these pages, but I can't claim "authorship" in the traditional sense of the term. Despite the romantic notions most people have about the task of writing, this book didn't appear fully formed in my mind one day. Rather, it emerged over time as the product of an ongoing dialogue—a real-life, concrete, flesh-and-blood conversation that I have been privileged to have with countless friends, family members, colleagues, and ministry partners.

Of course, as someone who grew up in the evangelical subculture of the '80s and '90s, it would not be an overstatement to say that I've been involved in this particular conversation for pretty much my entire life. But even though the question of how the church understands singleness and marriage was always in the air, it took on a greater sense of urgency during the time I served as a pastor to students and then later to emerging adults. What I always sensed but couldn't quite articulate during my time in pastoral ministry was that the Christian community was somewhat confused and at times even conflicted about its conceptions of marriage, singleness, and sexuality. Presently, as I train Christian leaders of all kinds in a seminary setting and also serve on the ministry board for my local church, my on-the-ground observations about church life and culture remain largely unchanged. The only difference is that we have now reached a cultural-ecclesial tipping point. So in a very real sense, this book is simply a reflection of my pastoral response to the increasingly complex situations in which countless men and women of faith find themselves. It exists not because I've always wanted to write about marriage, but because of my life's calling to love and serve the people of God. And sometimes (maybe even most of the time) that calling leads me into territory I would not have chosen on my own.

Chief among those who have joined me on this (unexpected) journey are the Fuller Theological Seminary alumni, faculty, staff, and spouses that authored the personal vignettes included throughout the text. I am incredibly thankful for their desire to partner with me on this project, for their willingness to be vulnerable, and for the creative energy and encouragement they provided all along the way. This collection of contributors did more than simply put their stories into written form. They quite literally wrote the book with me. Not only did they read and respond to numerous rough drafts, but during our frequent lunch-hour meetings they also helped me discern which avenues to pursue and which would likely be dead ends. If only everyone had a team of advisors who all had terminal degrees in theology and biblical studies! I simply cannot overstate their contributions to the book. Thank you, Tawanna Benbow, Jennifer Graffius, Lindy Williams, Michael Beardslee, Debi Yu, Sarey Martin, Marsha Lee, Claire Crisp, Colton Simmons, and Dei Thompson.

Among this group, a special word of thanks goes to Joshua Beckett, who also wrote chapter six. Joshua not only was able to say what I could never say as an old married guy (at least not with any real credibility), but he said it far better than I could have. The book is much stronger because of his commitment to the project, and that even goes for the sections he didn't write. In fact, he's the one who convinced me early on to focus on pop music along with film and TV in my cultural analysis section. Joshua's critical engagement with even the most harebrained of my ideas was both insightful and gracious. I am honored to call him a friend and a brother in Christ.

I also owe a debt of gratitude to colleagues who read early drafts of the manuscript in its various stages. Robert K. Johnston, Tommy Givens, Claire Crisp, Mark Finney, Joel Willitts, John Goldingay, David Downs, and Trevecca Okholm each offered me feedback and expert advice. I am humbled and overwhelmed by the caliber of what became my de facto editorial team.

Speaking of editors, many thanks to David McNutt and the great team at IVP. David has been a supportive and encouraging voice throughout, and his instincts about the overall shape of the project were always spot on. It says a great deal about David's approach that he would take the risk of letting an academic try to say something intelligible to a general audience. After all, we aren't usually very good at that kind of thing.

Each of these individuals played a key role in making this book far better than anything I could have produced on my own. Indeed, much of it wouldn't even exist without their contributions. That being said, I take full responsibility for all its shortcomings—whether theological, pastoral, cultural-critical, or otherwise.

I also want to thank my family, with whom I have shared numerous conversations about all manner of things over the years—marriage, singleness, and sex being just a few of them. I have learned a great deal about these matters from each of my siblings: Kamdon, Kassidy, Katon, Kolt, and Jon. In truth, though, the simple fact that we can speak so openly and honestly about the many complexities of life is largely due to the influence of my parents, Kinne and Kathy. In and through their marriage, they modeled for us a prior and more fundamental commitment to the One who is the origin and ultimate end of their love for each other. I am blessed to have grown up with such a life-giving vision of marriage—one that my parents embodied (and continue to embody) on a daily basis.

Finally, I want to thank my amazing wife. I am dedicating this book to her. My ability to commit time and energy to projects of this nature is only made possible by her ongoing love and support. There really are no words to express how much credit she deserves for the books that I write. If our daughters one day find themselves called to the difficult task of being a spouse, my prayer is that they are blessed with the kind of partner that my wife is to me. I love you dearly.

CONTRIBUTORS

Michael Beardslee is a PhD candidate at Fuller Theological Seminary and an affiliate professor at Southwestern College in Winfield, Kansas. He splits time between studying theology, spending time with his amazing family, and catering to his inner geek. He believes that the study of God is best done humbly and with a spirit of discovery. He likes to gather around coffee and talk long about theology, philosophy, and most things geek related.

Joshua Beckett is a PhD candidate in Christian ethics at Fuller Theological Seminary. His research focuses on the intersection of social criticism, justice, and reconciliation. Joshua likes the idea of writing more than the writing process itself, and his primary form of self-expression is song.

Claire Crisp is a writer, educator, and advocate for children with narcolepsy. Her blog (claireccrisp.com/blog) and her book *Waking Mathilda* explore the challenges of raising a child with special needs and its impact on marriage, which led to her being granted the 2015 National Patient Awareness Award. When not speaking at conferences, Claire can be found at home in Pasadena where she lives with her husband, Oliver, and their three children.

Jenn Graffius is the associate director of the Center for Vocational Ministry and an adjunct ministry professor at Azusa Pacific University. She has experience in church and campus ministry, including leadership in chapel ministry at Fuller Theological Seminary and Princeton University and five years as a church youth pastor. She is ordained and a graduate of Princeton Theological Seminary (MDiv) and is currently pursuing a doctor of ministry in Christian leadership at Duke Divinity School.

Marsha Lee is a native of Philadelphia who has worked for several years with InterVarsity Christian Fellowship and Fuller Theological Seminary. Lee is committed to issues of reconciliation and developing young leaders. Lee graduated from Fuller in 2005 with a master of arts in theology. Currently she works in Fuller's Office of Development and serves on the executive board at Evergreen Baptist Church of Los Angeles.

Sarey Martin resides in Los Angeles with her chihuahua named Eight. She has a master of arts in theology from Fuller Theological Seminary and is part of a church-planting team at Missio Dei Church in Silver Lake. On the side she likes to write and produce films. Find her on Instagram @doctormonalisa.

Colton Simmons is a graduate of the Theology and the Arts program at Fuller Theological Seminary and has studied the intersection of comedy and religion extensively. His current passion project is a podcast called *The Back Pew* (available on iTunes), which he cohosts with humorist and former missionary kid Dan Prevette. Together they facilitate uncensored conversations about topics too often ignored by the church and create a safe, comedic space for those hurting or curious about the spiritual side of life.

Lindy Williams is a vocational advisor for Fuller Seminary. She spends most of her free time studying for her PhD in Hebrew Bible, but when not doing that she's riding her bike in the Colorado Mountains.

Debi Yu was born in Seoul, Korea, but was raised mostly in Los Angeles, at least for the last thirty-five years or so. Currently working at Fuller Theological Seminary in the Doctor of Ministry office, Debi hopes to follow in the footsteps of Dr. Kutter Callaway and teach in seminary one day, preparing people for the manifold ministries of Christ! (That's Fuller's mantra, by the way.)

NOTES

INTRODUCTION

[1]Richard Scarry, "Is This the House of Mistress Mouse?," in *Richard Scarry's Best Story Book Ever: 82 Wonderful Stories for Boys and Girls* (New York: Golden Books Publishing, 1968), 140.

[2]Scarry, "Is This the House?," 150-52.

[3]James Davison Hunter, *To Change the World: The Irony, Tragedy, and Possibility of Christianity in the Late Modern World* (New York: Oxford University Press, 2010).

[4]The actual marriage and divorce rate in the United States is incredibly difficult to nail down with any kind of accuracy. Some estimate that over 50% of marriages end in divorce, while others suggest it is closer to 35%. Although the 50% statistic is not strictly true, if marriages ending in separation are included, the statistic holds up fairly well. According to the National Center for Health Statistics and the United States Census Bureau, 20% of all marriages end within 5 years, 32% end within 10 years, 40% end within 15 years, and a full 48% end within 20 years. See National Center for Health Statistics, "Marriage and Divorce," www.cdc.gov/nchs/fastats/marriage-divorce.htm (accessed June 28, 2016); and Jamie M. Lewis and Rose M. Kreider, "Remarriage in the United States," American Community Survey Reports, March 2015, www.census.gov/content/dam/Census/library/publications/2015/acs/acs-30.pdf.

[5]The notion that marriage is central to the proper functioning of society is often linked to the rearing of children. "Marriages have always been the main and most effective means of rearing healthy, happy, and well-integrated children. The health and order of society depend on the rearing of healthy, happy, and well-integrated children. That is why law, though it may take no notice of ordinary friendships, should recognize and support marriages. There can thus be no right for nonmarital relationships to be recognized *as marriages*. There can indeed be much harm, if recognizing them would obscure the shape, and so weaken the special norms, of an institution on which social order depends." Sherif Girgis, Ryan T. Anderson, and Robert P. George, *What Is Marriage? Man and Woman: A Defense* (New York: Encounter Books, 2012), 7, emphasis original.

CHAPTER 1: DISNEY PRINCESSES,
TAYLOR SWIFT, AND *THE BACHELOR*

[1]It's also not a book about gay marriage, or the role of children in marriage, or egalitarianism versus complementarianism, or patterns of healthy communication in marriage. For anyone looking for those kinds of resources, I highly recommend the following: Cameron Lee, *Marriage Path: Peacemaking at Home for Christian Couples* (Pasadena: Fuller Institute for Relationship Education, 2015); Andrew Christensen and Neil S. Jacobson, *Reconcilable Differences* (New York: Guilford Press, 2002); John Gottman, *The Seven Principles for Making Marriage Work: A Practical Guide from the Country's Foremost Relationship Expert* (New York: Harmony Books, 2015); Sue Johnson, *Hold Me Tight: Seven Conversations for a Lifetime of Love* (New York: Hachette Book Group, 2008); and Howard Markman and Scott Stanley, *Fighting for Your Marriage: Positive Steps for Preventing Divorce and Preserving a Lasting Love* (San Francisco: Jossey-Bass, 2010).

[2]Jonathan Grant, *Divine Sex: A Compelling Vision for Christian Relationships in a Hypersexualized Age* (Grand Rapids: Brazos Press, 2015), 20.

[3]*The Little Mermaid*, Ron Clements and John Musker (Walt Disney Pictures, 1989).

[4]*Beauty and the Beast*, Gary Tousdale and Kirk Wise (Walt Disney Pictures, 1991). I owe this insight into Belle's character to Elijah Davidson, codirector of Fuller's Reel Spirituality.

[5]*Little Mermaid.*

[6]*Frozen*, Chris Buck and Jennifer Lee (Walt Disney Pictures, 2013).

[7]I owe this insight into the internal workings of Disney's various departments and John Lasseter's immediate rejection of the Merida makeover to Tamara Khalaf.

[8]Ian Crouch, "Haters Gonna Hate: Listening to Ryan Adams's '1989,'" *The New Yorker*, September 22, 2015, www.newyorker.com/culture/culture-desk/haters -gonna-hate-listening-to-ryan-adams-1989.

[9]Taylor Swift, "Love Story," *Fearless* (Nashville: Big Machine Records, 2008).

[10]Taylor Swift, "We Are Never Ever Getting Back Together," *Red* (Nashville: Big Machine Records, 2012).

[11]Taylor Swift, "Style," *1989* (Nashville: Big Machine Records, 2014).

[12]Taylor Swift, "Wildest Dreams," *1989* (Nashville: Big Machine Records, 2014).

[13]Taylor Swift, "Bad Blood," *1989* (Nashville: Big Machine Records, 2014).

[14]Swift, "Bad Blood."

[15]Taylor Swift, "Blank Space," *1989* (Nashville: Big Machine Records, 2014).

[16]Taylor Swift, "Shake It Off," *1989* (Nashville: Big Machine Records, 2014).

[17]A number of recent television shows explore the many struggles and joys of modern relationships with depth and complexity. Among others, *Catastrophe*,

Modern Family, *The Detectorists*, and *Master of None* each develops characters and narrative worlds that are equal parts winsome and honest. For anyone interested in a theological engagement with television and televisual culture, see Kutter Callaway, *Watching TV Religiously: Television and Theology in Dialogue* (Grand Rapids: Baker Academic, 2016).

[18]Kristin Dos Santos, "How *The Bachelor* Did the Impossible: Got Better Than Ever in Season 19," *E! News*, February 23, 2015, www.eonline.com/news/626824 /how-the-bachelor-did-the-impossible-got-better-than-ever-in-season-17.

[19]Mark Regnerus and Jeremy Uecker, *Premarital Sex in America: How Young Americans Meet, Mate, and Think About Marrying* (New York: Oxford University Press, 2011), 192.

[20]NPR Staff, "'Anything That Connects': A Conversation with Taylor Swift," *All Things Considered*, October 31, 2014, www.npr.org/2014/10/31/359827368/anything -that-connects-a-conversation-with-taylor-swift.

[21]In its most basic form, this narrative defines the cultural moment in which we find ourselves. As Grant suggests: "One of the most influential myths nourished by the culture of authenticity is that we will be 'saved' or made complete when we meet the right-shaped soul, the perfectly complementary person who can fulfill all of our needs and desires.... The problem is that we are likely to experience a keen sense of frustration and despair as this paragon fails to materialize. Some personality trait or quirk always mars our idealized image.... This search [for the perfect soul] ... locks us into a quest for a sanctuary that does not exist." Grant, *Divine Sex*, 48.

CHAPTER 2: THE INTERNAL NARRATIVES
OF CONTEMPORARY EVANGELICALISM

[1]Emily Joy Allison-Hearn, "Getting Married Made Me Angry," *The Mirror*, April 6, 2016, www.gradient.is/getting-married-made-me-angry.

[2]Andrew Marin, "A Revolution's Broken Promises," in *Perspectives on Marriage: A Reader*, ed. Kieran Scott and Michael Warren (New York: Oxford University Press, 2007), 169.

[3]Charles Taylor, *The Language Animal* (Cambridge, MA: Belknap Press, 2016), 43.

[4]Taylor, *Language Animal*, 43-44.

[5]"Conservative evangelicals rely on much the same cultural script for imagining and responding to social problems [and other moral commitments] as they previously have." James S. Bielo, "Act Like Men: Social Engagement and Evangelical Masculinity," *Journal of Contemporary Religion* 29, no. 2 (2014): 234.

[6]Bielo, "Act Like Men," 239.

[7]Bielo, "Act Like Men," 245.

[8]Stephen Arterburn and Fred Stoeker, *Every Man's Battle: Winning the War on Sexual Temptation One Victory at a Time* (Colorado Springs: WaterBrook Press, 2000). This was the first book in what would eventually become an incredibly successful line. The series now includes *Every Woman's Battle*, *Every Young Man's Battle*, *Every Man's Marriage*, and *Preparing Your Son for Every Man's Battle*.

[9]Darrin Patrick, vice president of Acts 29 at the time, stated in a promotional video for a book he authored, "This church had a man crisis. . . . That's probably what happened to this church and that's definitely what's happening in our churches." Cited in Bielo, "Act Like Men," 239.

[10]Tony Anderson, "Our Story," www.unearthedpictures.org/our-story, author's transcription (accessed June 16, 2016).

[11]"True Love Waits," Lifeway Christian Ministries, www.lifeway.com/n/product-family/true-love-waits (accessed June 16, 2016).

[12]The "sex is great!" chant is described in detail by Christine J. Gardner, *Making Chastity Sexy: The Rhetoric of Evangelical Abstinence Campaigns* (Berkley: University of California Press, 2011).

[13]Gardner, *Making Chastity Sexy*, 61.

[14]Gardner elaborated on this point in her interview with *Christianity Today*. Sarah Pulliam Bailey, "The Rhetoric of Chastity: Making Abstinence Sexy," *Christianity Today*, November 18, 2011, www.christianitytoday.com/ct/2011/november/making-chastity-sexy-interview.html.

[15]Bailey, "Rhetoric of Chastity."

[16]John Eldredge, *Wild at Heart: Discovering the Passionate Soul of a Man* (Nashville: Thomas Nelson, 2001), 9.

[17]John and Stasi Eldredge, *Captivating: Unveiling the Mystery of a Woman's Soul* (Nashville: Thomas Nelson, 2005), 8.

[18]Eldredge, *Wild at Heart*, 180-82.

[19]James Dobson, *Bringing Up Girls* (Carol Stream, IL: Tyndale House Publishing, 2010), 118.

[20]Dobson, *Bringing Up Girls*, 120.

[21]Namely, I take issue with their view of gender stereotypes as not only "natural" but an essential part of what it means to be male and female and thus a reflection of God's purposeful intentions for humanity. Their view of gender distinctions is problematic not only because it offers a limited vision of what it means to be a "real" man or woman, but also because it purports to be theologically grounded.

[22]Eldredge, *Wild at Heart*, xi (italics original).

[23]Eldredge and Eldredge, *Captivating*, 42.

[24]Eldredge, *Wild at Heart*, 185.

[25]See especially chapter three in Joshua Harris, *I Kissed Dating Goodbye: A New Attitude Toward Romance and Relationships* (Sisters, OR: Multnomah Books, 1997).

[26]This is the way Harris interprets Rebekah and Isaac's marriage arrangement in Genesis. I will offer a somewhat alternative reading in the following chapter. Harris, *I Kissed Dating Goodbye*, 167-70.

[27]Harris, *I Kissed Dating Goodbye*, 152.

[28]Eric and Leslie Ludy, *When God Writes Your Love Story: The Ultimate Guide to Guy/Girl Relationships* (Sisters, OR: Multnomah Books, 2009). This book was originally published in 1999, but was popular enough to go through two more editions (2004 and 2009).

[29]Joshua Harris, *Boy Meets Girl: Say Hello to Courtship* (Sisters, OR: Multnomah Books, 2000), 77.

[30]Margaret Kim Peterson and Dwight N. Peterson, "God Does Not Want to Write Your Love Story," in *God Does Not: Entertain, Play Matchmaker, Hurry, Demand Blood, Cure Every Illness*, ed. Brent D. Laytham (Grand Rapids: Brazos Press, 2009), 83, 85. The Petersons qualify their read of contemporary Christianity in much the same way that I do, by continually reminding readers that "we are not making any of this up. Everything we have said about the Perfect Love Story is something that our students have told us that they expect or want in a relationship, or that they have been taught they should expect or want in a relationship. A good many of these things we have found explicitly stated in one Christian relationship-advice book or another. And these books are all very clear: this is all of God" (92-93).

[31]Harris, *Boy Meets Girl*, 11-12.

[32]The effect of pornography culture on both single people and married couples is a concern not only for those in the church but also for society as a whole. As Belinda Luscombe pointed out in a cover article for *Time* magazine, "A growing number of young men are convinced that their sexual responses have been sabotaged because their brains were virtually marinated in porn when they were adolescents. Their generation has consumed explicit content in quantities and varieties never before possible, on devices designed to deliver content swiftly and privately, all at an age when their brains were more plastic—more prone to permanent change—than in later life. These young men feel like unwitting guinea pigs in a largely unmonitored decade-long experiment in sexual conditioning.... It's not merely that so many young men are unprepared for marriage. They are unprepared for dinner and a movie. We have sown to the wind. We are reaping the whirlwind—especially our daughters, who are less likely than ever to find a man who hasn't been corrupted by this." Belinda Luscombe, "Porn and the Threat to Virility," *Time*, March 30, 2016, www.time.com/4277510/porn-and-the-threat-to-virility.

[33]Both of these prominent evangelical leaders are asking all the right questions, although with slightly different audiences in mind. What if my prince never comes? What if I don't want one? What if I like princesses? Is celibate singleness even possible, much less desirable? And if this is my calling, is the Christian community still committed to my flourishing? Moreover, what does it mean if I'm no longer sexually "pure"? Or, in contrast, what if I'm just not that into sex in the first place? And what if I'm already married, but "happily ever after" hasn't turned out to be so happy? In other words, is the church still a place for me even if I don't fit the marriage mold?

MORE THAN JUST A LABEL

[1]Portions of Debi's story were originally published as "More Than a Label," *Inheritance Magazine* 30 (March 2015): 16-19. Used with permission.

CHAPTER 3: BONE OF MY BONES
AND FLESH OF MY FLESH

[1]Martin Luther, *Letters of Spiritual Counsel*, trans. and ed. Theodore G. Tappert, Library of Christian Classics (Philadelphia: Westminster, 1955), 274. As quoted in Laura A. Smit, *Loves Me, Loves Me Not: The Ethics of Unrequited Love* (Grand Rapids: Baker Academic, 2005), 251.

[2]We will return to Luther, but for now it is enough to say that while he did overcorrect in terms of making marriage an imperative for the Christian, he also demonstrated the very justice-oriented kind of marriage we will consider in chapter five.

[3]It is important to point out that, as my editor David McNutt reminded me, Luther also appealed to marriage as a metaphor to explain justification, which is a helpful alternative to the legal language most often invoked by Protestants.

[4]For a great example of the former, see Sherif Girgis, Ryan T. Anderson, and Robert P. George, *What Is Marriage? Man and Woman: A Defense* (New York: Encounter Books, 2012). For an example of the latter, see Max Stackhouse, *Covenant and Commitments: Faith, Family, and Economic Life* (Louisville: Westminster John Knox, 1997).

[5]On a popular or pastoral level, two rather different versions of this argument can be found in Francis Chan and Lisa Chan, *You and Me Forever: Marriage in Light of Eternity* (San Francisco: Claire Love Publishing, 2014), and Timothy Keller, *The Meaning of Marriage: Facing the Complexities of Commitment with the Wisdom of God* (New York: Penguin Books, 2013). For more academic arguments concerning why the church needs to move away from the marriage norm, see Smit, *Loves Me, Loves Me Not*, and William Loader, *Sexuality in the New Testament: Understanding the Key Texts* (Louisville: Westminster John Knox, 2010).

[6]David T. Lamb, *Prostitutes and Polygamists: A Look at Love, Old Testament Style* (Grand Rapids: Zondervan, 2015).

[7]Following the lead of Old Testament scholar John Goldingay, I am using the language of "First Testament" rather than "Old Testament" in part because one of my central claims is that we need to treat the Hebrew Bible as something that speaks to our present situation, and not as something that is "old" and thus irrelevant. Too often contemporary Christians operate as functional Marcionites without the courage of their convictions, and this is especially the case when it comes to marriage.

[8]For a helpful summary and a list of additional bibliographic resources on marriage documents in the ancient Near East, see R. K. Bower and G. L. Knapp, "Marriage," in *The International Standard Bible Encyclopedia*, vol. 3, ed. Geoffrey W. Bromiley (Grand Rapids: Eerdmans, 1986), 261-66.

[9]John Goldingay, *Old Testament Theology*, vol. 1, *Israel's Gospel* (Downers Grove, IL: InterVarsity Press, 2003), 107.

[10]Goldingay, *Old Testament Theology*, 1:107.

[11]For Simon, the "covenant view" is the central organizing lens, without which the others become distorted. Thus "[the covenant] view is integral to the Christian faith in its traditional forms, as well as to some other religious traditions. This view sees full sexual expression as an embodiment of the lifelong uniting of two individuals within one new shared identity. For this reason, sexual intercourse should be reserved for marriage, and both premarital and extramarital sex fall short of God's intentions for human sexuality." Caroline J. Simon, *Bringing Sex into Focus: The Quest for Sexual Integrity* (Downers Grove, IL: InterVarsity Press, 2012), 15.

[12]David Allan Hubbard, "When Man Was Human, Pt. 1," *His Magazine*, October 1971, 2.

[13]Ellen Davis, *Proverbs, Ecclesiastes, and the Song of Songs* (Louisville, KY: Westminster John Knox, 2000), 231.

CHAPTER 4: LIKE A VIRGIN

[1]Colin Campbell, "Mike Huckabee Launched His Presidential Campaign with a Fiery, Religious Speech," *Business Insider*, May 5, 2015, www.businessinsider.com/mike-huckabee-launched-his-presidential-campaign-with-a-fiery-religious-speech-2015-5.

[2]Campbell, "Mike Huckabee."

[3]Laura A. Smit, *Loves Me, Loves Me Not: The Ethics of Unrequited Love* (Grand Rapids: Baker Academic, 2005), 251. Smit notes two primary side effects of the church's misguided assumptions about marriage: (1) the creation of unnecessary barriers between the church and single people, and (2) a complete loss of credibility

when advising heterosexual or LGBTQ brothers and sisters concerning their call to celibacy.

[4]This is the view of J. Harold Ellens, *Sex in the Bible: A New Consideration* (Westport: Praeger, 2008), 46.

[5]Although Loader is somewhat sympathetic to the views of scholars like Ellens who posit an age of "holy promiscuity," he cannot finally affirm this reading because it not only envisions Jesus as setting biblical law aside, but also overlooks the fact that Jesus' comparison to angels is most likely a reflection of the common assumption that angels were celibate. See William Loader, *Sexuality in the New Testament: Understanding the Key Texts* (Louisville, KY: Westminster John Knox, 2010), 98.

[6]Timothy Keller, *The Meaning of Marriage: Facing the Complexities of Commitment with the Wisdom of God* (New York: Penguin Books, 2013), 40.

[7]Peter Rollins, *The Divine Magician: The Disappearance of Religion and the Discovery of Faith* (New York: Howard Books, 2015), 67.

[8]Rollins, *Divine Magician*, 98.

[9]Rollins, *Divine Magician*, 98.

[10]I want to acknowledge that the question of Paul's singleness is a matter of some debate, especially in light of 1 Cor 9:5. But regardless of whether he was single, a widower, or even married, his point about marriage and singleness remains the same.

[11]I owe this insight regarding mutuality to Tommy Givens.

[12]For example, Ladd seems to agree with C. H. Dodd and D. E. H. Witeley, who attribute Paul's early teachings on marriage in 1 Corinthians 7 to his expectation of Christ's imminent return, which eventually gives way to a more favorable take on marriage in Ephesians 5 when the apostle realized the Day of the Lord might be delayed for some time. George Eldon Ladd, *A Theology of the New Testament* (Grand Rapids: Eerdmans, 1993), 696.

[13]Caroline J. Simon, *Bringing Sex into Focus: The Quest for Sexual Integrity* (Downers Grove, IL: InterVarsity Press, 2012), 75.

[14]Smit, *Loves Me, Loves Me Not*, 77.

[15]I owe this insight to Wesley Hill and his discussion of Aelred of Rievaulx. Wesley Hill, *Spiritual Friendship: Finding Love in the Church as a Celibate Gay Christian* (Grand Rapids: Brazos Press, 2015), 31.

[16]Augustine, *The Confessions of St. Augustine*, trans. John K. Ryan (New York: Image Books, 1960), 43.

[17]Rollins, *Divine Magician*, 79-80.

[18]This is the way that Francis and Lisa Chan frame the purpose and value of marriage in their recent book. See *You and Me Forever: Marriage in Light of Eternity* (San Francisco: Claire Love Publishing, 2014), 73, 78. Given the reach of the Chans'

ministry and their influence on contemporary Christianity, it is important to understand their approach to the topic. I don't want to misrepresent their overarching argument here, but there is a sense in which their book is not really about marriage at all, but rather about "eternity." Marriage seems to have little purpose in its own right or without reference to the great "hereafter." While it is true that marriage—like every aspect of our present lives—has an "end" (a *telos*) to which it is directed, the danger in the Chans' approach is that by locating its significance in "eternity," they risk robbing marriage of its value in the here and now. It thus directs us away from the world instead of toward a loving embrace of the world.

CHAPTER 5: THE CALL OF MARRIAGE

[1]For the notion of the kingdom as "event," see John Caputo, *The Weakness of God: A Theology of the Event* (Bloomington, IN: Indiana University Press, 2006) and *The Folly of God: A Theology of the Unconditional* (Salem, OR: Polebridge Press, 2016). However, I have taken the categories of the unconditional (justice, gift, forgiveness, hospitality, and love) from Caputo's *What Would Jesus Deconstruct? The Good News of Postmodernism for the Church* (Grand Rapids: Baker Academic, 2007).

[2]It is interesting to note that, long before he was married, Lewis considered marriage and justice to be intertwined: "Before we consider this modern view [of marriage] in its relation to chastity, we must not forget to consider it in relation to another virtue, namely, justice. Justice, as I said before, includes the keeping of promises. Now everyone who has been married in a church has made a public, solemn promise to stick to his (or her) partner till death. The duty of keeping that promise has no special connection with sexual morality: it is in the same position as any other promise. If, as modern people are always telling us, the sexual impulse is just like all our other impulses, then it ought to be treated like all our other impulses; and as their indulgence is controlled by our promises, so should its be. If, as I think, it is not like all our other impulses, but is morbidly inflamed, then we should be especially careful not to let it lead us into dishonesty." C. S. Lewis, *Mere Christianity* (New York: Macmillan, 1952), 96-97.

[3]C. S. Lewis to Arthur Greeves, October 30, 1955, in *The Collected Letters of C. S. Lewis*, vol. 3, *1950–1963*, ed. Walter Hooper (San Francisco: Harper San Francisco, 2007), 669, as cited in Mary Stewart Van Leeuwen, *A Sword Between the Sexes? C. S. Lewis and the Gender Debates* (Grand Rapids: Brazos Press, 2010), 197.

[4]Lewis's decision to marry Davidman is especially interesting given that he had written quite extensively about Christian marriage as an indissoluble covenant and, at least on a theoretical level, was an opponent of remarriage after divorce. See Lewis, *Mere Christianity*, 92-93.

[5]Caputo, *What Would Jesus Deconstruct?*, 70.

[6]Thanks to Mark Finney for this insight.

[7]Martin Luther, "Judgment of Martin Luther on Monastic Vows (1521/22)," as quoted in Christopher C. Roberts, *Creation and Covenant: The Significance of Sexual Difference in the Moral Theology of Marriage* (New York: T&T Clark, 2007), 115. Along with this quote, my reading of Luther as a whole has been greatly helped by Roberts's insightful analysis of the significance of sexual difference within the development of the theological tradition.

[8]Roberts, *Creation and Covenant*, 121.

[9]For a helpful discussion of Luther's marriage to Katharina, see Michelle DeRusha, *Katharina and Martin Luther: The Radical Marriage of a Runaway Nun and a Renegade Monk* (Grand Rapids: Baker Books, 2017).

[10]Erin Dufault-Hunter, personal email correspondence, March 17, 2016.

[11]Numerous evangelical marriage books, especially those written from perspectives that assume complementarianism, suggest that the husband's primary role is to "prepare" his wife to "meet Jesus," which means that husbands are responsible for both "disciplining" and "training" their spouses to become their best selves. Given how significantly I disagree with this way of framing marriage, I find it difficult to respond charitably to these and similar arguments, so I hesitate to cite specific examples. However, one prominent example can helpfully sum up the others: "If you are to love like Christ, then you must also concern yourself with your wife's sanctification. Though Jesus has already taken all of her sin on the cross, you still have a real responsibility. You are to love, lead, and sacrifice in such a way that it results in your wife's sanctification. The most loving thing you can do is to lead your wife closer to Jesus, to become more like Him. Practically speaking, this will mean encouraging her in her time alone with God. Sacrifice to make sure she has time. It will mean reminding her not to love the world or the things of the world. Keep her focus eternal. It will mean guiding her towards acts of love that will result in eternal reward. Men, have you ever considered your role as a husband in these terms? This is huge." Francis Chan and Lisa Chan, *You and Me Forever: Marriage in Light of Eternity* (San Francisco: Claire Love Publishing, 2014), 78.

[12]Caputo, *What Would Jesus Deconstruct?*, 75-76.

[13]As Caputo points out, "'hospitality' means to welcome or admit the '*hostis*,' which in Latin means the stranger, who is the guest (of a 'host' in a 'hotel'); but a *hostis* is sometimes the stranger who is alien or 'hostile.'" Caputo, *What Would Jesus Deconstruct?*, 76.

[14]Alain Badiou, *In Praise of Love* (New York: The New Press, 2009).

[15]James K. A. Smith, "Marriage for the Common Good," *Comment*, July 17, 2014, www.cardus.ca/comment/article/4247/marriage-for-the-common-good.

[16]Smith, "Marriage for the Common Good."

[17]Alain de Botton, *Religion for Atheists: A Non-believer's Guide to the Uses of Religion* (New York: Vintage Books, 2013), esp. 77-79.

[18]I am referring here specifically to Badiou's *In Praise of Love.*

[19]For a wonderful elaboration on the thought of Augustine and Gregory, see Sarah Coakley, *God, Sexuality, and the Self: An Essay 'On The Trinity'* (New York: Cambridge University Press, 2013).

CHAPTER 6: DESIRE IN SINGLENESS

[1]This was a topic of deep reflection for other monks as well. When another brother, a British man in his mid-thirties, asked me if I was married, I said, "No . . . I sing 'God alone fills us' [a powerful Taizé chant with themes of longing for and trust in God], and sometimes I even believe it." He chuckled to himself and then responded soberly, "I think it's taking me a lifetime to believe that—so I keep singing it."

[2]One exception was my youth pastor James, who saw his primary job as helping high school students fall in love with Jesus, not keeping them from having sex. He located sexual holiness within the broader context of God's radical love, not as a legalistic end in itself.

[3]Since this is a chapter about desire in singleness, rather than sexual ethics, I will not rehearse these arguments here. Additionally, I wish to reiterate that although we differ vastly on matters of great significance, I continue to hold my non-celibate (partnered) gay Christian friends in great esteem, affection, and gratitude.

[4]Although many of the resources that I incorporate are written by other gay celibates, I believe that most of the content that follows is also profoundly relevant for all single Christians, regardless of sexual orientation. Relatedly, it is my hope to foster collaborative conversation with married Christians as well, for the sake of our mutual transformation.

[5]The book of Ruth, set during the time period of Judges, offers a beautiful and fascinating picture of how these different levels of relationship interacted with one another.

[6]With Taylor, I mean "secular" not as the opposite of "sacred" or as "neutral," but as a description of the reality of our age: belief in God is no longer dominant but contested.

[7]Charles Taylor, *A Secular Age* (Cambridge: Harvard University Press, 2007), 543.

[8]Taylor, *Secular Age,* 38.

[9]The immanent frame is not the only factor that has contributed to this decline, and Christian communities have not fully bought into it (after all, each week we gather together to remind each other that God exists and is active in our lives and in our world!). Still, I am convinced that Christians have been more

pervasively affected and profoundly malformed by the immanent frame (leading to "functional atheism") than we realize.

[10]James K. A. Smith, *Imagining the Kingdom: How Worship Works* (Grand Rapids: Baker Academic, 2013), 27. In fact, one of Smith's latest publications (which reprises his proposals from *Desiring the Kingdom* and *Imagining the Kingdom* for a nonacademic context) is titled *You Are What You Love: The Spiritual Power of Habit* (Grand Rapids: Brazos, 2016).

[11]James K. A. Smith, *Desiring the Kingdom: Worship, Worldview, and Cultural Formation* (Grand Rapids: Baker Academic, 2009), 41.

[12]Smith, *Imagining the Kingdom*, 61 (emphasis original).

[13]Smith, *Imagining the Kingdom*, 62.

[14]Smith, *Desiring the Kingdom*, 79.

[15]William Dyrness, *Poetic Theology: God and the Poetics of Everyday Life* (Grand Rapids: Eerdmans, 2011), 5.

[16]Dyrness, *Poetic Theology*, 5.

[17]William Dyrness, *The Earth Is God's: A Theology of American Culture* (Eugene, OR: Wipf & Stock, 2004), xv.

[18]Dyrness, *Poetic Theology*, 254.

[19]Sarah Coakley, *God, Sexuality, and the Self: An Essay 'On the Trinity'* (Cambridge: Cambridge University Press, 2013), 10.

[20]Coakley, *God, Sexuality, and the Self*, 58-59.

[21]Coakley, *God, Sexuality, and the Self*, 10. Scripture is filled with reminders of God's powerful love for humanity, at times even using the language of strong desire. For example, at the Last Supper Jesus tells his disciples, "I have earnestly desired to eat this Passover with you before I suffer" (Lk 22:15). Even more pointedly, James 4:5 asks, "Or do you think the scripture means nothing when it says, 'The spirit that God caused to live within us has an envious yearning'?"

[22]Coakley, *God, Sexuality, and the Self*, 52.

[23]Coakley, *God, Sexuality, and the Self*, 24. Put more starkly, Coakley writes that contemplative engagement with the Spirit "is both to risk having one's human desires *intensified* in some qualitatively distinct manner, and also to confront a searching and necessary *purgation* of those same human desires in order to be brought into conformity with the divine will" (13).

[24]Matt Jones, a celibate gay Christian blogger, describes the challenge of speaking authentically about this ache: "By all means I want to speak honestly about pain and struggle (which also requires I admit when I experience neither) and give others the opportunity to speak honestly about theirs, but I'm not sure honesty pairs well with ceaseless metaphors about 'some kind of flaming/icy/abyssal/dark serpent/ dagger/monster/dementor crushing/piercing/rupturing/devouring my heart/brain/ bowels/soul.' Pain can be too important a thing to devalue with dramatic excess."

Matt Jones, "Speech-Act, Part II," *A Joyful Stammering* (blog), September 10, 2013, www.matthewfranklinjones.com/2013/09/10/speech-act-pt-2.

[25]Brother Roger of Taizé, *The Sources of Taizé: No Greater Love* (Chicago: GIA Publications, 2000), 54.

[26]Tushnet, "Romoeroticism," *Crisis Magazine,* June 29, 2009, www.crisismagazine .com/2009/romoeroticism. In this regard, Protestants can still learn much from our Catholic sisters and brothers today!

[27]Dyrness, *Poetic Theology*, 278.

[28]Smith, *Desiring the Kingdom*, 54.

[29]Wesley Hill, *Spiritual Friendship: Finding Love in the Church as a Celibate Gay Christian* (Grand Rapids: Brazos Press, 2015), 80-81.

[30]Henri Nouwen, *Clowning in Rome: Reflections on Solitude, Celibacy, Prayer, and Contemplation* (New York: Image Books, 1979), 46. He continues, "The celibate person is a witness and a sign reminding others of their source and their goal. We are children of God first and we all belong to God first." Similarly, in *Reaching Out,* Nouwen writes of turning a desert of loneliness into a garden of solitude. See Henri Nouwen, *Reaching Out. The Three Movements of the Spiritual Life* (New York: Image Books, 1975).

[31]Coakley, *God, Sexuality, and the Self,* 52.

[32]Coakley, *God, Sexuality, and the Self,* 48. When my younger sister got married, she asked me to give a speech at the reception. I chose Nouwen's theme, testifying to our mutual need to offer one another these reminders: the importance of community and the space that God alone can fill.

[33]Dyrness, *Poetic Theology*, 244.

[34]Steve Holmes, "Taking Sin Appropriately Seriously: Marriage (and Singleness) as Ascesis?" (presentation given at the Evangelical Theological Society, Atlanta, GA, November 21, 2015). Available on his blog, *Shored Fragments,* as "Sex, Death, and Marriage," December 3, 2015, www.steverholmes.org.uk/blog /?p=7570.

[35]Augustine, *The Confessions of St. Augustine,* trans. John K. Ryan (New York: Image Books, 1960), 150.

[36]Augustine, *Confessions*, 17.

CHAPTER 7: SEX, SAINTS, AND SINGLENESS

[1]In particular, see Debra Hirsch, *Redeeming Sex: Naked Conversations About Sexuality and Spirituality* (Downers Grove, IL: InterVarsity Press, 2015); Wesley Hill, *Spiritual Friendship: Finding Love in the Church as a Celibate Gay Christian* (Grand Rapids: Brazos Press, 2015); and Laura A. Smit, *Loves Me, Loves Me Not: The Ethics of Unrequited Love* (Grand Rapids: Baker Academic, 2005).

[2]See, for example, Christena Cleveland, "A Liberation Theology for Single People," April 11, 2016, www.christenacleveland.com/blog/2016/4/a-liberation-theology -for-single-people.

[3]Cleveland, "Liberation Theology for Single People."

[4]See vignette 8 above.

[5]*God Is the Bigger Elvis*, Rebecca Cammisa (New York: HBO, 2012).

[6]*God Is the Bigger Elvis.*

[7]Alain de Botton, *Religion for Atheists: A Non-believer's Guide to the Uses of Religion* (New York: Vintage Books, 2013).

[8]Though this extension actually follows quite naturally from Hill's project: "I'm praying for it [i.e., friendship] not just for myself but also for others—single, married, gay, straight, and otherwise—in the church today. I'm convinced that all of us could benefit from a recovery of friendship as a genuine love in its own right. We've largely forgotten it, but I'm praying we can find it again." Hill, *Spiritual Friendship*, 22.

[9]Hill, *Spiritual Friendship*, xiii.

[10]Hill, *Spiritual Friendship*, xv.

[11]Hill, *Spiritual Friendship*, 41.

GENERAL INDEX

Acts 29 network, 60-63, 252

Adams, Ryan, 37-38, 41

adventure, 31, 67, 70

aesthetics, 202-3, 206, 227-28

　　See also beauty

Aladdin (film), 29-30, 38

Anderson, Tony, 61-62

Arterburn, Stephen (*Every Man's Battle*), 62, 83, 252

attraction, 9, 26, 32, 69, 103, 152, 193-96, 205-7

　　same-sex, 9, 193-96, 205-7

Augustine of Hippo, 147, 186, 200, 210

Bachelor/Bachelorette, The (TV series), 9, 23-24, 38, 42-46, 76, 182

Badiou, Alain, 182, 185-87

Barth, Karl, 91

battle, 26, 62, 67, 70, 82-84, 93, 103, 146

beauty, 17, 26-29, 36, 49, 67-71, 178, 189, 193-96, 200-206, 210, 223

　　See also aesthetics

Beauty and the Beast (film), 29-31, 38, 45

Bielo, James, 60-61, 251

Bonhoeffer, Dietrich, 224

Brave (film), 34-35

Brother Emile of Taizé, 193, 195, 200, 205

Brother Roger of Taizé, 204-5

calling, 6-7, 78, 81, 87, 94, 98, 102, 133, 144, 161-90, 193, 199, 217, 220, 254

　　See also celibacy; marriage; vocation

Caputo, John, 163, 172, 257-58

Catholicism, 49, 174, 205, 226, 261

celibacy, 4, 9-10, 61, 78, 127, 131-43, 147-48, 173, 193-211, 221, 224-32, 239, 254-56, 259-62

　　See also marriage; singleness; vocation

Chan, Francis and Lisa, 254, 256-58

chastity, 142-50, 173, 195, 204, 221-28, 257

Cinderella (film), 27-28, 33, 45, 68, 75

Cleveland, Christena, 82, 218-19

Coakley, Sarah, 202-4, 207, 259-60

community, 4-18, 23, 25, 30, 47-48, 51-54, 56-60, 62, 69, 73, 75-79, 81-82, 91-96, 105-8, 114, 116-17, 120, 124-27, 135, 137-52, 155, 160, 165, 167-75, 178, 182-88, 193-96, 202-10, 215-23, 225-40, 254, 261

complementarianism, 250, 258

courtship, 59, 72-77

　　See also dating

covenant, 9, 81, 96-107, 117-19, 130-32, 171, 197-200, 204, 208, 217, 229-32, 255, 257

　　See also family; friendship; marriage

culture, 2-4, 8-12, 17, 23-48, 53-77, 83, 87, 91-93, 96-105, 125, 135, 144-47, 165, 185-88, 191, 194-202, 205, 213-16, 225-28, 236, 243-45, 251, 253

　　countercultural, 8, 110, 138, 161, 188, 226

　　See also narratives

dating, 8, 22, 43-44, 49, 55, 72-75, 150, 159, 182, 237

　　See also courtship

Davidman, Joy, 170-71, 257

Davis, Ellen, 119

de Botton, Alain, 185-87, 227

desire, 2, 6, 9-10, 13-14, 24, 26-36, 40, 42, 45, 52, 61-72, 77-80, 112, 118, 120,

125-26, 130, 133-42, 146-50, 152, 155,
     163, 166-67, 173-74, 176-77, 182-88,
     192, 193-211, 221, 225, 227-28, 232, 251,
     259, 260
  divine, 149-50, 202-3, 209, 260
  sexual, 13-14, 40, 52, 61-62, 66,
     78-80, 126, 130, 136-42, 173-74,
     184-86, 201-3, 206, 221, 225, 227
Disney, 9, 23-39, 45-46, 53, 67-69, 223,
     250
divorce, 12-15, 64, 99, 103-7, 109, 119-21,
     130-32, 144, 146, 159, 162, 170-71, 200,
     213, 230, 237, 249, 257
Dobson, James, 69-70, 72
Dufault-Hunter, Erin, 175
Dyrness, William, 201-3, 205-6, 209
egalitarianism, 167-68, 250, 252
Eldredge, John and Stasi, 67-72, 194
ethics, 61, 79, 93, 102, 106, 143, 193-96,
     240, 259
eunuchs, 131, 136, 196-98
evangelicalism, 9, 16, 47, 51-84, 91-93,
     125, 162, 170, 193-94, 215-38, 243, 251,
     254, 258
family, 4, 13, 16, 21, 31-33, 62, 74, 98,
     101-3, 110, 119-21, 125, 133, 150-52,
     155-56, 176-77, 183, 191-92, 197-98,
     206-10, 213, 230-41
  new, 110, 177, 233-38
  nuclear, 13, 16, 62, 183, 197, 213
femininity, 25-36, 60-72
forgiveness, 156, 163, 177-81, 184, 186,
     190, 239-40, 257
friendship, 75, 189-90, 195, 207, 228-32,
     249, 262
Frozen (film), 31-34
Gardner, Christine, 64-66, 81, 252
gender, 30, 48, 67-72, 109-15, 131-32,
     167-68, 195, 202-3, 205, 252
  stereotypes, 67-72, 252
  See also femininity; masculinity
generosity, 41, 142-43, 146-47, 163,
     172-77, 183, 186, 208, 221, 236-37, 239

Givens, Tommy, 188-90
Goldingay, John, 110, 254-55
Grant, Jonathan, 23-24, 46, 251
Harris, Joshua, 72-76, 253
Hart, Dolores, 225-27, 232, 234
Hill, Wesley, 82, 206-7, 217, 229-30, 233,
     262
Hirsch, Debra, 217, 261
holiness, 80-81, 194, 198, 207, 210, 241,
     259
Holmes, Steve, 209-10
Holy Spirit, 16, 202-4, 210
hospitality, 163, 181-84, 186, 208-9,
     234-36, 239, 257-58
Hubbard, David Allen, 113
Huckabee, Mike, 123-24
Hunter, James Davison, 10
identity, 8, 28, 31, 49, 60, 71, 84, 88, 124,
     215, 255
idolatry, 78, 125, 133-35, 146, 177, 192,
     194, 200-204, 216
independence, 29-30, 35, 116, 143, 183,
     206, 210, 233
interdependence, 7, 94, 116-17, 183, 197,
     206-10, 222, 232
Jesus Christ, 95, 106, 109, 115, 121,
     128-37, 142-45, 147-50, 160-63, 168,
     175-76, 178, 184, 190, 193, 195, 198,
     204-6, 225, 229, 233-34, 237, 239-40,
     256, 258-60
  body of, 8, 15, 140, 144-45, 149, 178,
     183, 208, 210, 222, 228-40
  bride of, 10, 110, 149, 168, 215, 234,
     240
  disciple of, 4, 7-10, 52-53, 74, 78, 87,
     91, 127, 131-32, 137, 147, 160-62,
     177-78, 260
Jones, Matt, 260
justice, 89, 104-8, 163-76, 184-86, 202,
     206, 210, 237-39, 254, 257
Keller, Timothy, 254
Ladd, George Eldon, 256
Lamb, David, 95

lament, 121, 200, 204

leadership, 5, 51, 57, 62, 82, 196, 208, 216-17, 237

Lewis, C. S., 170-71, 257

Little Mermaid, The (film), 29-31, 33, 36, 38, 61

liturgy, 182-83, 200, 205

Loader, William, 129, 254, 256

Lobster, The (film), 213-15

loneliness, 1-2, 5, 13-14, 39, 45, 52, 108, 117, 121, 190, 199, 203-7, 223, 261

love, 5, 9, 11, 25-46, 52-53, 57, 65, 67-78, 81, 87-89, 101, 118-19, 125, 133-34, 139-43, 145, 147-50, 163-66, 168-70, 173, 175-76, 179-80, 184-92, 195-96, 201-10, 214-15, 217-19, 220, 223, 229-30, 233, 240-41, 259

    divine, 88-89, 119, 123, 142-43, 149-50, 175, 195, 202, 206-8, 218-19, 240, 259

    erotic, 40, 42, 52, 118-19

    romantic, 9, 25-46, 53, 57, 65, 67-78, 134, 163-66, 169-70, 176, 188, 191-92, 195, 214-15, 217, 223

    self-giving, 11, 65, 81, 87, 119, 139-41, 168, 173, 179-80, 184-90, 191, 196, 206-10, 220, 223, 229, 241

Ludy, Eric and Leslie, 75, 253

Luscombe, Belinda, 253

Luther, Martin, 92-94, 173-74, 199, 254, 258

Marin, Andrew, 56

marriage, 2-18, 21, 23-24, 27-29, 31-36, 38-39, 42, 44-49, 51-82, 87, 91-111, 114-18, 120-21, 123-30, 132-50, 152, 155-56, 159-99, 193-200, 204, 207-11, 213-23, 226, 228-30, 232-34, 237-40, 249-50, 253-58

    "biblical" definitions of, 16, 63, 105, 218

    same-sex, 195, 250

    See also celibacy; covenant; family; sex, sexuality; singleness

masculinity, 63, 70, 191

monasticism, 193, 204, 225-28, 232, 234, 259

narratives, 1-9, 16, 25-48, 51-82, 84, 91-150, 166, 188, 199-200, 204, 215-25, 251

    biblical, 7, 91-150, 166

    cultural, 25-48

    evangelical, 51-82

norms, normativity, 3-8, 11-15, 23, 29, 32, 35, 47, 53-60, 68-69, 72-83, 92-97, 109, 125, 127, 143, 146, 160, 175, 197, 200, 209, 214-21, 226, 234, 237, 239-40, 249, 254

Nouwen, Henri, 207-8, 224, 261

Peterson, Margaret and Dwight, 253

Plato, 117-18

practices, 3, 6, 10, 23, 54, 57, 59, 69, 71-73, 75, 78, 81, 91-92, 101, 110, 120, 138, 144-48, 169, 183, 185, 187, 196, 200-209, 216, 218, 224, 226-29, 234, 237, 239-40

Princess and the Frog, The (film), 31-34

Protestantism, 92, 125, 170, 173, 199, 205-6, 215, 217, 224-25, 254, 261

    Reformation, 93, 199

purity culture, 59-66, 72, 81, 194

Regina Laudis (monastic community), 225-28, 232, 234

resurrection, 115, 128-34, 144, 147, 198, 200, 204, 209

Rollins, Peter, 134-35, 148

Scarry, Richard, 1-3

secularism, 64, 187, 199, 259

sex, sexuality, 4-5, 9, 13, 24, 35-36, 38-47, 49-53, 55-56, 59-66, 69, 71, 73-74, 77-81, 83-84, 91-92, 96, 101-5, 110-19, 121, 124, 126-50, 160, 165-66, 173-75, 177-80, 183-88, 193, 193-207, 214, 217, 220-22, 224-28, 232, 239-40, 253-55, 257-58

    and abuse/violence, 105, 107, 151, 165, 180

and fulfillment, 5, 22, 35, 39, 52,
    79-80, 101, 107, 117-18, 133-36,
    141, 148, 162, 175-76, 186, 196-97,
    201, 221, 225-28, 251
  LGBTQ, 9-10, 193-96, 205-7,
    229-30, 250, 255, 259-60
  See also desire; love; marriage
Silver Ring Thing, 63-65, 81, 221-22
Simon, Caroline, 112-13, 143, 255
singleness, 2-11, 14-17, 22, 24, 35-54,
    56-59, 62-67, 71-74, 77-82, 87-89, 91,
    93, 95, 107-8, 114, 117, 124-27, 132-33,
    136-48, 150-52, 160-63, 173-74, 190,
    195-200, 203-10, 213-41, 253-56, 259
  See also celibacy; marriage
Sleeping Beauty (film), 27-28, 68
Smit, Laura, 125-26, 144, 217, 254-55
Smith, James K. A., 183-84, 200-201,
    203, 206, 210, 259-60
Snow White (film), 25-28, 36
solidarity, 208-9, 232
  See also interdependence
solitude, 207-10, 261

  See also loneliness
Stoeker, Fred (*Every Man's Battle*), 62,
    83, 252
Story of Us, The (film), 159-60
Swift, Taylor, 9, 23-24, 36-42, 45-46, 66
Taizé (monastic community), 193, 204,
    259
Tangled (film), 31-34, 36
Taylor, Charles, 58-59, 68, 199-200, 259
Thomas, Gary, 80
True Love Waits, 4, 63-65, 81
Tushnet, Eve, 205
virgins, virginity, 69, 83-4, 105, 127,
    136-39, 144, 148, 173, 196-200
  See also celibacy; purity culture
vocation, 6-7, 10, 15, 133, 142-48, 156,
    178, 180, 182, 188, 193, 196, 199, 207,
    209, 215-16, 223-24, 227, 238
  See also calling; celibacy; marriage
widows, 104, 107, 136, 145-46, 165-66,
    171, 196-97, 200, 213, 230, 237, 256
  and orphans 165, 171, 197
You've Got Mail (film), 5, 190-91

SCRIPTURE INDEX

OLD TESTAMENT

Genesis
1, 111, *132*
1–3, *109, 114, 116, 128*
1:26-27, *111*
1:27, *109, 114*
1:28, *115, 204*
2, *113, 130*
2:8, *116*
2:18, *113, 117*
2:23, *110, 113, 114*
2:23-24, *116*
2:24, *109, 110, 115, 130,*
    204
3:15, *197*
3:16-19, *116*
3:21, *116*
4:1, *115*
12, *98*
12–50, *97*
12:1-3, *98*
12:3, *197*
12:10–20, *99*
16:3-5, *99*
16:9-15, *99*
20:12, *98*
21:1-2, *197*
24, *73, 100*
25:19-26, *100*
30, *100*
33, *101*
33:5, *101*
38, *96*
41, *96*

Exodus
2, *96*
21:7-11, *104, 164*

Leviticus
18, *103*
18:16, *104*
18:18, *103, 164*
20:21, *104*

Deuteronomy
17:17, *103*
21:10-14, *104, 164*
22:28-29, *105*
22:29, *105, 164*
24:1-4, *103*
25:5-6, *104*
33:29, *113*

Ruth
3:10, *166*
4:9-12, *166*

1 Samuel
1:10-20, *197*

2 Samuel
12:8, *126*
13, *97*

Psalms
27:9, *113*
34:8, *195*

Proverbs
5:15-19, *204*
18:22, *107*
21:9, *108*

Ecclesiastes
4:7-12, *189*
4:12, *222*

Song of Solomon
2:4, *204*
2:16, *204*
8:4, *52*

Isaiah
54:1, *197*
54:5, *118*
56:3-5, *198*

Jeremiah
3:20, *118*

Ezekiel
16:1-63, *118*

Hosea
13:9, *113*

Micah
6:8, *104, 165*

Malachi
2:14-15, *118*
2:16, *106, 107*

NEW TESTAMENT

Matthew
10:39, *176*
12:50, *198*
18:22, *179, 240*
19, *130, 132, 133*
19:3-9, *109*
19:4, *131*
19:6, *130*
19:8, *106*
19:9, *131*

19:10, *160*
19:11, *132*
19:11-12, *131*
19:12, *136*
19:16-30, *178*
22:1-14, *148, 184*
22:23-32, *128*
22:30, *198*
25:1-13, *149, 184*

Mark
2:18-20, *149*
3:31-35, *233*
10:1-12, *130*
10:5, *106*
10:6-12, *109*
10:17-31, *178*
12:18-27, *128*
12:25, *129*
12:31, *220*

Luke
2:36-40, *144*
5:34-35, *149*
18:18-30, *178*
20:27-40, *128*
20:34-35, *128*

John
15:13, *229*
15:15, *229*

Acts
21:8-9, *144*

Romans
5:12-15, *136*
8:26, *204*

1 Corinthians
1:25, *172*

1:27, *172*
6:9-18, *141*
7, *121, 140, 194*
7:1-3, *138*
7:2, *204*
7:4, *138*
7:5, *138*
7:6, *137*
7:7, *136*
7:8-9, *137*
7:9, *174, 204*
7:12-16, *144*
7:29-31, *198*
7:32-35, *199, 206*
9:5, *144*
12:12-31, *139*
13:12, *142*
15:20-28, *136*
15:42-49, *136*

2 Corinthians
11:2, *149*
12:9, *121*

Galatians
6:10, *198*

Ephesians
5, *139, 140, 167*
5:1, *240*
5:5, *141*
5:21, *140*
5:21-23, *139*
5:22, *140*
5:25, *168*
5:27, *241*
5:29-32, *149, 184*
5:31, *109*
5:32, *110*

Philippians
2:4-8, *168*

Colossians
1:15, *135*
3:5, *141*
3:18–4:1, *139, 140*
4:15-16, *144*

1 Thessalonians
4:3, 141

1 Timothy
3, *146*
3:8, *146*
4:1-5, *145*
5:10, *146*
5:11, *146*

Titus
1:6, *146*
2:1, *145*
2:2, *145*
2:4-5, *145*
3:3, *146*
3:8, *146*

Hebrews
13:4, *198*
13:4-7, *144*

1 Peter
2:9-10, *198*
2:12, *145*
3:1-5, *145*
3:8, *145*

Revelation
19:6-10, *149, 184*
21:1-14, *149, 184*

Finding the Textbook You Need

The IVP Academic Textbook Selector
is an online tool for instantly finding the IVP books
suitable for over 250 courses across 24 disciplines.

---

ivpacademic.com
